DISPATCHES FROM THE FREUD WARS

Dispatches from the Freud Wars

Psychoanalysis and Its Passions

JOHN FORRESTER

HARVARD UNIVERSITY PRESS

Cambridge, Massachusetts
London, England
1997

Second printing, 1997

Library of Congress Cataloging-in-Publication Data

Forrester, John.
    Dispatches from the Freud wars : psychoanalysis and its passions /
John Forrester.
        p.   cm.
    Includes bibliographical references (p.   ) and index.
    ISBN 0-674-53960-5 (alk. paper)
    1. Psychoanalysis.   2. Psychoanalysis—History.   3. Psychoanalytic
interpretation.   4. Freud, Sigmund, 1856–1939.   I. Title.
    BF175.F646   1997
    150.19'5—dc20   96-38678

For Katrina,
without whom this book would have been
finished much sooner

And for Lisa,
without whom this book would never have been
finished at all

CONTENTS

DISPATCHES FROM THE FREUD WARS

INTRODUCTION

The Freud Wars have been raging for some years now, with serious historical argument and abstract philosophical criticism neatly dovetailed with name-calling, ill temper, and vitriol. From television to the daily newspapers, from the weekly reviews to museum exhibitions, from books and articles published by scholarly presses to professional conferences and debates—all these open spaces for the public expression of opinion have become arenas of contestation. More private spaces are no doubt equally infused with sniping and surprise offensives, sometimes even the search for an armistice—at least they are in my experience. Leaving the necessarily more intractable private spaces to one side for the moment, how do questions as abstruse as different philosophical approaches to confirmation in the sciences or as gossipy as Freud's relationship with his sister-in-law become regular concerns of national newspapers? Why, in other words, do the Freud Wars matter to our culture at large?

For those less involved in the day-to-day skirmishes than the combatants necessarily are, Freud's place in twentieth-century culture—scientific, philosophical, literary, cultural, and religious—is uncontested. "We live," Mark Edmundson writes, "at least according to numberless commentators, in the Age of Freud, a cultural moment in which the critical and descriptive terminologies readiest to use sound with unmistakeably Freudian resonances."[1] George Steiner, Philip Rieff, Jacques Derrida each confirms his judgment. The list of "Eminent Freudians" will inevitably open with different names in different places, depending on our own particular cultural horizon and history; Edmundson's opens with Empson, Burke, and Trilling, but we could just as easily start with Mann, Wilson, and Sartre, to finish with Cavell, Kristeva, and Habermas. And any list should be capacious enough to include Claude Lévi-Strauss and Woody Allen, Sir Aaron Klug and Brian de Palma, Richard Rorty, A. S. Byatt, and even the enigmatic French soccer player Eric Cantona. Each of these would probably assent to Rorty's perception that, in the domain of moral reflection, of the creation (rather than recognition) of the self and in the arena of sex, there is as little chance of going back to pre-Freudian beliefs as there is of going back to pre-Copernican beliefs.[2] There is something irreversible about what Freud has done to twentieth-century culture. The vitriolic debates are simply an index of coming to terms with that transformation, with no more real prospect of undoing it than militant greens have of restoring the planet to the *status quo ante* the automobile. Which does not require us to accept without question the effects on our lives of either Freud or the Volvo.

Certainly in the twenty-five years or so that I have been concerned with psychoanalysis, with its history and philosophy, with its conceptual structure and its social practices, there has never been a time when it was not contested or viewed with suspicion. In the 1970s, the feminist critique of psychoanalysis associated with Friedan, Millett, Greer, and many others was as splenetic and furious as any of the present entanglements.[3] In 1971, when pulling out from a bookshelf a volume of the *Standard Edition* whose title interested me, by this "Freud" whose name I of course knew but had never read, I had been admonished by a close feminist friend that Freud was not worth reading because he was of all writers the most male chauvinist. The injunction, it may be thought, had precisely the opposite effect. "What is so threatening and so dangerous about this writer that one should make sure not to read him?" Much of 1970s feminism was virulently anti-psychological, fearing that inquiry into motives and inner worlds inevitably entailed a strategy of divide and rule: divide the women into their individual inner worlds so as to remove the possibility of their recognition of what was social and therefore common, in its banal ordinariness, to every oppressed woman. It was rape, not fantasy, that began to concern feminists; and, from the late 1970s on, it was the sexual abuse of children, not the Oedipus complex, that became a new crusade for many feminists. Freud and all the institutions of psychoanalysis became deeply suspect for having highlighted fantasy and desire, rather than brute reality and sexual exploitation.

The vilification of Freud by feminists has undoubtedly provided a stable cultural framework over the last thirty years for much discussion of psychoanalysis. A second principal theme in the overall critique of psychoanalysis has been its status as a source of scientific authority and therapeutic promise. This critique is considerably older than the feminist critique, dating back to the beginnings of psycho-analysis; it is—and this is a very important feature of the cultural and scientific location of psychoanalysis—the constant companion of psychoanalysis, as much a part of its history as its infiltration and co-optation by the movie industry. The letters of Freud, Jung, Jones, Ferenczi and all the early adherents of psychoanalysis are catalogues of the campaigns fought on behalf of psychoanalysis against its critics. These critics have been stationed somewhat, but finally not fundamentally, differently from the current wave: psychiatrists, bi-ologists, social scientists, academic psychologists, cultural critics, newspaper reviewers, novelists, philosophers, and health insurance managers (formerly known as asylum superintendents). One does not need to rely on Freud's concept of a generalized and universal cultural resistance to the difficult truths of psychoanalysis to realize that the proponents and opponents have been conducting trench warfare over the same piece of territory for nigh on a hundred years.

What are we to make of this unceasing struggle? It may be educational to think of the battle between Freud and his critics as akin to the contest between an analyst and his patient. Whose side you are on in this unholy mixture of seduction and strife—whether you think the analyst should be treated with all the suspicion we might reserve for a priest who uses the weapons of the intellectual terrorist, a Grand Inquisitor for our time, or whether you think the analyst might have something useful to say to his patient—can be set aside for a moment. Consider whether Freud's description of that dialogue may not be helpful: "If in the course of a battle there is a particularly embittered struggle over the possession of some little church or some individual farm, there is no need to suppose that the church is a national shrine, perhaps, or that the house shelters the army's pay-chest. The value of the object may be a purely tactical one and may perhaps emerge only in this one battle."[4] Recognizing that the battle over the phallocentrism of psychoanalytic theory and practice, or the battle over the scientific pretensions—as if it were a shrine—or over the therapeutic efficacy—as if it were the pay-chest—may only be tactical, we are obliged to ask: what is the war itself being fought over?

The war is over far larger issues than either Freud's critics or the professionals who are identified as Freud's defenders and progeny—the analysts, the therapists, the "mental health professionals," as they are dolefully known—are willing to accept. Freud speaks to much larger cultural issues in the twentieth century than, say, Frederick Crews's tripartite division of issues raised by psychoanalysis into questions of therapeutic efficacy, questions of scientific explanation, and questions concerning Freud's scientific probity. Even Crews admits as much when he asks: "Where, then, are Freud's authenticated contributions not to ethics or mores or literary criticism but to actual knowledge of the mind?"[5]—implying that Freud has made "authenticated contributions" to ethics, mores, and literary criticism. Leaving aside the perplexity provoked by the assumption that ethics or mores might not involve actual knowledge of the mind, it is clear that even for Crews, ethics, mores, and literary criticism have been clearly marked by Freud, and we can effortlessly add the following to this list of cultural endeavors irreversibly stamped by Freud:

politics, the social sciences, literature itself—not just literary criticism—and the arts in general. We have to take seriously the suggestion that debates about psychoanalysis should not be couched in the form: is it an art or a science? But rather: what changes in our general categories are required by recognizing that psychoanalysis is both an art *and* a science? Not just the old-fashioned sense of art, as when we say that medicine is an art and a science, in order to remind ourselves that, no matter how scientific medicine becomes, its primary obligation is always to curing the individual, which requires the practical wisdom, the *phronesis*, associated with any deliberate action in (as opposed to knowledge of) the world. But also the recognition that psychoanalysis has produced in the analyst a cultural figure whose work is aesthetic as much as it is investigative (in the style of the research scientist or of the private detective) and has made available to the patient the opportunity to render his or her life a work of art, a narrative of chance and destiny as well as a thriller, whether psychological or otherwise. Freud, thus, must not only be considered alongside Darwin or Einstein, but also as a combination of Darwin with Proust, Pasteur with Picasso, or even Weber with H. G. Wells. Or, for those somewhat less impressed by Freud than these names would imply, at the very least a combination of bogus second-raters: say, Salvador Dali with the suspect scientist Paul Kammerer.

The essays in this book range widely, tracking areas in which Freud's influence has been undeniable, often unexpected and usually controversial. Chapter 1 arose from considering one single sentence of Freud's in which he suggested a surprising and original interpretation of the biblical Judgment of Solomon. The necessary context for inquiring into that sentence turned out, however, to be much broader than biblical texts, implicating the distinctive psychoanalytic transformation of our views of the relations between politics and the individual and between morality and the emotions. What place does an emotion such as envy have in our view of politics if the very constitution of the political subject may be affected by the experience of envy—or, by implication, of other intense passions which may influence, may even provide the basis for, our view of the social world and our relations to others? What effect does psychoanalysis as a result have on political theory in general, and how should psycho-analytic political theory be appraised in that connection? Does psy-choanalysis imply the demise of a theory of political agency which calls on universal categories of justice and rationality? Must our model of judicial rationality now be based not so much on ideals of equality and rationality but on the crass reality of the behavior of judicial plaintiffs squabbling over a newborn baby or, in an equally modern mode, of a husband and wife using the justice of the courts to take their revenge on each other?

Certain critics, in their demand on psychoanalysis to make good its claim to be a science, insist that in order to be scientific it must remove every element of subjectivity. While appreciating that objec-tivity, in the sense of the absence of biased and self-interested claims, is something to be admired under certain circumstances, such as making judgments in court or in the dispensation of funding for charitable or cultural causes, it has always seemed to me an inappro-priate goal in psychoanalytic treatment. Treatment, after all, is part of life, and the relationship a patient develops with his or her analyst is as passionate, as intimate, and maybe even as lengthy as many a modern marriage. To demand objectivity of both patient and analyst under these circumstances seems as sensible as asking married cou-ples to be objective and rational in their relations with their spouses.

One may well object to this analogy: marriage is real life, psycho-analytic treatment is only make-believe. From one point of view that is true; but from the point of view of the patient, the line between make-believe transference and real passions is inevitably, if only temporarily, erased. Freud's view of transference-love, that it was as real and as normal as any other instance of that pathology we call love, is clear on this point. It is the foundation of psychoanalysis, and its inevitable and irremediable scandal, that patients develop passionate relations to and with their analysts. The scandal becomes a double scandal, rather like those operatic comedies in which a double marriage brings to a close the dramatic action, when the passions of life have added to them the pursuit of scientific truth and professional achievement. Such was the double scandal of Freud's relationship with Sándor Ferenczi and Ferenczi's relationship with his mistress Gizella Pálos and her daughter Elma. How the analysts and colleagues, Freud and Ferenczi, negotiated their ways through the minefield of love and truth, psychoanalysis and science, is the concern of the second chapter, "Casualties of Truth," where I present the view that psychoanalysis is distinctive in its practice because of its resolute lack of concern for ethical principles. Milan Kundera writes of the western novel in its development since Rabelais that "suspending moral judgment is not the immorality of the novel; it is its *morality.*"[6] Something very similar could be said of psychoanalytic practice. No doubt at a deeper cultural level the possibility and the cultural fertility of both the novel and psychoanalysis are linked. And, just as the novel may appear to be the vehicle for the values of honesty and character, of truth and courage, while its very form is irony, indirection, and playful mimicry, so a similar tension inhabits psychoanalysis: one between the ethic of honesty which its theory promotes and the practice of play-acting, the carnival of masks, that its practice consists in.

Those who seek the values that psychoanalysis promotes or embodies have sometimes pointed to the stern bourgeois habits and values of its founder as a firm indicator. To round off the image evoked by alluding to Freud's taste for classical German literature and realist novels, what could be more clinching than the paean of praise to conventional values proclaimed by the collection of classical antiquities that Freud amassed over some forty years as a collector? In Chapter 3 I take a new look at the lessons about psychoanalysis to be learned from Freud's collecting activities, starting with the obvious but usually overlooked fact that Freud collected much more than archaeological objects of contested aesthetic value—what a connoisseur of ancient art, who on the face of it spends his life totally outside the war zones associated with psychoanalysis, recently informed me was a second-rate collection put together by a typical Viennese philistine. Freud was a preeminent collector of *scientific* objects as well as of objets d'art. Having recognized this, what more do we learn about psychoanalysis and its place in twentieth-century culture once we accustom ourselves to viewing Freud as an original if eccentric collector of unconventional objects devoted to a scientific end? The realization slowly dawns on us that the properly analyzed patient is not necessarily a second-hand Oedipus, Hamlet, or even Marcel. The fully analyzed person may well be just someone who is finally capable of doing a somersault.[7]

Certainly Freud's masterpiece, *The Interpretation of Dreams*, bears witness to his acute awareness of the audience for those collectables. In Chapter 4, "Dream Readers," I attempt to answer the most fundamental question concerning the development of psychoanalysis as a practice and as an institution, a question succinctly posed by Jacques Derrida: "How can an autobiographical writing, in the abyss of an unterminated self-analysis, give birth to a world-wide institution?" How does Freud create a science out of a self-analysis? How does he disarm, seduce, persuade, and finally manufacture his readers out of such unlikely materials as the meanderings of a dreamer as he recounts those dreams to an audience? How, in other words, does Freud transform the dream into a proper object for science and its methodical procedures of inquiry? And how does Freud, at the same time, induce the reader—the follower, the critic, the disciple, even the "educated and curious-minded reader" of whom Freud writes— to enter into that intimate, jousting relationship with him, the first skirmish in this century's long-drawn-out Freudian campaign, that his masterpiece initiated?

Chapter 5, "A Whole Climate of Opinion," is devoted to a chronicling of that long campaign in its wider context, the historiography of psychoanalysis in the twentieth century. Beyond the studies of Freud as a personal, historical, or intellectual figure, beyond the conceptual history of psychoanalysis as a set of doctrines and theories, the chapter points toward the necessity for a history of psycho-analytic cultures. Those cultures are multifaceted: part medical, part scientific, part pop, part avant-gardist. The many faces of Freud's offspring, sometimes working together, sometimes in tension or in conflict, require a more subtle history than we have yet been offered. The chapter presents guidelines and guesses for such histories, drawing on figures as diverse as Michel Foucault, Alasdair MacIntyre, Ernest Gellner, Peter Swales, and Bruno Latour.

British readers will remember how the classic work *1066 And All That* depicts English history as so many risible attempts, each doomed to failure, to answer the Irish Question. My final chapter, which gives this book its title, addresses a range of offensives in the recent cultural interrogation of the Freud Question. From Stanley Fish to Frederick Crews, via Adolf Grünbaum and Frank Sulloway, the chapter explores the terrain on which the critiques are played out. Some of the observers on the sidelines come away, like Pierre Bezuhov from the Battle of Borodino, convinced that the only way to bring peace is to do away with the General, the invader, the villain of the piece—Freud himself. "We don't need bloody Freud to tell us *that!*" commented a doyen of the contemporary wave of criticisms of psychoanalysis, Frank Cioffi, when interviewed for a TV program in 1993.[8] Killing the messenger is one of the most hallowed of strategies for dealing with unwanted news. Freud called it disavowal, foreclosure, or repudiation. In the recent intensification of hostilities around Freud and psychoanalysis, repudiation—treating the events as *non arrivés*—is to be found on both sides. For the Cioffis and the Crewses, there is no mistaking, despite their repeated protestations to the contrary and their gratuitous slurs on their opponents and critics, their heartfelt wish that Freud might never have been born or, failing to achieve that end, that all his works and influence be made as nothing. (In the Epilogue to this book, an apocryphal Freud gets to comment on this strategy.) The classic maneuver asserts that whatever Freud said that is true is *either* banal and commonplace *or* can be found in writers and thinkers, such as Shakespeare, Pascal,

Hobbes, Dostoevsky, and Nietzsche, who predate him (and sometimes both). And whatever he says that is novel and revolutionary is false and misleading. In other words, if what he says is right, he stole it from somewhere else, sometimes even passing off the universal wisdom of mankind as his own discovery—"Was it really Freud who first disclosed such commonplaces?" asks Crews.[9] On the other hand, if what he says is wrong, it belongs entirely to him and it is we who are the fools if we believe it. Take another typical example of Crews in benign mood, noting the cultural durability of Freud's achievements: "Freud will survive because his essentially medieval (spirit-possession) and romantic (little elves make deeper selves) conceptions, combined with his emphasis on sex, his facile symbolic code, and his courageous-looking but essentially egocentric and prurient encouragement to look for low motives in everyone but oneself, still pack an emotional wallop."[10] This hilarious passage, clearly completely devoid of any intention to "pack emotional wallop," conveys a limpid sense of the issues for Crews and the spirit in which the Wars should be fought. But, to be fair and accurate, there is no mistaking the complementary visceral reactions of fear and rage on the other side, of the apologists of psychoanalysis, when confronted with the intemperate tone and the wounding criticisms generated by Freud's opponents.

Despite—could it really be because of?—the fact that Freud has been dead for close on to a lifetime, it is clear that there is an incessant to-ing and fro-ing between attacking him and his work and attacking large-scale intellectual and clinical movements which are attributed, in one way or another, to him, as if victory on one front will increase the chances of capitulation on others. Hence there is an incessant oscillation between the widely spaced terrains of battle: between Freud as a person and Freud as the founder of a cultural practice, between Freud as a scientist-cum-priest and psychoanalysis as an institution and cultural presence, between therapy itself as a personal venture, eccentricity, or "confidence trick" (Medawar's verdict on psychoanalysis) and therapy as a fact of twentieth-century life—a movement with as many subvariant products as the modern consumer expects from cable TV. Each of these individual battlefields will be taken to stand for the whole war. Each shot that is fired, let alone seen to hit its mark, in one zone is expected to bring victory across the whole front.

This constant confusion between "Freuds"—as embodied in the "life," the "work," Freudiana, Freud's writings, Freud's theories, classical psychoanalytic theory, orthodox psychoanalytic practice, psychoanalysis as a cultural movement, therapy as a professional practice—is made easy by a strange fact: everyone knows, from a very young age, what "Freud" said and what "Freud" stands for. I remember one day in 1979 bumping into a close friend and his 11-year-old daughter; when I told her that I had just finished writing a book about Freud, she exclaimed: "Freud, yuk! He's horrible!" Very much in the same tone as she might have said: "The Bay City Rollers, yuk! They're horrible!" There is a difficult piece of cultural history to be written in this domain, the domain of Freud as a received idea of the twentieth century. The first entry of Flaubert's *Dictionary of Received Ideas* reads:

ABELARD.   No need to have any idea of his philosophy, nor even to know the titles of his works. Refer discreetly to the mutilation inflicted on him by Fulbert. The grave of Abelard and Héloïse: if someone proves to you that it is apocryphal, exclaim: "You are robbing me of my illusions!"

For Freud's entry, in the late twentieth century, we might wish to write:

FREUD.   No need to have any idea of his philosophy, nor even to know the titles of his works, because everyone already knows all that. Refer discreetly *either* to the fact that he slept with his sister-in-law (after all, the man who invented modern sexuality must have had some kind of illicit sexual passions, preferably of the unacceptable kind) *or* to the fact that he made everything up (after all, people like you and me don't spend all their time thinking about sex, do we?). But preferably not both at once. In uncertain company, it's always good manners to say he's rather *passé*, though he once had something useful to say to our parents' generation (see PSEUDOSCIENCE). But be prepared to backtrack and defend the power of his eternal insights into human nature. If feeling forceful and required to be up-to-date, declare how shameful it is that we've only recently learned about all those scandals. And there are still more to come . . .

Not only does everyone know what Freud wrote and what everything Freudian "really means," everyone also knows what all the fuss is really about. So the process of writing about Freud must always be one of uneducating one's readers. I stand on common ground with some of Freud's critics on this issue, since at least some of them believe in reading and thinking closely about his work and its historical context. But, unlike these critics, it is my wager that the more one knows about Freud—the more one has unlearned what one was culturally hard-wired to know about him—the more interesting and surprising and thought-provoking he becomes. The final answer to Freud's critics is that many intelligent men and women—and maybe even children—have recognized and continue to recognize this.

I

JUSTICE, ENVY, AND PSYCHOANALYSIS

An illiterate man went up to Aristides, whom he had never seen before, and asked him to write the name *Aristides* on a potsherd, so he could vote for his ostracism. Aristides asked him: "What harm has Aristides done you?" The illiterate man answered: "None. And I don't know him, but it bothers me hearing everybody call him Aristides the Just." Without more ado, Aristides wrote his own name on the potsherd.

Plutarch, *Life of Aristides*

In the third chapter of the book of Kings, two harlots come before King Solomon to ask for his judgment. They have been living together and have both given birth to sons a short time before. While sleeping, one of the women inadvertently crushed her child and then secretly exchanged the dead baby for the living one of her friend. On waking, the friend was certain that the dead child lying beside her was not her own son and tried to take the live baby from the other woman. Both women disputed the other's version of the events.

To resolve the dispute, Solomon says: "Bring me a sword . . . Divide the living child in two, and give half to the one, and half to the other." The King James Bible continues:

Then spake the woman whose the living child was unto the king, for her bowels yearned upon her son, and she said, O my lord, give her the living child, and in no wise slay it. But the other said,

Let it be neither mine nor thine, but divide it.

Then the king answered and said, Give her the living child, and in no wise slay it: she is the mother thereof.[1]

When I was young, I thought the point of the judgment of Solomon was to demonstrate the chutzpah of the King. It was a detective story, demonstrating the skill and acumen of the hero-detective. Solomon's strategy is a case study in how the master dialectician acts, as he ostensibly sets off in precisely the opposite direction to his actual goal, knowing that the other actors will ineluctably carry him back to that goal. He, the King and absolute Master, orders the baby to be cut in half precisely so that the baby will not be cut in half. We could also call this the Zen master reading of the parable.

My second reading of the parable, when I was a little older and had decided that such stories were less about the intelligence of men than about the tragedy of life, emphasized the selfless and poignant action of the true mother, who gives up her claim on her beloved child and, in order to preserve its life, is prepared never to see it again. Perhaps her child means more to her than her own life—perhaps she would, given the choice, substitute herself for the child and die in its place. In giving up her claim, then, she gives up something more valuable than her own life: she gives up her motherhood in order to save her baby's life. Her conscious motive is thus paradoxical in a similar way to Solomon's: she acts in the opposite direction to her ostensible goal. In order to save her child, she abandons it. In this way, the judgment also becomes a parable of the relationship between mother and child—of how the mother gives life to the child, succors and protects that life with her own, to the point of exchanging her own life for that of the child.

I was entirely blind to a third possible reading until I came across it in Freud's *Group Psychology and the Analysis of the Ego*, in a chapter where he discusses the hypothesis of a primary herd instinct in human beings:

What appears later on in society in the shape of *Gemeingeist, esprit de corps,* "group spirit," etc., does not belie its derivation from what was originally envy. No one must put himself forward, every one must be the same and have the same. Social justice means that we deny ourselves many things so that others may have to do without them as well, or, what is the same thing, may not be able to ask for them. This demand for equality is the root of social conscience and the sense of duty. It reveals itself unexpectedly in the syphilitic's dread of infecting other people, which psycho-analysis has taught us to understand. The dread exhibited by these poor wretches corresponds to their violent struggles against the unconscious wish to spread their infection on to other people; for why should they alone be infected and cut off from so much? why not other people as well? And the same germ is to be found in the apt story of the judgement of Solomon. If one woman's child is dead, the other shall not have a live one either. The bereaved woman is recognized by this wish.[2]

Freud's reading of the judgment of Solomon focuses neither on Solomon nor on the true mother of the baby, who gives up her claim on her own child. Instead, he focuses on the woman who maintains her claim against the other woman. Freud's simple interpretation is something of a shock. Focusing on the third party, the woman who maintains her claim, reveals how it is *we,* and not Solomon or the true mother, who are led away, by the narrative structure of the parable, from her. The parable-work, to coin a term along the lines of the dream-work and more proximately the joke-work, conceals the fact that it is the second woman, the woman who maintains her claim on the child, who is the principal actor.[3] We have been duped by the structure of the parable.[4]

Freud's interpretation has textual support in the Bible. Uncannily repeating the lofty impartiality of King Solomon, the envious mother says: "Let it be neither mine nor thine, but divide it." Freud generalizes this principle in the following rather dry way: "Social justice means that we deny ourselves many things so that others may have to do without them as well." This is the joke-work of political theory. The high ideal of social justice tendentiously cloaks something altogether more individually self-interested: the envious woman is not truly interested in half a baby, as if half a baby were better than none. Her true aim is to ensure that the other woman has no baby, just like her. For her, no baby is better than one. Her idea of justice, then, is not stably redistributive, nor is it entirely impersonal, despite the iron logic of equal shares for equal subjects; its motivations and its manifestations are destructive and personal, aimed not at any *general* other, but at any *specific* other who has the thing she does not have.

To highlight the personal and specific aspect here, we can contrast the woman who wishes to see the baby cut in two with the woman who gives up her claim on the baby, rather than see it cut in two. You do not have to be the baby's mother to wish to see its butchery avoided at any cost—it does not take a specifically *maternal* love to withdraw a claim under such circumstances. Any ordinary human being would prefer the child to live rather than see it cut in two. Therefore what requires explanation is why any human being would *maintain* her claim under such circumstances. Freud's explanation shows that the parable's structure misleads us into thinking that love of the baby is the center of the dispute, whereas it is more fundamentally the envy of one mother for what the other woman has that provides its motor. Do not forget that the mother who wishes to see the baby cut in two is in mourning for her own baby. The dispute is primarily an attack on the other woman, not a desperate expression of love. We are, after all, observers of a dispute; and when it is love that leads to war, we begin to suspect that there are other motives mixed in that are not entirely visible. Paris is undoubtedly known as the man who wished to possess Helen, but he does not figure high on the list of the world's great lovers.

Freud is not the only theorist to draw attention to the peculiar behavior of the mother who maintains her claim. Jon Elster views Solomon's action as being that of a judge presiding over the first child custody case. So, in his reading, Solomon's ruling to cut the child in two set a test for the two parents competing for custody of a child; in reacting to the test by maintaining her claim, one of the two competing parents revealed herself to be unfit for child custody: "By making certain claims, or by acceding to certain proposals, one can reveal oneself to have a character that has a bearing on the resolution of the dispute. In Solomon's case, the woman who was willing to have the child cut in two thereby revealed herself ineligible for custody."[5] What interests Elster is how one can deduce from the behavior of one of the litigants facts about her suitability as a parent. That this may produce paradoxes, and demonstrate the limitations of legal rationality, is what makes the judgment interesting. But at no point is the actual content of the character—the envy Freud attributes to the litigating parent—referred to. Elster—like Rawls, as we shall see—does not connect the actions of the mother of the dead child to the very foundation of judicial rationality. Viewing Solomon's judgment solely as a diagnostic tool presupposes that the rational judgment that follows diagnosis is independent of that which has been diagnosed, as if the concern with the rationality of public action must necessarily bracket off any concern for the passions that underlie such action, even in a writer as sensitive as Elster has consistently been to the limits of rational decision-making.

Before turning to the larger issues contained in the relation of envy to justice, we should pause to consider the remarkable fourth interpretation of the judgment of Solomon to be found in Jean Carbonnier's classic, *Flexible Droit*. Carbonnier notes a historically contextual motive for the mother of the dead baby claiming the live one as her own: archaic laws may well have required the death of the mother of the dead baby on the grounds of infanticide. "The mothers are not only pleading for their possession, but for their innocence, maybe even for their lives."[6] Note that under these circumstances, both mothers would have the same motive for claiming the child as their own: fear of execution. Solomon's judgment would then be an even more arduous test of maternal love: the woman who

17

ceded her claim on the live child might well have expected that her act would be equivalent to signing her own death warrant. Greater love hath no woman . . .

Brecht offers a parallel displacement of the frame of the judgment in *The Caucasian Chalk Circle*. The judge rules that the woman who can pull the child out of the chalk circle will have it; twice, Grusha, the poor woman who has raised the child, refuses to pull on the child, whereas the biological mother is willing to do so: she has come to claim her child from Grusha only out of avaricious motives, since under changed legal circumstances, the child will bring with it a vast estate. Both Brecht and Carbonnier "normalize" the motivations of the woman who is willing to see the child divided equitably, one by giving her the motivation of greed, the other by imputing to her a fear for her own life. Unlike Freud, they do not see in the structure of the parable a myth of the origin of justice out of envy.

Carbonnier goes on to suggest an even more provocative interpretation of the meaning of the parable: namely, that it does not have a "deep" meaning, does not depict a set of motives to be discovered and subtle strategies for their uncovering. Rather the naive reading of Solomon's judgment, to which the "deep" reading opposes itself, is that the essence of justice itself is to be found in the verdict: "Divide the living child in two." Solomon wields the sword of justice in order to cut the Gordian knot of all civil conflicts; and he does it with total disinterestedness, blind as justice must be. Carbonnier points to other ancient Hebrew variants of the parable (Josephus) that endorse this conception of what justice requires: Solomon commanded that both the live baby and the dead baby be cut in two.[7] The judgment of Solomon is thus that justice is simply the blind observance of the principle of equal division of the objects over which the parties are disputing, as in the rabbinical advice that, when two parties dispute over two apples, the apples should both be cut in two and each party receive two halves. The truth contained in the judgment of Solomon is the ruthlessness with which justice pursues its own ends, a ruthlessness that must, in order to be true justice—

that is, pure equity—outstrip the ruthlessness with which the civil parties pursue their own interests. No legal system, Carbonnier notes, employs the rule that a proposition A or B can be derived from A/2 + B/2. "But was law invented to assure the victory of logic or the reign of peace on earth?"[8]

Carbonnier continues, in more pessimistic mode: do not ask what the justification is for this "instinct for authoritative division":

> If it appears to answer to the need for peace, which is itself a need for order, it may also be a means of inciting conflict and war by awakening the hope of partial recompense in partitivity. *Obiter dictum:* bear in mind the illusions brought with them by those who, in our era, wish to found a politics, even a theology, on the idea of equal division, without realizing that, behind this idea derived from the law, there are demons, not angels, at work.[9]

And we should pause over Carbonnier's reinterpretation of the aim of justice in general:

> The judgment of equity seem to us to be judgment in its pure state, judgment which does not seem capable of becoming a rule ("sans tirer à conséquence," the Parlements of the Ancien Régime would say). This judgment in no sense is less of a law, but not in the form of a general rule, rather as an individual solution. The bringing to an end of litigation, the resolution of conflict: bringing peace between men is the supreme goal of law; and the smoothing of ruffled feathers, the compromises, the accommodations, the deals are just as much law, if not more so, than all those ambitious norms.[10]

Freud's discussion of envy and Solomon's judgment formed part of an attack on the plausibility of a herd instinct. Freud wished to show that, in contradiction to Trotter's theory of the herd instinct, human beings are not by nature social animals.

For a long time nothing in the nature of herd instinct or group feeling is to be observed in children. Something like it first grows up, in a nursery containing many children, out of the children's relations to their parents, and it does so as a reaction to the initial envy with which the elder child receives the younger one. The elder child would certainly like to put his successor jealously aside, to keep it away from the parents, and to rob it of all its privileges; but in the face of the fact that this younger child (like all that come later) is loved by the parents as much as he himself is, and in consequence of the impossibility of his maintaining his hostile attitude without damaging himself, he is forced into identifying himself with the other children. So there grows up in the troop of children a communal or group feeling, which is then further developed at school. The first demand made by this reaction-formation is for justice, for equal treatment for all. We all know how loudly and implacably this claim is put forward . . . If one cannot be the favourite oneself, at all events nobody else shall be the favourite.[11]

For Freud this argument clinches his case against the assumption of a primary, innate social feeling: "Thus social feeling is based upon the reversal of what was first a hostile feeling into a positively-toned tie in the nature of an identification."[12] At the core of this argument is the demonstration that the call for justice and equality is founded upon the transformation of envy. One of the exemplars of such a transformation might be the generation of the institution of exclusive, monogamous marriage out of the envy of the son (or the excluded male) for the father's cornucopia of women. Put generally: without envy, not only would there be no *need* for a judicial apparatus, there would be no *desire* for justice.

It is this conclusion, this link between an emotion and a principle for the organization of society, which I want now to explore further. Before I do so, I want to make a few digressionary remarks—remarks which, I hope, will show the interest of this inquiry.

Envy as a fundamental fact of psychic life is well known in two different psychoanalytic theories, both of which have had rather mixed fortunes. The first is Freud's thesis that a little girl becomes a woman via the transformation of penis envy into the wish for a baby. Aligning his theory of general social envy with the specific theory of penis envy reveals immediately their closeness of fit, if I can put it like that. The primal scene of penis envy is very similar to the primal scene of envy in general: the girl, like the sibling, *sees* the other child with an object that she thinks gives him complete satisfaction and she falls prey to envy.[13] The closeness, for Freud, of the scene of penis envy to that of general envy is confirmed when we note that the little girl is never envious of her *father's* penis, but only of the penis of her peer, her potential equal. And the envy she feels acts as an intrusion upon her dyadic relation with her mother, retroactively reinforcing the already existent feelings of disappointment with the mother, including what Freud calls the "jealousy of others whom the mother loves."[14] "Girls hold their mothers responsible for their lack of a penis and do not forgive her for their being thus put at a disadvantage."[15] This lack of forgiveness is linked to the child's later reproach that her mother did not give her enough milk as a baby—the child "never gets over the pain of losing its mother's breast."[16] The very language that Freud employs to describe the dislodging of the girl from her undisturbed intimacy with her mother indicates the links with later claims for justice and equality: the child is, he writes, "dethroned, despoiled, prejudiced in its rights"[17] by the other sibling. So the image of the mother's body as full of goodness, this image of the original Eden, the utopia which we can retrieve through the reign of perfect justice, is implicitly characterized as the body full of enviable goods—of milk and of penises to be dispensed to only some of her children. Freud's theory of the retrospective promotion of the lost object provides the structure within which such utopias are created: "A young man who was a great admirer of feminine beauty was talking once—so the story went—of the good-looking wet-nurse who had suckled him when he was a baby: 'I'm sorry,' he remarked, 'that I didn't make a better use of my opportunity.' I was in the habit of quoting this anecdote to explain the factor of 'deferred action' in the mechanism of the psychoneuroses."[18] The other half of the theory is supplied by the envy which provides the motivating force for the stabilization of the ideal object.

What is missing when Freud discusses envy of the penis compared with envy in general is the explicit highlighting of the subsequent reaction-formation: the identification with the other child and the clamorous demand for equality—though some of his remarks concerning the motivations for feminism indicate that he envisaged such an outcome for penis envy. And, as Teresa Brennan astutely points out,[19] Freud's theory of justice should mean that women have stronger superegos than men, not weaker as he asserted: "The fact that women must be regarded as having little sense of justice is no doubt related to the predominance of envy in their mental life; for the demand for justice is a modification of envy and lays down the condition subject to which justice can be put aside."[20] This argument has as its hidden premise the notion we have been examining, that the demand for justice is derived from envy that has been repressed. Yet it does not explain why women do not repress their envy and thus transform it into a very strong sense of justice. One would have thought that the plausible conclusion to draw is that women, with the added motivation for general envy of a lack of a penis, should thus be *more* just than men. Instead Freud notes that adult women manifest envy in their mental life and links this to their indifference to justice without asking why women do not transform, as just men do, their envy into the demand for justice.

Before leaving to one side this theory of penis envy—a secure part of our intellectual mythology, even when it is regarded as entirely implausible, worthless, and dangerous—it is worth asking the question: in the debates that Freud's notorious account started, which element of the concept of penis envy aroused the most passion—the penis or the envy?

The other psychoanalytic theory centered on envy is contained in

22

Melanie Klein's short book *Envy and Gratitude*. Klein advances the hypothesis "that one of the deepest sources of guilt is always linked with the envy of the feeding breast, and with the feeling of having spoilt its goodness by envious attacks."[21] Beneath the Oedipus complex, which in Klein's view manifests itself principally in the primal scene of the parents making love, enjoying each other endlessly, there is a deeper fantasy: that of the breast endlessly feeding itself on the good things contained in it—including the father's penis.[22] If there is any failure in the relation to the breast, if there is any frustration, then the child's response is envy of the breast and the attempt to spoil what is good.

Klein's theory sees envy as a direct derivative of the destructive impulses, the death instinct. The destructive impulse attaches itself immediately to the first object of love, the breast, which is the immediate object of destructive impulses precisely because it is loved.

> Yet each man kills the thing he loves,
> By each let this be heard,
> Some do it with a bitter look,
> Some with a flattering word.
> The coward does it with a kiss,
> The brave man with a sword!

Destroying what you love most: this fundamental response to the world, expressed so well in Oscar Wilde's poem, is summarized in the emotion of envy.

Klein's theories have received an uneasy response, in part because the theory looks very like a psychoanalytic version of the doctrine of original sin. Appropriately enough, St. Augustine, with whom original sin is always associated, perceived the relation of the child to the breast in exactly the same way as Klein, and made clear that the envy of the child confronted with the feeding breast supports the doctrine of original sin:

23

Who can recall to me the sins I committed as a baby? For in your sight no man is free from sin, not even a child who has lived only one day on earth . . . I have myself seen jealousy in a baby and know what it means. He was not old enough to talk, but whenever he saw his foster-brother at the breast, he would grow pale with envy. This much is common knowledge. Mothers and nurses say that they can work such things out of the system by one means or another, but surely it cannot be called innocence, when the milk flows in such abundance from its source, to object to a rival desperately in need and depending for his life on this one form of nourishment? Such faults are not small or unimportant, but we are tender-hearted and bear with them because we know that the child will grow out of them. It is clear that they are not mere peccadilloes, because the same faults are intolerable in older persons.[23]

In Lacan's commentary on this passage, he accentuates one feature, a feature that is only implicit in Klein. Lacan affirms that the object of envy is not something useful to the subject—the child no longer has need of the breast as he watches his brother feeding. The object of envy is not what I desire, but rather what satisfies the other with whom I compare or identify myself. It is the image—and it is important for Lacan that envy is a sin of looking, *invidia,* of looking outward—of the other's plenitude closed in upon itself, of another gaining satisfaction through enjoyment of an object, that is the scene of envy. At the very inception of envy, the object is separate from and outside the subject. Included in the very idea of envy is a throwing outward, a projection.[24] It is then the dialectic of inner and outer that characterizes envy. The very concept of the subject's interiority depends upon the subject's attention being directed primarily to the other, in the moment when the subject perceives the other being satisfied by the object of envy. A lack is installed in the subject at the very moment of perceiving the fullness of the object possessed by the other.

One further way in which the topic of envy can be linked to psychoanalysis is to point out, as Helmut Schoeck does, how certain key psychoanalytic concepts, in particular the concepts of identification and incorporation elaborated in *Group Psychology and the Analysis of the Ego*, cover the same ground as the more traditional language of emulation and vindictive spoiling associated with envy.[25] The fruitfulness of this link between identification, contagion, and envy can be seen in recent work by Diana Fuss.[26] Schoeck also argues, somewhat less plausibly, that sadism and masochism are modern psychoanalytic substitutes for the traditional thematics of envy. Such an approach, less tied to the term *envy*, would demonstrate much about the links between the "modernist" psychoanalytic theory and the traditional discourse of the sins and the passions. As the rest of this chapter, and in particular the absolute centrality of envy in modern political theory, will demonstrate, however, one does not need to go so far as to show the tentacles of envy making their way into the heart of other psychoanalytic concepts. That these tentacles are at work I do not deny.

At this point I wish to turn to Nietzsche's genealogy of morals to explore a parallel analysis which, in my view, proves to be very similar to Klein's analysis of the original sin of envy. It is these passages that also form the starting point for Max Scheler's influential essay on *ressentiment*.

Nietzsche's *Genealogy of Morals* sets out to analyze the development of the concepts of good, bad, and evil. He counterposes two fundamentally different principles, associated with two different peoples: the aristocrats and the Jews. The aristocrats' morality consists in a "triumphant self-affirmation"—though Nietzsche questions whether such a principle of self-affirmation can ever give rise to what *we* call morality. But the morality of the Jews—and by Jews Nietzsche obviously (also) means Christians—develops from their *ressentiment* or rancor, which is derived from their vengeful feelings for and hatred of the noble aristocrat. Out of their hatred grows that "deepest and sublimest of loves" as expressed in the "ghastly paradox of a crucified god." With the universalization of this slave morality, the people, the slaves, the herd have triumphed over noble values.

25

Slave ethics . . . begins by saying *no* to an "outside," an "other," a non-self, and that *no* is its creative act. This reversal of direction of the evaluating look, this invariable looking outward instead of inward, is a fundamental feature of rancour. Slave ethics requires for its inception a sphere different from and hostile to its own . . . the "enemy" as conceived by the rancorous man . . . is his true creative achievement: he has conceived the "evil enemy," the Evil One, as a fundamental idea, and then as a pendant he has conceived a Good One—himself.[27]

In his commentary on Nietzsche's genealogy of the slave morality, Scheler characterizes the envy that so often leads to the attitude of *ressentiment* toward the world as arising from a sense of impotence.[28] The awareness of the object envied and the awareness of one's own failure, one's own emptiness, go hand in hand. They are inseparable. Envy thus turns out to be the most "sociable" of the passions.[29] Envy reveals one's fundamental failure in relation to the world, at the very causally dependent moment when it reveals the success of another.

From envy Freud derives the sense of justice: "If one cannot be the favourite oneself, at all events nobody else shall be the favourite." In a more pungent tone, Nietzsche called this attitude "world-destroying": "This man fails in something; finally he exclaims in rage: 'Then let the world perish!' This revolting feeling is the summit of envy, which argues: because there is *something* I cannot have, the whole world shall have *nothing!* the whole world shall *be* nothing!"[30] For Klein, envy's effect is on the one hand to undermine gratitude toward a good object and on the other to encourage indiscriminate spoiling and destroying of the objects in the world. For Nietzsche, the man of *ressentiment* embodies the reactive, negating attitude of the slave, of the common man, of democratic man. As Bertrand Russell put it in an uncharacteristically Nietzschean moment: "Envy is the basis of democracy."[31] Thus Nietzsche, Freud, and Klein each offer a genealogy of the social and moral world as derived from envy.

It is this project of conjoining an affective state to a configuration of the social world that interests me. Nietzsche characterized the foundation of part of the project as follows: "Moralities are also merely a *sign language of the affects*."[32] Freud derives considerably more than a moral stance, or a moral universe, from the affect of envy; he also derives a socio-political regime, one that has been severely criticized by modern commentators. To measure the extent to which this is an unwelcome project, I want now to consider a theory of justice that vigorously rejects Freud's genealogy of justice.

—————

The most influential recent account of justice, that of John Rawls, betrays a certain unease in relation to the passions.[33] Having elaborated the fiction of an "original position" from which social actors are to choose the fundamental principles of justice—a position characterized by ignorance both of the specific social world the actors will actually have to inhabit and of their individual dispositions and place in that social world—Rawls eventually fills in his account by elaborating a moral psychology, in which both moral and natural attitudes must play a part:[34] "a theory of the moral sentiments . . . setting out the principles governing our moral powers, or more specifically, our sense of justice."[35] His account is explicitly teleological, "founding the account of moral learning explicitly upon a particular ethical theory" (p. 496), that of his contract doctrine.

Rawls distinguishes between moral sentiments, such as guilt and resentment, which are dependent upon a background set of principles or ideas of justice, and natural aptitudes, such as anger and rancor, which arise independently of moral principles. He is quick to point out that some forms of envy fall into this second category, and thus are not moral: "It is sufficient to say that the better situation of others catches our attention"; "we are downcast by their good fortune and no longer value as highly what we have" (p. 533).[36] Recognizing that such forms of envy, even though not moral in the sense of arising from the prior principles of justice, may be "excusable" (p. 534) and are certainly common, Rawls seeks to determine whether this fact puts into question the principles of justice derived from the original position which, it should be remembered, had explicitly excluded consideration of such attitudes or passions.

Even while he recognizes that envy is not a product of *moral* principles, Rawls emphasizes the *social* derivation of envy: "although it is a psychological state, social institutions are a basic instigating cause" (p. 536). Rawls looks to the well-orderedness of a society based on his (or similar) principles of justice to mitigate the envy-producing effects of disparities of wealth, endowments, and so forth: the well-orderedness will "reduce the *visibility,* or at least the painful visibility, of variations in men's prospects" (p. 536; emphasis added); various features of social organization will mean that these "discrepancies" will not "attract the kind of attention which unsettles the lives of those well placed" (p. 537). He goes on to say that "taken together these features of a well-ordered regime diminish the number of occasions when the less favored are likely to experience their situation as impoverished and humiliating" (p. 537). Rawls concludes that "the problem of general envy anyway does not force us to reconsider the choice of the principles of justice," even though he has not given an argument for this, but rather has pointed to social conditions that will mitigate any possible effects of envy.

Rawls is by no means alone in finding in the *visuality* of envy a crucial element in its potential destructiveness; we have already seen such a focusing on the visual field in Augustine, Lacan, Klein, and in Freud's theory of penis envy. Put walls around the havens of contentment, set up barriers between the rich and the poor, between the well endowed and the rest, and, with luck, envy will not arise. But Rawls's response to the danger of the invading envious gaze—surely a plausible candidate as the original form of the evil eye—is ironic and salutary. The gesture aiming to ward off the envious gaze repeats the founding gesture of his argument: the positing of an original position in which subjects have a veil of ignorance drawn both between them and the outside (the society in which they will have an as yet unknown place) and between them and the inside (those specific and individual desires, dispositions, and aptitudes with which they will in reality be endowed). The original position is "a situation in which everyone is deprived of this sort of information. One excludes the knowledge of those contingencies which set men at odds and allows them to be guided by their prejudices" (p. 19). The final chapters of Rawls's book thus cannot keep from creeping back into the social arrangements for a harmonious society exactly that element that Rawls built into the hypothetical original position only to discard it once the principles of justice had been firmly established, that is, agreed to by those who would, in a real world, prove vulnerable to envy (both as subjects and objects). The fiction of the original position excluded *ab origine* the potentially destructive passions of envy, rancor, and spite (p. 538), and this initial exclusion eliminates all primary social sentiments: "Presuming [in the original position envy's] absence amounts to supposing that in the choice of principles men should think of themselves as having their own plan of life which is sufficient for itself" (p. 144). But Rawls also hoped to show how his entirely individualistic starting point would allow the emergence of a primary social sentiment: "the combination of mutual disinterest and the veil of ignorance achieves the same purpose as benevolence" (p. 148). In this way, Rawls hoped that the primacy of benevolence would secure the well-ordered society from the destructive effects of envy, spite, and rancor. But at the beginning of his book, in the original position, and at the end, when he finally confronts, like Hercules, the many-headed hydra of rancor, spite, envy, grudgingness, and jealousy, Rawls has one basic strategy to save the principles of justice: place a veil between oneself and the primordial object of envy.

Having asserted that envy does not constitute a threat to his principles of justice, Rawls turns to confront the arguments of others which assert that it does. The first argument is a skeptical and pessimistic one: it doubts whether any society in which discernible differences of wealth, prestige, and goods exist can be proof against envy. Rawls admits that a specific form of envy, that directed at specific, rather than general, kinds of goods, is "endemic to human life; being associated with rivalry, it may be associated with any society" (p. 537). But he maintains that a well-ordered society, one based on secure principles of justice, will manage the problem of envy. And this first argument does not put in doubt the concept of justice, since it conceives of envy as being external to justice. The second hostile argument Rawls confronts is potentially much stronger: it maintains that the very principles of justice are themselves *based* on envy, so that justice is simply envy in disguise and that envy is internal to the very possibility of justice. It is here that Rawls recognizes Freud as a principal opponent (pp. 539–541).[37]

To counter Freud's "conservative" views, Rawls runs a number of different arguments. The first is the strongest, but also the argument that distances Rawls's theory most from getting a grip on a substantive rather than a hypothetical account of justice. Rawls asserts that the principles of justice remain untouched even if the actual motivations for all or most people holding to principles of equality are derived from envy. Here, he is responding to the need, felt by many theorists such as Lyman,[38] for principles of justice that are entirely independent of the passions, since where there is no clear criterion of justice, demands will often be attributed to envy. Similarly, the response to the implications of the disparaging phrase "the politics of envy" is thought to be the discovery of some means of grounding justice and fairness outside of any motivations attributable to envy. This is what Rawls's first argument attempts to do.

Second, Rawls notes that many arguments that appear to derive justice from envy in fact derive it from resentment; and, since resentment is already a moral feeling founded on a sense of justice and injustice, justice is actually being derived from itself.

The strongest attack that Rawls mounts on the view that envy is the foundation of demands for justice is the following:

> In order to show that the principles of justice are based in part on envy it would have to be established that one or more of the

conditions of the original position arise from this propensity . . . But each of the stipulations of the original position has a justification which makes no mention of envy. For example, one invokes the function of moral principles as being a suitably general and public way of ordering claims. (p. 538)

In other words, Rawls is attempting to show that all the elements of justice are independent of envy, and that therefore the argument that justice is derived from envy is conceptually erroneous. Rawls is confident that the envy-thesis cannot extend into the constitutive elements of the original position.

This underestimates some of the implicit force of Freud's argument. Freud is principally concerned to show how social feeling derives from the identification of children with each other, the motives for which are in turn derived from original hostility and envy. Thus when Freud notes that "the first demand made by this reaction-formation is for justice, for equal treatment for all," he is observing something more than simply a demand for equality. Freud is accounting for the principles which Rawls explicitly holds up as having nothing to do with envy: the formal constraints on the concept of right, among which there are two principal constraints, that principles should be general, and that they should be universal in application (pp. 130–132). In other words, Freud is claiming that the very concepts of universality and generality are derived from the sequence of defenses against the original envy and hostility. In a quasi-Durkheimian move, what he calls "*Gemeingeist, esprit de corps*, 'group spirit'" or the "herd instinct" is this predicate of potential universalizability in action. And this predicate stems from the initial defense of "identifying himself with the other children,"[39] giving rise to "a positively-toned tie in the nature of an identification."[40] So Rawls overlooks Freud's specific challenge to his basic assumption that the formal constraints on the concept of right are formulated without reference to envy. Freud would argue that assenting to universalizable and generalizable principles of any sort is already a reaction-formation to the passion of envy, albeit a formal one. One might reply that this is a matter of semantics: what Freud calls a reaction-formation, Rawls calls a formal constraint of universality and generality. But Freud's usage points to the possibility, not considered by Rawls, that the formal constraint of universalizability may itself be defensive in character, and cannot simply be regarded as a formal characteristic.

I mention this *formal* aspect because Rawls recognizes the interest of Freud's argument when it comes to describing the motivational *forces* at play in the development from envy to the call for equality. He expounds with great clarity this aspect of Freud's argument: "Freud means to assert more, I believe, than that envy often masquerades as resentment. He wants to say that the energy that motivates the sense of justice is borrowed from that of envy and jealousy, and that without this energy, there would be no (or much less) desire to give justice" (p. 540). Rawls's response to this, which he takes to be the strongest version of the Freudian argument concerning the derivation of justice from envy, is to assert that the argument derives its persuasive force from the conflation of envy and resentment. When Freud describes the elder child as wishing "to put his successor jealously aside, to keep it away from the parents, and to rob it of all its privileges," Rawls maintains that this desire is derived from resentment, not envy; and when "we resent our having less than others, it must be because we think that their being better off is the result of unjust institutions, or wrongful conduct on their part" (p. 533).[41] So resentment, being a moral feeling, requires that a moral principle be cited in its explanation: the principles governing injustice. Rawls thus accuses Freud of a *petitio principii,* of smuggling the principle of justice into his account of "envy" by having falsely renamed "resentment" as envy, and then deriving the demand for justice, for equal treatment for all, from the covert accusation of injustice which we call resentment.

The difference between Rawls and Freud is now easier to describe. Rawls wishes to affirm that a child's demands on its parents for love and attention at the expense of the other child's are often justified, and are within the boundaries of that which could in principle be justified:

> If children compete for the attention and affection of their parents, *to which one might say that they justly have an equal claim,* one cannot assert that their sense of justice springs from jealousy and envy. Certainly children are often envious and jealous; and no doubt their moral notions are so primitive that the necessary distinctions are not grasped by them. But waiving these difficulties, we could equally well say that their social feeling arises from resentment, from a sense that they are unfairly treated. (p. 540; emphasis added)

One is tempted to quote Augustine to Rawls: "surely it cannot be called innocence, when the milk flows in such abundance from its source, to object to a rival desperately in need and depending for his life on this one form of nourishment?"[42] Rawls wishes us to recognize that the moral principles underlying resentment are already present in the nursery, and accuses Freud of smuggling them back there but claiming he hasn't, by conflating envy and resentment. Freud, on the other hand, wishes us to recognize the passion of envy at work in the "adult" moral principles of justice and fairness. They work in opposite directions—Rawls to eliminate the childish from the adult world of moral principles, Freud to demonstrate the domination of the adult by the forgotten childish. Rawls implicitly refuses to accept the Freudian assumption that we often, if not always, continue well into adulthood to employ the original template of childhood experience, whose guiding shape and ruling configuration can be perceived in ghostlike form in the adult world. An indication of this refusal can be found in his discussion of guilt, where he is quite explicit about the necessity to eliminate the "childish" form of guilt that derives from disobeying authority from an account of the properly moral guilt-feelings (pp. 481ff).[43]

But Rawls does go so far as to admit that principles of justice that do not follow from his own argument based on the fiction of the original position may derive from envy: "To be sure, there may be forms of equality that do spring from envy. Strict egalitarianism, the doctrine which insists upon an equal distribution of all primary goods, conceivably derives from this propensity" (p. 538). Rawls thinks that he has protected the argument by which he derives the principles of justice from the subversive corrosion of envy and the other passions (his "special psychologies," which he also revealingly calls "envy and other aberrant propensities"; p. 548). He thus thinks he has shown that there *could* be a motivation for justice that is not derived from envy. But he does not show that, in the actual world, there ever has been or is at present a demand for justice that is not based on envy. He himself leaves up in the air this empirical question: "None of these remarks is intended to deny that the appeal to justice is often a mask for envy" (p. 540). And he ends his discussion of envy reflecting, in all fairness: "I believe, though I have not shown, that the principles of justice as fairness pass this test" (p. 541).

———

Political discourse was not always so reticent about or mistrusting of the passions. One of the founding questions of sociology requires that one pay attention to the development of discourse on the passions: Max Weber, Ernst Simmel, R. H. Tawney, and others trace one of the political foundations of modernity to the transformation in the Church's attitude toward business, commerce, and banking. Put crudely, although not altogether falsely, avarice became transformed from one of the seven deadly sins into the foundation stone and guarantee of stability of the new social order. Alongside the thesis of religion and the rise of capitalism is the thesis of passion and the rise of capitalism.

One longstanding transformation of theology into political philosophy has regarded the passions as effects of external social and political arrangements, rather than as causes of these. As we have seen, Rawls thinks that a well-ordered society can reduce the general level of envy to manageable proportion. Or, to quote a much earlier example, from Winstanley in the 1640s: "I speak now in relation between the Oppressor and the oppressed; the inward bondages I meddle not with in this place, though I am assured that if it be rightly searched into, the inward bondages of minde, as covetousness, pride, hypocrisie, envy, sorrow, fears, desperation and madness, are all occasioned by the outward bondage, that one sort of people lay upon another."[44] The contrasting of inner with outer, of the passions with the social relation of oppression, is the radical twist on a millenarian theme. The passions are themselves the products of man's fall from grace, of his expulsion from Eden. The restoration of that Eden, in the form of equitable social relations, will bring a revolution in the inner world—freedom from the bondages of the passions.

It is also clear that these passions—Winstanley's covetousness, pride, hypocrisy, envy, sorrow, fears, desperation, and madness, Rawls's envy, anger, spite, jealousy, and rancor—overlap considerably with the Christian table of the seven deadly sins.[45] Elaborated gradually from the fourth century on, given some stability by Gregory the Great, the seven sins provided a way of organizing a discourse of the passions which subordinated worldly to eschatological concerns. Christianity always gave the discourse of the sins and thus of the passions an individualistic bent; one can see stark evidence of this in St. Augustine's conviction that one should never tell a lie, not even one that might save another person's life, since what did another person's earthly life count when put in the balance against the fate of one's own immortal soul?[46] Yet the revival of classical learning and its routinization in the universities allowed what came to be known as morals to fuse the Aristotelian study of practical philosophy—ethics, politics, and household management—with consideration of the passions in human affairs. More concretely, a less formal consideration of the foundations of politics did grow up within the courts of the European states, from Machiavelli onward.[47] And it was in the courts that the new moralism of the seventeenth century analyzed the place of the passions in a secular context.[48] The theory of the state came to depend upon a depiction of man as he really is.

In his stimulating essay entitled *The Passions and the Interests,* Hirschman has traced the development of the discourse of the passions into the theory of the interests from the late seventeenth century to the end of the eighteenth century. As well as being threats to one's state of grace, the passions were threats to political and moral stability. Hirschman outlines three theories within which the necessary controlling and disciplining of the unruly and dangerous passions were envisaged: first, their coercion and repression; second, their being harnessed, moderated, and refined by the action of civilization, of civil society; third, the principle of the countervailing passion, the idea that one of the passions becomes the principal ally of the social order in disciplining the others. Gradually, the general framework of benign passions being capable of molding and containing the malignant passions was developed. The court and salon societies which gave rise to the merciless dissection of human motivation by La Rochefoucauld, Nicole, and La Bruyère produced the conviction that self-love is the one founding and unshakeable passion.[49] As a more mercantile society became the frame of reference, self-love could become transformed into self-interest, which could be assayed as the stable element in the taxonomy of motives for human action. Marcel Mauss dates the introduction of the concept of individual interest to the turn of the eighteenth century, after Mandeville's *Fable of the Bees.*[50] And it was avarice, the love of money, the most constant and dogged of all passions, Dr. Johnson's "uniform and tractable vice,"[51] that could be granted the position of universal and perpetual passion, in contrast with envy and revenge, which, according to Hume, "operate only by intervals, and are directed against particular persons."[52]

Avarice and greed, the "calm desire of wealth,"[53] thereby became officially sanctioned, benevolent, and innocuous passions, the master passions with which anger and sloth, envy and pride could be tamed without recourse to religiously founded precepts. Hirschman dates the decline of the doctrine of the countervailing passion to Adam Smith's *Wealth of Nations,* which established a powerful economic justification for the untrammeled pursuit of individual self-interest, rather than the political and moral account that the story of the passions and the interests previously gave. Yet the search for an underlying master-principle that is universal, that is unifying, that is rationalizing, is characteristic of the nineteenth-century sociologies from the utilitarian calculus of pleasure and pain, via Marx to Weber, Durkheim, and the Frankfurt School. Tentatively, I would suggest that the key document here is the chapter on money in Marx's *Capital,* which demonstrates the way in which the specific qualities of things are transformed by the inner logic proper to money into quantity; we find its echoes in the internal logic of rationalization that Weber and Simmel perceive in modern society. What is eliminated—most conspicuously in the eighteenth-century mechanical algebra of utilities,[54] and in the rational decision theoretic calculations of "interests" developed and criticized by Elster[55]—is the specific color and force of the passions. The passions become epiphenomena, mere effects of the underlying shifts of interests, mere signs of conflicts and clashes of interests, particularly of different self-interests; or else they are privatized, and only retain their own character and flavor in the separate world of the family.

In the early Marx we find a further flourish of this transformation of passion into social principle, when he describes the bestial form that primitive communism, the ultimate generalization of the critique of private property, takes on when it attacks marriage as private property and turns women into communal property, "universal prostitution."

> This communism, inasmuch as it negates the *personality* of man in every sphere, is simply the logical expression of the private property which is this negation. Universal *envy* constituting itself as a power is the hidden form in which *greed* reasserts itself and

37

satisfies itself . . . in the form of envy and the desire to level everything down; hence these feelings in fact constitute the essence of competition. The crude communist is merely the culmination of this envy and desire to level down on the basis of a *preconceived minimum*.[56]

And it is in the family that Freud and Klein find them again. The archetypal scene of envy, remember, is of two children, one at the breast, the other looking on. Or, in the Freudian drama of the sexes, there is a girl who looks, sees, and is instantaneously seized by envy. Unlike the sociologists, however, psychoanalysis blithely takes no notice of the logic of money, or even of self-interest—although part of that concept's force is recaptured by psychoanalytic theory in the new principle of universal narcissism, albeit in a form which is much less easily assimilable to the arithmetic of financial self-interest. And this is why the social theory generated by psychoanalysis so often has an archaic tone to it. Quite clearly, psychoanalysis harks back to the eighteenth-century principle of the countervailing passion. The story of superego, ego, and id is a new morality play, in which one sin is pitted against another, one passion is subverted by another. For analysis, it takes the always passionate and vindictive superego to curb the unruly passions of envy and greed. The narcissistic pride of the ego can only be tempered by the fear of loss, itself akin to the *acedia* or withdrawal from connection to the world of the early Christian Fathers. "Anomie" might be the best modern translation for the sin of *acedia* (or sloth).[57] So, in the psychoanalytic morality play, it might well be the balance of pride and anomie that determines the true sources of moral action, while envy gives us justice.

Thus, if psychoanalysis can be said to contain a discourse of the passions, that discourse shares some similarities with the moral and political thought associated with the French moralists of the seventeenth century and with certain strands of "establishment" political theory of the Enlightenment, before the legitimation of capitalism and the stability of the social order could be attributed to the invisible hand of the money market. Freud and Nietzsche are on common ground here, seeking in a genealogy of the passions and the principle of the countervailing passion the only possible derivation of so-called higher principles, such as the concept of equal rights, of justice, or of a universalized morality such as "Love thine enemy." They would endorse Mandeville's vision of private vices being transformed into public benefits, and add that one should not expect people to be attached to such benefits without their private vices somehow being satisfied in the process.[58] In the conservative Freud and in Nietzsche, that "masterly debunker of our liberal fallacies"[59] as Auden called him, we find arguments concerning the origins of morality and society which bypass the structures arising out of the inner rationality of money. In particular, the passion of envy is the source of a society founded on the idea of justice and of individual rights.

Finally, we must return to the question of penis envy. Given the more general context I have now supplied for thinking about the concept of envy within psychoanalytic theory, it is possible that the criticisms of the theory of penis envy are as much directed at Freud's more general project of locating the cement of the social fabric and its institutions (such as the requirement of social justice) in the vicissitudes of the passions, in particular of envy, as they are against the image of the penis as the dominant symbol of the good, the achieved, the fulfilled. I want to make three final comments about this.

My first comment stems from this image of the full penis, the enviable penis. It is the envying subject who encounters this image of plenitude, who experiences impotence, that impotence that Max Scheler located as the source of envy, in the face of this image. The impotence or lack upon which this image in the other is founded is remarkably similar to the account of desire that we find in Lacan's work: the fundamental lack upon which desire is based, and the axiom that desire is always desire of the other.[60] Isn't this concept of desire remarkably like envy? The linking of envy, *envie*, and desire in Lacan's texts is clear in his early seminars:

At first, before language, desire exists solely in the single plane of the imaginary relation of the specular stage, projected, alienated in the other. The tension it provokes is then deprived of an outcome. That is to say that it has no other outcome—Hegel teaches us this—than the destruction of the other. The subject's desire can only be confirmed in this relation through a competition, through an absolute rivalry with the other, in view of the object towards which it is directed. And each time we get close, in a given subject, to this primitive alienation, the most radical aggression arises—the desire for the disappearance of the other in so far as he supports the subject's desire.[61]

If this near-identity of desire and envy is the case, then Freud's penis envy and Lacan's general formula of desire are one and the same. One might point out that this smoothing out of any distinction between envy and desire is made easier by the French language, in which *j'ai envie* means "I want, I desire"; but the structuration that Lacan gives to *désir* is precisely that which the German-speaking philosophers and analysts have given to *Neid* and those who speak English have given to "envy."

Second, I want to come back to Rawls's original position. The subject behind the veil of ignorance does not know anything about its attributes, nor about its position in society; remember, though, that the subject does possess its "own plan of life which is sufficient for itself" (p. 144). What kind of subject can this be, which has a self-sufficient plan of life? Can it, for instance—though I assure you that this is not an example taken at random—be a sexed subject in any sense that matters? Does it matter if it is a man or a woman who is behind the veil of ignorance? One fundamental constraint that Rawls was obliged to build into the original position was what he called the savings principle, which preserves justice between generations. The subjects behind the veil of ignorance might decide to favor their generation by refusing to consider the next generation; this problem, Rawls notes, "subjects any ethical theory to severe if not impossible tests" (p. 284). By fiat, Rawls demands that "no generation has stronger claims than any other . . . Thus imagining themselves to be fathers, say, [the persons in the original position] are to ascertain how much they should set aside for their sons by noting what they would believe themselves entitled to claim of their fathers" (p. 289). And, as with his discussion of envy, Rawls waves aside Herzen's and Kant's perplexity over the chronological unfairness of human history, whereby those who live later profit by the labor of their predecessors without paying the same price, by declaring: "This situation is unalterable, and so the question of justice does not arise" (p. 291).

But what if the original object of envy is intimately connected with this problem of the relation between generations, which Rawls solves with the "just savings principle"? What if we take our cue from Freud's well-known equation of feces = penis = baby? Feces fit very well with the just savings principle—as the accumulated results of past production and consumption, but also as money, that sediment of exchange which, as Rawl hopes, continually effaces its own history. The penis as I've portrayed it here, the full penis, the principle of fertility, was for Lacan the very emblem of generativity. And I do not need to emphasize that the baby is itself what we mean by future generativity. Thus we have, in the series feces = penis = baby, the past, present, and future of the object which connects the generations together and thus demands special treatment beyond the principles of justice.

The consequence of these remarks is the following. What if, instead of a neutered individual subject with a self-sufficient life plan, the Rawlsian subject behind the veil of ignorance is a son who envies the primal father his possession of all the women, or a girl who envies her brother's penis, or the mother of a dead baby? Let us grant them ignorance: this is a son who does not know to whom he owes his debt; a girl who does not know to what lack the presence of her envy/desire attests; a mother who does not know if her baby is alive or dead.[62] Each of these exemplary Freudian subjects is, as a virtual subject, the ruination of the Rawlsian scheme, since each would install envy behind the veil of ignorance. Yet each of them is a human subject whose specific attributes—the son, the girl, the mother—cannot be reduced down to the neutered, self-sufficient, individualistic subject without denying the very problem of the relation between generations which Rawls, in his honesty, recognizes must be solved. Behind Lacan's veil of Maya is always the phallus; behind the Rawlsian veil of ignorance there is a subject the object of whose envy is beyond the veil—perhaps on our side of this veil. I do not need to commit myself to Lacan's phallocentric ontology; it is sufficient to recognize that a live baby may be the object of envy.

Finally, I want to ask why the Freudian account of the derivation of the sense of justice from the passion of envy is regarded with such suspicion. Is the very idea of the countervailing passion, the idea that we are protected from one malignant passion by the force of another, an implausible one? I presume we all find plausible the idea that we can be shamed out of acting upon cruel impulses, or restrained by fear from making love to someone we love. Bear in mind the moral of the story, derived from early Teutonic law, of four brothers who take out a suit for recovery of a dowry against their widowed mother on account of her adultery. On hearing from the judge that their mother has agreed to admit to her adultery, and will also make known which of the brothers is the fruit of her adultery, the litigants agree to withdraw their suit.

Or is it, as Klein suspected, that we still hanker for some higher foundation for what we value in ourselves and our social worlds, something more like love than hate, something more like Adam Smith's "sympathy" or John Rawls's benevolence, something more worthy than envy or avarice? La Rochefoucauld noted that we are often proud of even the most criminal of our passions, "but envy is so cowardly and shameful a passion that we can never dare to acknowledge it."[63] To be noble is to be free of envy: "All the conspirators save only he / Did that they did in envy of great Caesar."[64]

There is one additional factor at work here. We may have become able to accept a base genealogy for religion and Christian morality; at the very least, the Freudian and Nietzschean critiques have habituated us to the idea that humility and brotherly love may be based on fear and resentment. But how relaxed are we about seeing our sense of justice based on envy? It seems that we are now accustomed to God being dead, but we would be reluctant to admit that social justice died from similar causes.

2

CASUALTIES OF TRUTH

Ne disons pas—*Autres moeurs que les nôtres,* disons: *Moeurs plus en honneur qu'aujourd'hui.*

Let us not say—*Other ways than ours,* rather: *Ways more honoured then than now.*

Charles Baudelaire, *Note sur Les Liaisons Dangereuses*

"Bereft of religion and betrayed by the spurious objectivity of so many sciences, the modern mind has found nothing so convincing as a science that is at the same time a casuistry of the intimate and everyday life."[1] Such is Philip Rieff's sketch of the appeal of psychoanalysis. Freud's science is a new middle way between knowledge and belief, between technique and ethics. The only imperative in the novel psychoanalytic ethos is the requirement of absolute honesty. "'Never forget that you have promised to be absolutely honest,'" Freud tells his patients, "'and never leave anything out because, for some reason or other, it is unpleasant to tell it.'"[2] There are no available opt-out clauses from this obligation: all names must be disclosed, the rights of third parties to privacy and discretion must be ignored:

> It is very remarkable how the whole task becomes impossible if a reservation is allowed at any single place. But we have only to reflect what would happen if the right of asylum existed at any one point in a town; how long would it be before all the riff-raff

[*Gesindel*] of the town had collected there? I once treated a high official who was bound by his oath of office not to communicate certain things because they were state secrets, and the analysis came to grief as a consequence of this restriction. Psycho-analytic treatment must disregard all such considerations, because the neurosis and its resistances are themselves so inconsiderate.[3]

Despite the stark social conservativism of Freud's choice of metaphor here, the period from 1905 to the Great War was undoubtedly the high point of Freud's liberal views both in sexual morality and in the extension of the psychoanalytic ethos of honesty to all cultural life. His important essay of 1908, "'Civilized' Sexual Morality and Modern Nervous Illness," ruthlessly exposed the hypocrisies—the wholesale lack of honesty—underpinning sexual morality: the Double Standard, the requirement that women bear the burden of concealing the unsatisfactory character of virtually all marriages. It was the tendency toward sexual moralism in the views of James Jackson Putnam, Freud's leading proponent in the United States, which elicited statements from Freud that leaned most clearly toward a libertarian sexual ethic. When Ernest Jones was required in 1913 to answer Putnam's queries about psychoanalysis and morality, Freud urged him in his quaint English not to give any ground: "I hope [you will engage in] no denial that our sympathies side with individual freedom and that we find no improvement in the strictness of american chastity. But you could remind him that advise plays no prominent part in our line of treatment and that we are glad to let everyman decide delicate questions to his own conscience and on his personal responsibility."[4] Again in 1915, Putnam elicited a radical response, this time directly from Freud: "Sexual morality—as society, in its most extreme form, the American, defines it—seems to me very contemptible. I advocate an incomparably freer sexual life, although I myself have made very little use of such freedom."[5]

"To talk now about sexual liberation seems cute, like talking about

45

the withering away of the state, or loving Great Literature,"[6] Adam Phillips writes. There is no doubt, however, that the historical destiny of psychoanalysis was bound up with the early twentieth century debates about sexual morality and sexual freedom. Freud negotiated his way through those debates with customary circumspection—that characteristic reluctance to venture beyond his own ground onto the ground of others, a reluctance born of a mixture of apprehension and calculation that told him no good would come to him or his science from any such trusting open-handedness. The doctrines of psychoanalysis—of the sexual etiology of the neuroses, of the poly-morphous perversity of children—pointed toward the toxic character of modern social arrangements. "It is one of the obvious social injustices that the standard of civilization should demand from every-one the same conduct of sexual life,"[7] Freud could write, putting the accent on the fundamental variety of men, women, and their sexual desires. But this diversity did not sanction sexual liberation and free-thinking licentiousness. Freud did not assent to that version of positivism which declares that what is natural is what is good. "If Freud takes side against culture, it is only for therapeutic purposes. He believed no more in instinct than in culture,"[8] Rieff observes accurately. It was the radical Freudians—Wittels, later Reich—who saw in psychoanalysis the scientific wing of that enthusiastic pro-claiming of utopia through sexual emancipation which has been a persistent current of twentieth-century social thought.

How curious it is, then, that the man closest to Freud during the crucial period in which psychoanalysis established itself as a scientific and international movement was an enthusiast for a society reformed on psychoanalytic principles, a proselytizer who unabashedly at-tempted, in the name of psychoanalysis, to convert a reluctant Freud to his vision of a society transformed by a generalized ethic of honesty. This close friend and colleague, Sándor Ferenczi, was the unexpected object of Freud's deep affection for two decades—a faithful affection as surprising in its way as that fateful precursor, Freud's love for Wilhelm Fliess in the 1890s. The eccentricities and implausibilities of Ferenczi's friendship with Freud have now been

46

much discussed: their collaborations and tussles over thought-trans-ference, over the variety of flexible psychoanalytic techniques that Ferenczi experimented with, over the biological speculations into which both of them were tempted by their psychoanalytic research. Yet the most sensitive episode of their relationship—Ferenczi's love-life and its intersection with his brief analysis with Freud—has not until recently been allowed to be given its due, owing to the remark-able sluggishness with which their voluminous correspondence has been published. With the publication of these letters, we can see more clearly the story of how Ferenczi and Freud bound together analysis, love, ethics, and knowledge.

Perhaps the key to their friendship is given in a basic character-trait, or libidinal position, of Ferenczi's. He was a man who fell in love with those to whom he told the truth. In this curious crisscross-ing of eros and knowledge, we catch an echo of that moment in the development of psychoanalysis when sexuality and knowledge were first intertwined, when a female patient withheld her secret and instead turned her passion to face the analyst. The intertwining and entangling of sex and knowledge is given the name of transference by all analysts, although it was Jacques Lacan who spelled out most clearly how transference involves three passions—love, hate, and knowledge—and that another name for the analyst in transference is the subject presumed to know.[9] With Ferenczi, Freud was introduced once again to the willful and enthusiastic confusion of love and truth. Whereas he accepted this complication, seemingly with reluctance, with his first patients in the 1890s, with Ferenczi he accepted it gladly and generously. The consequent interminable entangling of pleas-ures, misunderstandings, and disappointments in their friendship teaches us much about how psychoanalysis is situated in relation to love, truth, and ethics.

Freud's foremost Hungarian disciple, Sándor Ferenczi, was 34 when he first wrote to Freud in January 1908. They became friends quickly, Ferenczi always taking the position of the filial disciple whose privilege it was to be intimate with his master. Ferenczi also exercised the privilege of the disciple to take his master's ideas to what were in his view their logical conclusions and then to upbraid the master for his faintheartedness. Since Ferenczi believed that psychoanalysis as a world-view wiped out the boundary between the private and the professional, he soon came to challenge Freud about the limits that he perceived the older man imposed on friendship and psychoanalysis alike.

Perhaps not entirely coincidentally, the period 1908–1910 saw the crystallization of Freud's views on the close relation between paranoia and homosexuality.[10] Ferenczi was from the start a participant in the development of this theory—Freud's very first communications with Ferenczi had concerned a paranoid patient that Ferenczi asked him to see. In his reply to Ferenczi of February 1908, Freud had outlined for the first time his view that "it is a case of detaching the homosexual component of the libido."[11] A week later Freud shared this theory with Jung, with whom he had an intimate and trusting relationship dating from early 1907, but also revealed the source for this idea: "My one-time friend Fliess developed a dreadful case of paranoia after throwing off his affection for me, which was undoubtedly considerable. I owe this idea to him, i.e., to his behaviour. One must try to learn something from every experience."[12] Freud did not develop these ideas for publication as yet, but it is clear that he and Ferenczi discussed them often; their correspondence includes many scattered remarks, particularly on homosexuality, in the years 1908–1910. Thus both Ferenczi and Jung were early on made party to, as onlookers and disciples, Freud's attempt to show how the covert homosexuality of friendship could be turned into a theory of paranoia.

These were the honeymoon years of the friendship of Freud and Ferenczi, initiated in the summer of 1908 which Ferenczi spent with the Freud family at Berchtesgarten, when the thought certainly crossed Freud's mind of cementing his relationship with this favored disciple by marrying his eldest daughter, Mathilde, to him.[13] Ironically, Ferenczi and Mathilde did not conform to Freud's bourgeois fantasy of tying a young disciple by marriage into the family firm, but expressed that bond in the more Freudian mode of a friendship that included mutual analysis.[14] Given what was to happen later, one should underestimate neither Freud's willingness to mesh collegiality, friendship, and the bonds of marriage, nor Ferenczi's passive pride in being grateful for Freud's having wished him to become part of his family.[15] Though they were never to become father and son-in-law, their close collegial friendship was further cemented when Freud, Ferenczi, and Jung traveled to the United States together in the summer of 1909.

The three men were all equally knowing and equally coy about the homosexuality that bound them together—accepting as a matter of course that these homosexual bonds were of the greatest significance to them, without giving any sense of the actual content of their homosexual desires or fantasies. In April 1910 Ferenczi wrote to Freud: "one constantly vacillates back and forth between homosexual (public-communal) and (exclusive, private) heterosexual interests."[16] On the private side, the heterosexual side, Ferenczi placed his longstanding mistress, Gizella Pálos, a married woman with two grown daughters, Magda and Elma. Yet—and this is entirely characteristic of Ferenczi's inability and lack of desire to keep the private and the public separate—Gizella was Ferenczi's closest scientific colleague in Budapest. Ferenczi's letters to Freud in the period 1908–1911 grow ever fuller of his conversations with her, of her reading of his psychoanalytic writings, of her views on his patients.

Ferenczi, in fact, had considerable difficulty in liberating the public "homosexual" side of his life. In the period 1909–1912, his difficulties in working with colleagues and younger followers prevented him from the obvious next step of founding a Budapest Psychoanalytic Society. It was only when the anti-Jungian politics of Freud's international movement absolutely required affiliated societies of faithful Freudians that in 1913 Ferenczi, and following him later in the same year Jones, founded the Budapest and London

Psychoanalytical Societies.[17] But the more familiar index of this troubled "homosexual" side of Ferenczi's life is the convoluted father-son relationship that he developed with Freud, from the Palermo incident of the summer of 1910 onward. In this way, we see that Ferenczi's ideal relationship, which he hoped to develop both with Freud and with Gizella, was one in which the division between homo- and heterosexuality, between public and private, between scientific and erotic, was dissolved.

Unlike other women who became involved in the early days of the psychoanalytic movement, Gizella Pálos did not pass beyond the stage of the potent mixture of love and analysis to become an analyst in her own right. Nonetheless, like Sabina Spielrein, another of the women involved in intricate affective and intellectual relations with the early analysts, Gizella did make it clear that her attachment to psychoanalysis and to Freud was now deeper, in some sense, than her intimate relationship with her lover.

In July 1912, when Ferenczi felt he had lost her love through his own impulsive behavior, he wrote to Freud: "Frau G. wrote to me . . . that, even though she has lost me, she will eternally remain true to you and the cause."[18] Then in 1932, Ferenczi noted that she felt "attracted by the essence of psycho-analysis—trauma and reconstruction—but repelled by all analysts for the way they make use of it . . . She longs for an analyst who will be analytically as gifted as she is, who will be concerned above all with truth, but"—and what follows is Ferenczi's and possibly Gizella's criticism of Freud—"who will not only be scientifically true but also truthful regarding people."[19]

In contrast to Freud's broad range of female friendships and collaborations, Ferenczi's close intellectual relations with his mistress were to develop in an entirely different direction, in part because of his particularly enthusiastic and utopian reading of the value of psychoanalysis. Where Freud, with his courteous, intimate, yet always correct manner, found a way of making and retaining his sister-in-law Minna, Spielrein, and Lou Andreas-Salomé as colleagues, Ferenczi had, as we shall see, an altogether more ambitious conception of the values of psychoanalysis and the place of those values in the interweaving of science with sexual relations.

In the two primary relationships of his life in the period 1908–1911, those with Freud and Gizella Pálos, Ferenczi held up the absolute ideal of psychoanalytic sincerity to both his loved ones. The ideal first emerged as an ethical stance necessary to psychoanalytic practice: "no progress is possible in psychoanalysis without honesty."[20] Ferenczi went on to expound to Freud how the ideal and its realization tied him to Gizella, and in the process revealed his automatic assumption that one should make one's relations with intimates extensions of the psychoanalytic situation through the invocation of sincerity:

> As far as my feelings toward Frau Isolde [as he called her for a while] are concerned, I must say that the confession that I made to her, the superiority with which, after some reluctance, she correctly grasped the situation, and the truth which is possible between us makes it seem perhaps less possible for me to tie myself to another woman *in the long run* . . . Evidently I have *too much* in her: lover, friend, mother, and, in scientific matters, a pupil, i.e., the child—in addition, an extremely intelligent, enthusiastic pupil, who completely grasps the extent of the new knowledge.—Otherwise I am scientifically isolated.[21]

Three months later, in early 1910, Ferenczi's idealization of the relationship that psychoanalysis makes possible with the individual, personal other reached its peak. This time Freud was its target. In successive letters, Ferenczi lectured him on psychoanalytic honesty and its importance as a template for a transformation in human society:

> It is my unshakeable conviction, however, that these adherents [of psychoanalysis] are but the predecessors of all humanity.[22] . . . Once society has gone beyond the infantile, then hitherto com-

51

pletely unimagined possibilities for social and political life are opened up. Just think what it would mean if one *could tell everyone the truth,* one's father, teacher, neighbour, and even the king. All fabricated, imposed authority would go to the devil—what is *rightful* would remain natural. The eradication of lies from private and public life would necessarily *have to* bring about better conditions.[23]

It was with Gizella Pálos and Freud that Ferenczi attempted to realize this ideal. In a letter musing on his own thirty-seventh birthday and the inner revolution that Freud's "Ψ-analytic way of looking at things" had brought about in his inner life, Ferenczi wrote: "I believe that psychoanalytic honesty can be effected, not only among friends but also among life's companions of various genders. The analytic association with Frau G. is making decided progress, after at times overcoming very great resistances."[24] It is not clear if Ferenczi caught the ironic element in Freud's reply to this paean of praise for a life built around psychoanalysis: "I, too, gratefully acknowledge the elevation of life through psychoanalysis. A more complete view of life should certainly be based upon it. Now is not the time, in the fatigue of the end of the year."[25] The fatigue of the year was meant to be dissipated by the *Italienische Reise* that Ferenczi and Freud took together in September 1910.

In April 1910, Jung had told Freud enthusiastically about the *Memoirs of My Nervous Illness* written by Senatspräsident Schreber. With his Fliessian hypothesis about the homosexual root of paranoia ready to hand, Freud took the *Memoirs* on holiday with him when he and Ferenczi took off for a tour of Freud's beloved Italy that summer. Intending to work together on Schreber, Freud proposed that Ferenczi write down to Freud's dictation. Ferenczi refused, fearing that he would lose his independence and protesting against what he felt was Freud's too automatic assumption of intellectual ascendancy in the process of writing.[26] On every subsequent evening Freud worked on his own.

With this scene, which they subsequently called the incident at

Palermo, Freud dealt a crushing rebuff to Ferenczi's hopes of an equal and completely open relationship with him. Ferenczi would never forget the incident, and the two of them repeatedly referred to it in the coming decades, the younger man in particular trying to tease out the lessons he could learn from it.[27] The incident prompted Freud to write to Jung from Rome:

> My travelling companion is a dear fellow, but dreamy in a disturbing kind of way, and his attitude towards me is infantile. He never stops admiring me, which I don't like, and is probably sharply critical of me in his unconscious when I am taking it easy. He has been too passive and receptive, letting everything be done for him like a woman, and I really haven't got enough homosexuality in me to accept him as one. These trips arouse a great longing for a real woman. A number of scientific notions I brought with me have combined to form a paper on paranoia.[28]

Once back in Vienna, Freud confessed to Ferenczi that "I would have wished for you to tear yourself away from the infantile role and take your place next to me as a companion with equal rights . . . and that you had carried out more reliably your part of the task, the orientation in space and temporality. But you were inhibited and dreamy. So much for my educational efforts."[29] Ferenczi protested that he had felt forced back by Freud into the infantile role. He did admit that "I did, perhaps, have an exaggerated idea of companionship between two men who tell each other the truth *unrelentingly,* sacrificing all consideration."[30] Ferenczi aggressively insisted that this objective was not one that Freud could refuse:

> My ideal of truth that strikes down all consideration is certainly nothing less than the most self-evident consequence of your teachings . . . You once told me that ψA was only a science of facts, of indicatives that should not be translated into imperatives—the latter are paranoid. According to this conception there is no ψα worldview, no ψα ethics, no ψα rules of conduct . . . I believe that

you underestimate much too much the ennobling power of psychoanalysis if you don't believe that it makes people who have completely grasped its meaning absolutely worthy of trust.[31]

Freud's reply declined this invitation to be cast as the "psychoanalytic superman" that Ferenczi wished him to be. In his defense, Freud pointed to the countertransference which he had not surmounted and which, he implied, he did not *wish to* surmount: "I have not overcome the countertransference. I couldn't do it, just as I can't do it with my three sons, because I like them and I feel compassion for them in the process."[32] As so often, Freud attempted to set limits on the necessity, let alone the desirability, of psychoanalysis. But he argued further that it was the *success* of his analysis rather than its insufficiency that took him beyond Ferenczi's ideal of honesty and openness:

> Not only have you noticed that I no *longer* have any need for that full opening of my personality, but you have also understood it and correctly returned to its traumatic cause. Why did you thus make a point of it? This need has been extinguished in me since Fliess's case, with the overcoming of which you just saw me occupied. A piece of homosexual investment has been withdrawn and utilized for the enlargement of my own ego. I have succeeded where the paranoiac fails.[33]

Ferenczi's need for openness and equality, Freud implied, was due to his incompletely mastered homosexuality. In this argument Freud was opposing to Ferenczi's ideal of analytic honesty penetrating all spheres of life his own version of such interpenetration. The limitations of his relationship with Ferenczi were the fruit of his experience with Fliess, which, in the form of the piece on Schreber, he had been asking Ferenczi to write down. It was as if Freud had asked his new lover to scribe a final adieu to the old lover, an adieu which promised that he would never again love anyone the way he had loved him. No doubt Ferenczi understood this interpenetration of the

Fliess affair and the Schreber theory, since he had been in on it at the beginning. Freud underlined it for him, just in case he had missed the point: "My dreams at the time were, as I indicated to you, entirely concerned with the Fliess matter, with which, owing to the nature of the thing, it was difficult to get you to sympathize."[34]

Good-humoredly and half-seriously reasserting the claims of psychoanalysis, Ferenczi, "an incorrigible therapist"[35] as he called himself, replied by offering Freud his services as an analyst. Again he insisted on his ideal of honesty: "I do not wish to give up hope that you will let a part of your withdrawn homosexual libido be refloated and bring more sympathy to bear toward my 'ideal of honesty.'"[36] Freud did not take up Ferenczi's offer; instead, he continued writing his analysis of Schreber in the autumn of 1910, announcing in early December to Ferenczi that he had overcome an error that was holding him back in Palermo, so that by 16 December he could tell him: "I have now overcome Fliess"[37]—in other words, he had completed his Schreber case.[38]

In the course of the growing friendship between the two men, we find a clear statement by Freud of his differing view of the ethical questions raised by psychoanalytic knowledge in its relation to sexual relations. As a statement, it amounted to an intervention—the first of many—in Ferenczi's relationship with Gizella. It came in January 1910, before the Palermo incident, as the surge in Ferenczi's enthusiasm for the social and personal transformations to be expected from psychoanalytic honesty was beginning to mount. In a letter that has not survived, Ferenczi had recounted to Freud how he confessed to Gizella his sexual relationships with other women as well as certain impulses for which she reproached him. Here is how Freud commented on Ferenczi's attempt at a completely honest erotic relationship:

> As to what is real, I have to say that you were by and large undoubtedly correct with your disclosure to the beloved woman. It belongs to the ABC of our worldview that the sexual life of a

man can be something different from that of a woman, and it is only a sign of respect when one does not conceal this from a woman. Whether the requirement of absolute truthfulness does not sin against the postulate of expediency and against the intentions of love I would not like to respond to in the negative without qualification, and I urge caution. Truth is only the absolute goal of science, but love is a goal of life which is totally independent of science, and conflicts between both of these major powers are certainly quite conceivable. I see no necessity for principled and regular subordination of one to the other.[39]

Freud juxtaposed two great principles: science and love. In science, truth is the highest value; not so in love, which can be quite independent of truth. For Ferenczi, the value of truth overflowed from psychoanalysis into life. Such an intermingling would be to the benefit of both. In contrast, Freud separated the honesty that psychoanalytic science requires from the demands that love makes. In life, but not in science, truth may of necessity fall victim to the more pressing demands of love. To put it another way: Why make love, the most important thing in life, the victim of truth's callous disregard for human beings?

The difference of attitude between Freud and Ferenczi can be highlighted by considering the behavior of Freud in the early 1880s. Then, the young Freud craved the same truthfulness, the same tyranny of honesty, of himself and his fiancée Martha as Ferenczi was to demand of the whole of post-psychoanalytic society.[40] Early in their engagement, Freud had made clear to Martha what the stakes were: "It would be a ghastly loss for us both if I were compelled to decide to love you as a dear girl, yet not as an equal, someone from whom I would have to hide my thoughts and opinions—in short, the truth."[41] On another occasion, in the exhausting final months of that long engagement, the young Freud had repeated the theme—he would not sacrifice the requirements of honesty to the necessities of relations between the sexes, for fear of the consequences of departing from the narrow path of truth that was the only guarantee of a secure love: "I have always been frank with you, haven't I? I haven't made use of the licence usually granted to a person of the other sex—of showing you my best side. For a long, long time I have criticised you and picked you to pieces, and the result of it all is that I want nothing but to have you and have you just as you are."[42] Thus the young Freud was certainly as passionate a devotee of the absolute demands made by the goddess Veritas as Ferenczi was later to be. Had Freud acquired greater wisdom by 1910, when he gave his advice to Ferenczi? Is love of truth only a young man's infatuation? Or was it simply that he was no longer in the thrall of a passionate relationship, either with a woman or with psychoanalysis? In his relationship with Gizella, Ferenczi wished to live out the truth of psychoanalysis, to live his personal life in the blinding light of truth. He dreamed of creating a family which embodied psychoanalysis, one which was a perpetual psychoanalysis.

The Palermo incident undoubtedly constituted a setback to this ideal. The beginning of 1911 brought another warning note of what was to complicate this ideal. Ferenczi asked Freud to give advice to Gizella concerning her 24-year-old daughter Elma's "marriage and love affairs"; Ferenczi confessed that "I'm much too involved to be able to judge and act entirely coolly."[43] Despite these misgivings, Ferenczi took Elma into analysis in the early summer of 1911. In November, he belatedly confessed to Freud that he was more and more under the sway of fantasies of marriage with Elma, fantasies which had first emerged consciously in the spring of 1911.[44] Defiantly, in what he himself called his "letter of rebellion," he spelled out how his recent withdrawal from Freud and Gizella was his attempt at independence. Freud's response to Ferenczi, calling on him to discipline himself, probably did not help very much: "I would rather have an independent friend, but if you make such difficulties, I have to accept you as a son."[45] In two letters, in "fatherly speech"[46] designed to calm Ferenczi down, Freud addressed Ferenczi as "Dear son."

Events were now moving fast. Ferenczi found he could no longer represent his intimacy with Elma as either "the benevolence of the physician or of the fatherly friend."[47] What had aroused him most in Elma was her distress following the suicide in October 1911 of the most serious of her numerous suitors: "she badly needed someone to support her and to *help* her in her need."[48] But her needs had always been evident; what was pressing forward from its previous latency was Ferenczi's own need—"You know me, my wish for a family"[49]—which, he realized very quickly, was a "realization of the family romance."[50] It should be noted that for Ferenczi, the eighth of twelve children, this took the form of possession of his mother and sister together—"he is automatically swinging from his mother to his sister, as was once the case in his earliest years,"[51] Freud later wrote to Gizella. Something of his own: love, happiness, youth—and a baby. Freud ordered Ferenczi to break off Elma's analysis and come to Vienna. Ferenczi obeyed. After the two men had discussed the unfolding family drama and Ferenczi had returned to Budapest, Gizella asked Freud for an explanation of how things stood.

Freud opened the letter he wrote to Gizella by reminding her of Ferenczi's plight: attached to a woman too old to bear children, yet a woman of the highest quality in whom "he possessed incomparably more than what he had renounced."[52] With dramatic effect, Freud adopted the candid tones of an old gentleman—"I understand the tragedy of ageing; it is, after all, mine as well"[53]—addressing himself to an old lady: "The hard truth is that love is only for youth and that one must renounce; as a woman, one must be prepared to see one's sacrifices repaid with ingratitude. No reproach for the individual, a natural fate, as in the story of Oedipus."[54]

Even the 48-year-old Gizella might have felt that Freud was stretching things somewhat when he identified her with Jocasta and asked her to recognize the tragedy of Oedipus and Jocasta as a natural fatality that was hers—as if Antigone had been the seducer of Oedipus. Yet Freud was recommending to Gizella that she retire in favor of her daughter, and thus make Jocasta's family romance come true; he had already written in *The Interpretation of Dreams:*

> Occasions for conflict between a daughter and her mother arise when the daughter begins to grow up and long for sexual liberty, but finds herself under her mother's tutelage; while the mother, on the other hand, is warned by her daughter's growth that the time has come when she herself must abandon her claims to sexual satisfaction.[55]

So, having placed himself and Gizella as the old father and mother, just as Ferenczi had done in his letter of rebellion of the previous month, Freud could then position Ferenczi and Elma as the children, the young ones. To be precise, they were cast as brother and sister, both abandoning the mother for each other. He informed Gizella that his advice to Ferenczi had been quite tough-minded: "One has to leave the poor mother to her twofold suffering"[56]—the loss of both her lover and her daughter. Abandoning the older woman for the younger is, Freud implied, in the nature of things. On this score, Ferenczi's union with Elma had received a clear green light from Freud.

Before asserting the necessity of Gizella's pain, Freud had painted the scene in the following colors: "If it had been the case that the girl had fallen in love with her mother's youthful friend, pined for him, and suffered in the process until both of the others discovered the secret, it would have been a beautiful novel with a touching conclusion, as so often happens in real life; but neurosis would not have been allowed to play any role in it."[57] This scene is an entirely common, perhaps even a healthy one. It is certainly a classic scene of Freud's life and his epoch: the young man, uncertain of his choice between mother and daughter, a division that also intersects with that other axis, of sensuality and affection, of whore and mother, whose portrait Freud had painted two years previously in "A special type of object-choice made by men."[58] It is the key axis along which Freud's own adolescent passion for Gizella Fluss, which was recounted in his paper on "Screen-memories," had run: the 16-year-old Freud confessed that "it seems that I have transferred my esteem for the mother to friendship for the daughter . . . I am full of admiration for this woman whom none of her children can fully match."[59] Freud was to cast this slippage between the generations of mother and daughter in epic and theoretical mode in his final account of femininity, in the *New Introductory Lectures;* the fact of a man's love and a woman's love being a phase apart psychologically is to be attributed to the identification of a woman with her mother: "It is in this identification [with her own mother] too that she acquires her attractiveness to a man, whose Oedipus attachment to his mother it kindles into passion."[60]

Freud could also evoke the relation of mother and daughter strictly from the female point of view, in which case it became a ceaseless struggle, as in the case of paranoia in a woman that he described in 1915, a few years after the surfacing of the Gizella-Elma crisis:

> When a mother hinders or arrests a daughter's sexual activity, she is fulfilling a normal function whose lines are laid down by events in childhood, which has powerful, unconscious motives, and has received the sanction of society. It is the daughter's business to emancipate herself from this influence and to decide for herself on broad and rational grounds what her share of enjoyment or denial of sexual pleasure shall be. If in the attempt to emancipate herself she falls a victim to a neurosis it implies the presence of a mother-complex which is as a rule over-powerful, and is certainly unmastered.[61]

There was also, in another case, the interesting and surprising solution found by the female homosexual who retired in favor of her own mother, leaving the field of men entirely to her mother.[62]

Freud's letter to Gizella paints the scene of the young friend of the mature woman becoming the object of the daughter's secret desire as an altogether common state of affairs; the problem that requires addressing is the neurotic elements to be found on both sides, the man's and the daughter's. The man has persistently oscillated between mother and sister, Freud points out, so a single course of action is to be recommended: all parties should *wait*. The man will then discover if anything is left over once the displacement from mother to sister has been recognized and discounted;[63] the daughter will find out, through waiting, if she can put up with abstinence, if she can control her own bodily sensations. "If everything goes well, one can then venture to build the new reality on the old fantasies."[64] She—and the analytic observers—will also then establish if she wants anything more than to "repress her mother."[65] So the advice Freud had given everyone was: wait. For some of the parties, for Elma and implicitly for Ferenczi, this waiting would constitute a frustration, a quasi-analytic ploy, no doubt designed to produce regression. For others, in particular Gizella, this was the waiting that would bring mastery, if not victory. This is not the moment, Freud implied, for the lion to make its one spring.

Gizella did not have long to wait. According to Ferenczi, writing to Freud the day after Freud had written to Gizella: "Marriage with Elma seems to be decided. What is still missing is the fatherly blessing."[66] Did Ferenczi mean only the blessing of Elma's father, or was he seeking Freud's blessing as well? The paternal blessing certainly was not forthcoming from the psychoanalytic father in Vienna: "I have no more to say, perhaps I have said more than was justified, and I don't want to spoil your future completely."[67] It was the verdict of the real father, Géza Pálos, which—surprisingly, given his complete absence from the rest of the first volume of the Freud-Ferenczi correspondence—proved to be the real turning point:

At the last minute, when the already completed plan was presented to Elma's father, he made a few hesitant objections by alluding to Elma's earlier engagement, which had been called off a few years ago. At that, to my amazement, certain doubts crept into *Elma's* mind. That made me suspicious. I inquired further and learned from her (what I certainly should have learned in her analysis) that *every time* she wishes something especially strongly, she inwardly feels an inability to wish (as well as to hate) without reservation. *That* always made her so unhappy . . . But the scales fell from my eyes, and when, even after this scene, her presence did not fail to arouse feelings of tenderness in me, I had to recognize that the issue here should be one not of marriage but of the treatment of an illness. Of course, I myself cannot continue the treatment. After many bitter tears (which certainly had partly to do with her own fate) she consented to go to Vienna and enter treatment with you.[68]

Elma's father, who figured throughout the years of Ferenczi's correspondence with Freud only as a ghost, the phantom husband of Ferenczi's mistress, of superficially little significance for their emotional lives, produced an intervention that, judged by its effect on the "patient," was fully the equal of any interpretation of Ferenczi's, the young woman's analyst.

Freud replied that, if Ferenczi insisted, then of course he would accept Elma as a patient; but he was skeptical as to the wisdom of this course of action: "Just imagine under what unfavourable auspices I am supposed to begin. After withdrawing the bonus that can spur her on to recovery, with the knowledge that I was not in sympathy with her intentions, and with the vague desire for revenge against you, the one who is sending her into this treatment! Was ever woman in this humour woo'd?"[69] With this allusion to Shakespeare's *Richard III*, Freud delineates two noteworthy aspects of the analytic problem he was faced with. Richard, Duke of Gloucester, encounters Anne, whose husband, Prince Edward, and father-in-law, Henry VI, he has recently murdered. He sets about the task of courting her, so as to make her his wife. He is famously and, some have thought, implausibly successful. She leaves the stage and, with utter contempt for her, Richard reflects on the unlikely success of his seduction:

62

Was ever woman in this humour wooed?
Was ever woman in this humour won?
I'll have her, but I will not keep her long.
What! I, that killed her husband and her father,
To take her in her heart's extremest hate,
With curses in her mouth, tears in her eyes,
The bleeding witness of her hatred by—
Having God, her conscience, and these bars against me,
And I nothing to back my suit at all
But the plain Devil and dissembling looks,
And yet to win her, all the world to nothing!
Ha![70]

Clearly Freud's first response was to place himself in Elma's shoes and reflect: "if I were she, I would view being sent to Freud for analysis as equivalent to being sent to a man who has killed my husband and my father." And the job of the analyst will then inevitably be to seduce this woman. In other words, psychoanalysis, Freud assumes, is always simultaneously the site of seduction and the cause of the prohibitions and restrictions that hamper the subject as she or he enters it. In reality, it is Ferenczi and her father who are placing conditions on Elma's marriage; but once she reaches the analytic demolition-site in Vienna, she will make the analyst the immediate source of all these prohibitions.

It is striking that Freud at no point considered Ferenczi's request for him to analyze Elma as illicit or transgressive. Nor had he counseled Ferenczi against his earlier analysis of the daughter of his lover. In other words, Freud did not conceive of there being ethical conditions which bound or constrain decisions concerning analysis. We know that he certainly did not see such conditions as hampering his decision, some years later, to analyze his own daughter. In the case of Elma, what gave him pause for thought was rather the inauspicious *technical* circumstances of the case: he would be obliged to emulate the technical feats of Richard III, to emulate the technical prowess of a seducer. But his readiness to produce the literary model that fits the particular case—even when that model casts him as a man who, precisely because he has "nothing to back my suit at all / But the plain Devil and dissembling looks," feels justified in stopping at nothing in games of love and war[71]—shows just how far Freud was willing to push his thoroughly technical or pragmatic conception of analytic work.

Ferenczi, in counterpoint, assumed that he could use Freud's analytic technique in the way certain modern couples on the eve of their marriages use genetic testing laboratories: as an objective test of the aptness of the marriage. If there is something mysterious, unclear, unsettling in the chemistry of love, then one has recourse to a scientific laboratory to resolve the question. Once again, Ferenczi mixed, enthusiastically and indiscriminately, science and love.

So, at Ferenczi's insistence, Freud stepped into the seemingly unpropitious shoes of Richard III, and set out to seduce the young Elma. Just as for Richard in Shakespeare's play, the task did not turn out to be anywhere near as difficult as one might, taking things at face value, have expected. The center of Elma's psychic life was her early love of her father and his subsequent neglect of her, which then manifested itself in her "yearning to show herself naked, the sexual curiosity to see something male . . . She falls in love compulsively with doctors, i.e. with persons who see her naked, physically, and now mentally."[72] So the problem of resistance stemmed primarily from her wanting to be loved, wanting to be a good patient. After two months, Freud was satisfied that he had surmounted this feature of her paternal complex: "We are really in the narcissistic stage in which she behaves very self-sufficiently and actually refuses help. She is now herself . . . She no longer plays the part of the good patient at all."[73] A few weeks later, however, he had made no further progress with the murky question of her narcissism—"she doesn't want to get into the experience with you [Ferenczi] and doesn't seem to want to finish with me; i.e. because of the transference she wishes to extend her stay past Easter, which I don't want to do. So I am cooling off noticeably again."[74] Freud had his way; Elma returned to her mother and Ferenczi in April.

The strangest version of Ferenczi's psychoanalytic family now took shape:

> I also told her [Elma] candidly that Frau G. is indispensable to me as a friend and co-worker and that I have in her everything that I need, except for the youth which I had to seek in her (Elma).
>
> On the following evenings I was constantly in the company of both of them and was striving to establish the basis for a comfortable and harmonious life together . . . If *she* [Gizella] gives me to Elma and Elma to me, this marriage would seem to her to be the most beautiful and harmonious solution for the future.[75]

A further report indicates the division of labor the two women devised:

> I am spending my evenings with Frau G. and Elma and am attempting to live together experimentally, in a threesome, as it were. Elma is showing me her newly acquired mastery in the art of cooking and is using every opportunity that comes along to be tender with me; I am also friendly and loving toward her. I am conversing with Frau G. about scientific matters—Elma also listens, seems interested, and now and then makes some quite good remarks—of course, without that enthusiastic joy of recognition that Frau G. typifies.[76]

Elma was evidently Ferenczi's breeding stock. But the kaleidoscope of emotional positions soon changed again: Ferenczi grew stern. Ferenczi had taken Elma back into analysis in April 1912, using the threat of breaking off the engagement definitively as the stick with which "to educate Elma to freedom of speech with the aid of analysis."[77] His transformation of that haven of freedom and honesty, the analytic hour, into a workhouse where she should prove her virtues as a potential wife, became even more clear-cut: "If I were successful in educating her to be ruthlessly honest with me and with respect to herself, I would then have a certain guarantee that she will be reliable in marriage and not the plaything of dark drives, and then something could still come of the matter."[78] The cruelest moment in this analytic minuet came in August 1912. As a result of his incessant pressure, it became crystal clear to Ferenczi that

> she is subjecting herself to analysis against her will, solely because of her hoped-for and impatiently anticipated marriage, and her tendency is to withhold from analysis everything that might impede this plan. I explained . . . to her that under these circumstances, analysis was pointless. At the same time I made it comprehensible to her that the affective relations between doctor and patient usually fall victim to the analysis, so that the prospects for a marital union between us were minimal, even in the event that the analysis should continue. I told her at the same time that, if she comes to me as a *patient*, I will always gladly be at her disposal.—
>
> I did this with somnambulistic certainty, paying no heed to the painful uproar inside me.
>
> Elma was in despair; I accompanied her home and handed her over to her mother. Since then I haven't seen her; yesterday I heard from Frau G. that she had not yet recovered and is affirming her unchanged predilection for me.[79]

Freud's response was, as it had been for several months, laconic: "if in doubt, refrain."[80]

Ferenczi was never to make a definitive break with this triangular arrangement, this *folie à trois*. In May 1913, he reported to Freud how the separate members of the triangle had taken on very different roles, but the structure was still intact:

> As far as my psychic hygiene is concerned, the matter is as follows: I repeatedly tried to satisfy my erotic needs "outside," but (perhaps because of the inferiority of the material) with the sole result that

I quickly returned to Frau G. But Frau G. is, incidentally, working tirelessly on restoring relations between me and Elma. Up to now I have been resisting energetically. Elma herself is behaving well, rationally; according to Frau G. she is secretly longing for me, but remains silent and is "sponsoring" us (me and Frau G.), as it were.[81]

Elma, like Ferenczi, was making attempts to break away: she obviously wanted to get married at any price. At the end of October, she was preparing to pay a visit to Freud, to discuss her proposed marriage to a Viennese industrialist; Ferenczi had already given her his "permission." However, she did not marry this man, but instead became engaged to a Swedish-American journalist and writer, Hervé Laurvik, whom she did eventually marry in September 1914. Throughout the year of 1913, and virtually until her daughter's marriage date, Gizella "tirelessly championed Elma's cause . . . she sees in it the only possible and—as she says—favourable solution for all of us."[82] Clearly Gizella had not managed to "restrain the tender mother,"[83] as Freud had advised her to at the end of his letter of December 1911: she was firmly convinced that the path to her children's happiness, and her own, lay in the marriage of her lover to her daughter, and in her eternal control over them, whether as dual mother or "lover-in-law" *(belle amante)*.

As Freud suspected, once the *ménage à trois* had been established there was only one way to find satisfaction, and that was to escape from it. He had recommended as much to Ferenczi, but it was only Elma who appeared to have found a way to freedom. Meanwhile, Ferenczi had succumbed to a variety of physical illnesses, which, he reflected, served very well his need to tie Gizella back to him. Perhaps Ferenczi, like Ernest Jones, needed to have his women sacrificed, like a propitiatory offering, on the altar of Freud's couch, before he was ready to undertake an analysis himself.[84] Be that as it may, his first explicit demand to Freud for analysis came in December 1912.[85] And that analysis took place in three short, intense bursts, first in September 1914, then in June and July of 1916, and finally over two weeks in the autumn of 1916, bringing it to an end (by which "I [Freud] did not mean it was terminated").[86]

But neither Elma's marriage nor Ferenczi's analysis with Freud fundamentally altered matters.[87] "The double bond, *Frau G.* and *Elma,* has still not been dissolved in my unconscious fantasy,"[88] he wrote to Freud at the end of 1915. Whatever the cause—the increasingly lengthy duration of Ferenczi's attachment to Gizella, the sapping of Ferenczi's physical health through the psychosomatic complaints in which his indecision expressed itself, or the filling in of a transferential role that Freud could not shake off—Freud's impatience over Ferenczi's dithering was now sharply and consistently expressed. "So, act now, as swiftly and decisively as possible, and refrain from analysis now, or treat it as an extra enjoyment without real influence."[89]

Ferenczi went through the motions of decisive action, only to be rebuffed by Gizella's indecision. She wished to postpone any decision until Elma's return from America: "she promised to take her if she (Elma) didn't feel happy in marriage."[90] Ferenczi also wished to be free of Freud's influence in the matter of the decision, with its echoes of the Palermo incident, when he had refused to work with Freud for fear of coming too much under his influence and losing his independence of thought and judgment.[91] Again and again, Ferenczi's bodily ailments came between him and a clear view of his desire for Gizella. Freud responded sniffily and gruffly: "One must be able to decide whether one loves a woman or not even with stuffed-up nostrils. Of course, I know how difficult it is to differentiate between the psychic and the somatic in one's own person."[92]

The second section of Ferenczi's analysis occurred in June and early July of 1916. The question of his decision about marriage to Gizella was clearly central to these three weeks, which Ferenczi declared to be "the decisive ones in my life and for my life . . . Today I said to Gisella[93] that I have become another person, one who is less interesting but more normal."[94] But Gizella's position had not changed: she still wished to defer any decision till the return of her prodigal daughter from America. Once again, as in December 1911, she wrote to Freud to secure his advice on whether she was right or wrong to wait. Freud's reply purported to be itself indecisive about what advice to offer. But it contained a trenchant analysis:

> Are you thinking of waiting a half or 3/4 year longer, after one has already waited such long years, and for what? For this same daughter, who has already placed herself between the both of you and will do this immediately again both by her own will and by the consent of both of you. Does that mean something other than hiding the no behind a postponement, which will perhaps lead to a new motivation for the no?[95]

Having translated her desire to wait for Elma as a "no," he tried to divine her motive: "I am not unaware of the fact that you are simply propagating a role which your counterpart has, to your sorrow, conducted against you, and that such revenge is psychologically completely justified."[96]

Freud did make it clear that he had been working on Gizella's behalf for years:

> After containing myself for years with regard to our friend, I have finally come forward with advice, because I believe in the meantime to have arrived at the conviction that there is no other possibility, and because I am in general disposed to believe in the imminent end of all things—youth among them. Now I am becoming frightened and would still not like to have advised anything. Not out of cowardice about taking responsibility, but because I feel uncertain and am naturally much too engaged to be able to judge without error what is best.[97]

But he also did not overlook the necessity of including Elma in the equation, which he now felt was too complicated for him to solve: "Fate has tied a knot with Elma which someone on the outside will have difficulty loosening."[98]

In the period 1911–1912, it had looked as if Ferenczi was abandoning Gizella in pursuit of "youth (Elma, fertility, the blessing of children together)."[99] But from 1912 onward, it was Gizella who was convinced that happiness could be secured for her daughter by marriage to Ferenczi—perhaps in accordance with the model provided by Ferenczi's younger brother, who had married her younger daughter, Magda, a few years before Ferenczi fell in love with Elma.[100] Once Ferenczi had plucked up his courage and proposed to Gizella in the years 1916 and 1917, she persistently put him off with the excuse of Elma, intermittently raising the possibility that Elma's now decidedly unhappy marriage could be rectified with the revival of the plan to marry Ferenczi to Elma. Freud's letter to her seemed to have little effect, just as his various bits of advice to Ferenczi over the years had had little effect on him. Now it was Ferenczi's turn to insist on a decision from Gizella: "The resolute tone from yesterday in which I spoke to Gizella has had its effect. A crisis seems to be playing itself out in her, which says: finally to choose between me and Elma. More precisely: to give up the neurotic pampering— almost worshiping—of Elma (who did deceive her in concert with me) and to take cognizance of her real interests."[101]

This state of affairs—persisting after the final termination of Ferenczi's analysis in early October 1916—provoked Freud into his decisive and gruff tone, informing Ferenczi that it was quite evident that Ferenczi no longer wished to marry Gizella. Her reluctance to accept his proposal—which, Freud insisted, owed nothing to his influence over her—was unequivocal evidence that she saw this clearly as well.

Whether Ferenczi saw this or not, his response to the situation— before he received Freud's gruff letter—was to engage in that incestuous sexual activity which was the hallmark of his relation with Gizella—oddly enough, he called them his "compulsive attempts at flight"[102] when they were in reality innumerable ways of tying his bonds to this "family" even more tightly: "Yesterday afternoon— *before* receiving your letter—Saroltà [Gizella's sister] visited me in the matter of a theater ticket. I couldn't resist having my way with her, at least manually . . . That is typical of me. That's the way my actual neurosis before the trip to Rome began. I permitted myself intercourse with a prostitute—then with Saroltà—, the syphilopho-bia came as a punishment."[103] Gizella responded with her charac-teristic love and generosity—which others might have called altruistic surrender—to these events and their confession: "she finally made the suggestion that I should satisfy my sexuality elsewhere, only maintain friendship with her."[104]

Freud continued in his gruff and determined mood, insisting to Ferenczi that Gizella's refusal of the proposal of marriage, "which is definitely not neurotic,"[105] was now plain to see. Now determinedly convinced of the hopelessness of the plan for marriage, Freud in January 1917 spelled out to Gizella how he had done everything in his power to secure the marriage, but to no avail:

I have worked on the realization of this wish with the most varied means, directly and indirectly, in friendly intercourse and through analysis, carefully, so that my preambles would not produce recal-citrance in him, and with blunt demands, in order to bring my influence to bear. I have urged him to make himself free from you, as a test of whether he is capable of doing something else for himself, and then I referred him to you, after it became evident that he is incapable of doing without you and replacing you. I have really left nothing untried and have met with no success. Finally, I had to come out and tell him gruffly that he doesn't want to do anything decisive and that he is even misusing the analysis in order to conceal his no. It is not even a no; he just doesn't want to change anything, do anything, wait passively to see if something comes to his aid. Then this stupid, trifling, but nevertheless undeniable organic affliction, morbus Basedowi, came and has permitted him to free himself from the snare in which I was hoping to catch him. It troubles me deeply that he should have no more of you and of life than before. But I can do nothing.[106]

Was this a confession of failure, or one more turn of the wily analytic–cum–matchmaker's screw? Was rendering Freud entirely impotent the necessary condition for Ferenczi's and Gizella's marriage? One might have thought that these blunt letters to Gizella would have remained confidential, kept between Gizella and Freud. But Gizella refused to play at being the elderly wise parent that Freud always assumed she was (a woman of practically the same age as his own wife, Martha). She always showed his letters to Ferenczi: Freud would have done better to bet on the ethic of honesty with which Ferenczi always conducted his affairs with Gizella. Seemingly disconcerted, he wrote to Gizella in February 1917: "My last letter to you was meant for you only; it was too straightforward for him."[107] But was this also a ploy of Freud's? Was this transparent attempt to take sides with Gizella in her "non-neurotic" refusal of marriage and thus to separate her from Ferenczi the last twist in his scheme to force Ferenczi into an independent decision?

Ferenczi had certainly thought so in November 1916: "Naturally I thought (with the malicious distrust of all analysands) that it was a trick on your part when you gave your definitive view of my relationship with Gizella. You wanted to free me from the suggestive influence of your earlier view (to marry G.), so that I can decide freely."[108] But in early 1917, the news of Freud's determined detachment from all his cunning plans—and apparent despair at their ruin—seems to have had a different effect on Ferenczi. In a final twist, with an analytic joke that made fun of all Freud's protestations about his analytic and paternal neutrality, Ferenczi asked Freud to use his influence on Gizella so that she would accept his proposal of marriage. Ferenczi asked Freud, "the only authority in this matter," to explain to Gizella what her unconscious motives were for delaying her answer by "citing, upon Elma's return, the possibility that I would again fall in love with her (Elma)."[109] In other words, Ferenczi wished Freud to propose to Gizella on his behalf: "So, after so many aberrations, I return to where I have inwardly never gotten away from; even the fact that I want to get Frau G. by way of your mediation seems to have a symbolic significance."[110] Just as in December 1911, when Ferenczi asked Freud to accept Elma into analysis, Freud could not refuse this request: "Your will be done. I will write to Frau G. and will ask her not to hide her decision behind considerations for Elma, but I can't vouch for the outcome."[111]

It is moments such as this one, with Freud required by the bonds of friendship to consummate the function of analyst and friend by acting as amorous go-between, which make so plausible Jean Allouch's reading of the Freud/Ferenczi correspondence as an extended libertinage, as exemplified by the epistolary licentiousness of *Les Liaisons Dangereuses.* Allouch asks, is there any analysis in this relationship? Or is this just an extended seduction and exercise of transgressive free-thinking, with Freud cast as Madame de Meurteuil, the self-made woman who constructs her own ethical principles?

> The appearance of psychoanalysis gave rise, at the beginning of the twentieth century, to something akin to a return of a particular libertinage, one that was perhaps less daring than that of its great epoch in the eighteenth century, a libertinage which, in any case, does not identify itself as such but which is already recognizable (over and beyond the return of the epistolary novel) in the seesawing between analytic couch and bed . . . The trait by which we immediately recognize its libertine character is that, whatever happens, Ferenczi makes sure to keep Freud abreast of events in writing.[112]

Whether one can, as Allouch supposes, distinguish between libertinage and analysis is akin to supposing that one can distinguish between incest, family romance, and their analysis—between remembering and acting out, between transference and non-transference, between real and imaginary, between speech and action. Whether one can or not, Freud was certainly adept at working under conditions where such distinctions were merely academic—as witness this final climax of Ferenczi's courtship of Gizella.

Freud's proposal to Gizella asked her to "put aside considerations for your daughter, who can no longer play a role with him . . . It would be unnatural for you to sacrifice yourself for your daughter, to whom this sacrifice can bring no advantage . . . it is time to do the only serious thing to set matters straight."[113] To no avail: far from it. Gizella still held out for Elma's return from the United States and now revealed that she felt she had made an unspoken promise to her daughter of an imminent marriage to Ferenczi, if she wished it:[114] "since she was convinced that I could only be happy with one of the two of them (mother or daughter)—one of the two would have to be my wife. Now she requested her to return home as speedily as possible, in order to find the best solution for the three of us."[115]

Something was moving, though: Gizella had decided to seek an amicable separation from her husband. Over the summer of 1917, Freud, as so often traveling in his own threesome with Martha and Minna, spent some time in the Hungarian countryside with Gizella, from where he reported to Ferenczi: "In the background stands Elma, whose letters I have read a part of. My impression is the same, that you, because of your infidelity to Elma, have inflicted a deep wound on her and have confused the possible future with demonic dexterity. But nothing else can be done, and if Elma comes again, you must forget that you can be something other than a father to her."[116] The ambiguity of this letter—upon whom has the wound been inflicted, Gizella or Elma? whose futures have been so cleverly confused?—testifies to the solidity of the triangle that Freud was failing to resolve into simpler, more manageable elements. Just as in 1911, the situation was only resolved by Gizella's husband, who himself provoked a final break with his wife and agreed to a divorce.[117] The way was now clear for the marriage between Gizella and Ferenczi. Talk of Elma's return faded away. The couple entered into the protracted period of purdah that divorce laws of the period required. And, finally, as if to celebrate the prospect of entering into the legal married state, Ferenczi gave up being honest with Gizella:

In our infrequent intimate encounters, I often became unpleasantly aware of the duty-like character of the execution of this love. A progressive step, in contrast to before, was that I didn't share this with Frau G. (as I had done several times earlier sub titulo "honesty"). You were right again. It was difficult for me to get anything analytically; I had to be *really* obligated, as I am now, in order to bring about significant psychic progress.[118]

But such awareness of the lack of passion in their relations did not prevent the inexorable process now in train from coming to its planned end. Freud, however, still smarted from implied criticisms that he was foisting an old woman on Ferenczi:

Perhaps you think, since I myself have grown old and have no access to youth, that I am also wishing an old woman on you. No, I wouldn't have asked that of you, but it is not a matter of choosing a wife. She has already been that for fifteen years, became that when she was young and beautiful, has aged with you, and that should not be a motive for casting out one's wife after so many long years. It is now only a matter of transforming an uncomfortable marriage into a contented living together. Incidentally—she is today, with all the deficiencies of her—merely somatic—age, still worth incomparably more than most of the squeaky-clean and glossy women who get married. And finally—you know that yourself. What otherwise eludes you serves as a just punishment for you and, as such, will again satisfy an inner need.[119]

After the sorting out of the financial arrangements, the divorce finally came through in late 1918, amidst all the tumult of the end of the war and the series of political revolutions sweeping through the old Central Powers of Germany, Austria, and Hungary. Because of the disruption, Freud could not attend the wedding. Fate, that demon that Freud invoked often enough in discussing Ferenczi's marriage, still had a last word to say on that day. And as before, it

75

took the uncanny form of Géza Pálos, as Ferenczi indicated in a letter written on their wedding day, 1 March 1919:

> Our first greeting goes to you, whom we would so very much like to have chosen as a witness to our marriage.—
>
> It will interest you to know that our wedding day was disrupted by a tragic coincidence. Dr. Pálos, G.'s divorced husband, died suddenly of a heart attack on the same day; we already received the news before the ceremony.[120]

Two months later, Gizella and Ferenczi set up a permanent home together. As Ferenczi went through his old papers during the move, he sensed for the first time

> that, since the moment in which you advised me against Elma, I have had a resistance toward your own person which could not even be overcome by the attempt at a Ψa cure, and which was responsible for all my sensitivities. With the ucs. resentment in my heart, I, as a loyal "son," nevertheless followed all your suggestions, left Elma, again turned to my present wife, with whom I have stayed, despite countless temptations from other quarters . . . Yet the resistance seems to be gradually exhausting itself . . . It appears that I can be happy in life and content in work only when I can be and remain good, indeed, in the best relations with you. The realization that in Frau G. I have the best that could befall me— with my constitution—, is the first fruit of my inner reconciliation with you.[121]

Marriage to Gizella and reconciliation with Freud may have been Ferenczi's desires. But neither was to prove entirely without conflict. Periodically throughout the 1920s, Ferenczi was tormented by renewal of his desires for Elma. On Christmas Day, 1921—two years after his marriage to Gizella and virtually ten years to the day after he became engaged to Elma—Ferenczi wrote to his increasingly close friend Georg Groddeck about his relations with and analysis by

Freud; he complained in retrospect about Freud's maneuvering of the Elma episode in his life: "I did not want . . . an analytic interpretation, but something real, a young woman, a child."[122]

The desire for Elma resurfaced periodically, particularly in 1926–1927, when he and Gizella spent time in America with her. Once again, Gizella proposed to find the perfect solution, by divorcing him so that he could marry her daughter.[123] And the reconciliation with Freud would never be complete. Conflicts over his therapeutic experiments surfaced in 1924, again in early 1928, and, most famously, in the last years of Ferenczi's life, from 1930 to 1933.[124] It was Ferenczi's reproach, first hinted at in this letter written to Groddeck shortly after his marriage, and then made explicit in 1930, that Freud had failed to analyze him fully that stirred Freud to address the question of the efficacy of Ferenczi's analysis in "Analysis Terminable and Interminable" of 1937. There, in his valedictory to Ferenczi, Freud portrayed Ferenczi's brief but intense analysis as entirely successful: "He married the woman he loved and turned into a friend and teacher of his supposed rivals."[125]

This short summary by Freud of Ferenczi's struggles from 1911 to 1919 is tendentious. And Freud went on to rebut the charge that he should have paid attention to the negative transference by noting that, without any actual signs of it, "to activate it would certainly have required some unfriendly piece of behaviour in reality on the analyst's part."[126] If Ferenczi had been alive to read those words, he might have felt—as he had often felt, although how deeply and how persistently is difficult to judge—that Freud's espousal of the cause of the mother and his interdiction on the daughter amounted to just such an unfriendly piece of behavior. But he would then have had to ask: when were Freud's actions those of an analyst dealing with transference, and when were they those of his friend "in reality"?

If Ferenczi's marriage to Gizella did not put to rest for him the question of his triangle with Gizella and Elma, there is also evidence that Freud continued to reflect on it. The evidence is to be found in a paper, "Psychoanalysis and Telepathy," that Freud read to the six members of the Secret Committee, formed in 1913 to safeguard the future and orthodoxy of psychoanalysis, at their meeting in the Harz Mountains in September 1921. In this paper there is a curious echo, an uncanny repetition, of the Ferenczi-Gizella-Elma-Freud quadrilateral. Indeed, bearing in mind Ferenczi's functions as Freud's interlocutor on the topic of telepathy over many years,[127] one cannot but suspect that this paper was written principally for Ferenczi. Ferenczi would certainly hear more resonances than any other of the audience of Jones, Abraham, Rank, Sachs, and Eitingon in the third case study that Freud included in the paper—a case study added at the last minute, so Freud said, having left behind in Vienna the notes for the case he had originally intended to present.

It is an odd story to figure in a consideration of psychoanalysis and telepathy, since the telepathic phenomena under consideration are considerably less interesting than the analytic material. So it is clear that Freud used the material for a number of purposes: to show how the young man in analysis, through consulting the graphologist Schermann, is receiving two sets of "interpretations," one psychoanalytic, the other clairvoyant, thus providing a point of comparison between the successes of the analyst and those of the clairvoyant, as well as presenting the background material against which the clairvoyant's predictions may be judged. What interests us here is not so much the material relating to Schermann as the "family romance" of the patient at the core of Freud's account. Shrouding this particular family romance in a story about telepathy no doubt doubly intrigued Ferenczi.

The young man was in analysis with Freud because of his crippling dependence on a *demi-mondaine*. Analysis revealed that the *demi-mondaine* was a substitute for a woman he had been intensely involved with in his youth; he could take symbolic revenge on this woman through the tortures he inflicted on the generous and loving *demi-mondaine*. Having thus clarified the scene from the past that the young man was repeating, the analysis was able to progress further:

I detected from his dreams a plan that he was forming by means of which he would be able to escape from his relation with his early love without causing her too much mortification or material damage. She had a daughter, who was very fond of the young friend of the family and ostensibly knew nothing of the secret part he played. He now proposed to marry this girl. Soon afterwards the scheme became conscious, and the man took the first steps towards putting it into effect. I supported his intentions, since it offered what was a possible way out of his difficult situation even though an irregular one.[128]

However, both Freud's interpretations of the man's dreams and Schermann's interpretations of the young girl's handwriting signaled dangers in this plan:

The girl, who was by now regarded as the man's *fiancée*, behaved in a more and more contradictory manner, and it was decided that she should be analysed. As a result of the analysis the scheme for the marriage was abandoned. The girl had a complete unconscious knowledge of the relations between her mother and her *fiancé*, and was only attached to him on account of her Oedipus complex.

At about this time our analysis broke off. The patient was free and capable of going his own way in the future. He chose as his wife a respectable girl outside his family circle—a girl on whom Schermann has passed a favourable judgement. Let us hope that this time he will be right once more.[129]

The parallel between the young man's situation and Ferenczi's is clear: both had longstanding relations with a married woman, from whom they could not free themselves. Both sought their liberty in a compromise: marrying the mother's daughter. In Freud's 1921 case history, the dénouement of the young man's story centers on the question of her unconscious knowledge of sexual relations between her fiancée and her mother, the theme that had been brought to the fore in Freud's letter to Gizella Pálos of December 1911. In that letter, Freud had regarded it as evident that Elma's principal aim derived from the revival of an infantile desire to attack her mother, and that, as a consequence, she would be incapable of accepting the possibility that she is only a substitute for her mother, and a poor one at that: "The main difficulty is this: Does one want to build this alliance for life on concealing the fact that the man has been her mother's lover in the fullest sense of the word? And can one rely on the fact that she will take it well and overcome it in a superior manner when she knows it?"[130] In 1911, as in Freud's case of 1921, the stability of the entire arrangement depends on the unconscious of the young girl, irrespective of the man's desires.

The similarities between Ferenczi's story and that of Freud's patient are striking. Like the young man, in late 1915 Ferenczi even took refuge from his inability to choose between mother and daughter in the prophecies of card readers: "The double bond, *Frau G.* and *Elma,* has still not been dissolved in my unconscious fantasy.—A card reader yesterday 'prophesied' that I will marry *twice.* She also told me that I was supposed to have married recently, but that I pushed my bride away from me. Another, married woman 'worships me,' etc."[131] These similarities are so tempting that the historian wonders whether the story of the young man and the *demi-mondaine* is not a lightly fictionalized version of Ferenczi, Gizella, and Elma. Doesn't the packing of the fiancée off for a quick analytic once-over sound too much like Ferenczi's behavior toward Elma to be a coincidence? The more suspicious historian of psychoanalysis, of whom there have recently been so many, ready to regard psychoanalysis as implausible because psychoanalysts recount implausible life-stories of their patients, might suppose that the young man was a pure invention of Freud's, dreamed up to fill out the counterfeit annals of psychoanalytic cases. Others will be quick to see the young man as a disguised version of Ferenczi. As Freud had written to Gizella, the story of Elma and Ferenczi might well have turned out like "a beautiful novel with a touching conclusion, as so often happens in real life."[132] So might not the story of the young man and the *demi-mondaine* also be a novel? Might not psychoanalysis, even though, like truth, it is stranger than fiction, have only that strangeness in common with truth?

In this case, it turned out otherwise. In 1911, Elma Pálos was sent for analysis with Freud; the fiancée in Freud's telepathy paper was sent for analysis with Helene Deutsch, whose autobiography corroborates the authenticity of this Schnitzlerian story. However, it also reveals a remarkable fact about the case that Freud's account had concealed: the young girl was in fact the *niece* of the young man. Thus the mother with whom the man had been in love was his brother's wife. "The girl suspected that her uncle, to whom she was engaged, was not really her uncle but her father. The uncle, who was being treated by Freud, had actually once had a relationship with the girl's mother. The aversion that my patient felt whenever her fiancé approached her sexually was the expression of her horror that these might be the sexual advances of her own father."[133] Having started with figurative incest, we have finally arrived at something approaching literal, that is, theological or legal, incest. Freud's case of telepathy was a case of a young man having an affair with his brother's wife and intending to marry his niece, who believed her fiancé to be her father.

Even in this incestuous state of affairs, Freud did not think it analytically appropriate to intervene against the proposed incestuous marriage. Quite the opposite: he supported the young's man plan, even though he recognized it was an "irregular" one. Note that Freud characterized the solution as "irregular" even when he had not added in the important fact that the fiancée was the niece of his male patient; it is irregular, but perhaps a suitable solution for a "difficult situation," to marry the daughter of one's former lover. To Ferenczi, listening to this paper on telepathy, there was a hidden message here; yet again, Freud was required to intervene in an eternal triangle, required to plead the virtues of incest and the rights of amorous youth. Yet again, the incestuous plan of the central male character had come to nought; but yet again, Freud implied, this was not because of Freud's opposition to the plan. In the field of practical ethics, whether with patients or with colleagues, Freud's norms were anything but conventional.

Why did Freud conceal the fact that the young fiancée was the man's niece, his brother's daughter? Corresponding to this in Ferenczi's case was the fact that Elma was his brother Lajos' sister-in-law. In Freud's case history, the fact that the young man's lover is married to his brother is passed over in silence; similarly, in Ferenczi's letters and analysis, little that is concrete emerges concerning his brothers, and specifically the brother who was his lover's son-in-law.

And so we come back to the question of homosexuality, which for Ferenczi was oriented as much around his "brother-complex" as it was around the father-son axis. Freud even located Ferenczi's homosexuality as the principal driving force behind his desire for a baby and his thirst for revenge against the mother: "it is the case with *him* that his homosexuality imperiously demands a child and that he carries within him revenge against his mother from the strongest impressions of childhood."[134] Freud's references to Ferenczi's analysis often center on the figure of Géza Pálos, Gizella's husband and Ferenczi's rival.[135] But the other brother, the real brother Lajos, also had a part to play. When Ferenczi and Gizella's decision to press ahead toward marriage was finally taken in 1918, various members of the family drew up for battle. Elma gave her support to her mother, but "her sister—of a much more 'mundane' nature—trembles at the thought of what will come; her husband (my brother) is certainly also a bitter opponent. We must wait and see whether he also helps Pálos with legal arguments."[136] Yet again we stumble on a curious scenario: a man bitterly opposing his mother-in-law's intention to divorce his wife's father in order to marry his own brother. There were evidently incestuous forces at work between Ferenczi and his brother, alongside those more classically Freudian ones linking the young man with his lover and her daughter—not to mention the incestuous forces present in Ferenczi's sporadic couplings with Gizella's sister.

Ferenczi's case, and the young uncle's case, make it quite plain that Freud felt no horror of incest, whether it was sexual or psychoanalytic incest, whether its motivation was predominantly homosexual or heterosexual in character. Should we expect otherwise of the author of the following words? "It sounds not only disagreeable but also paradoxical, yet it must nevertheless be said that anyone who is to be really free and happy in love must have surmounted his respect for women and have come to terms with the idea of incest with his mother or sister."[137] These are the words Freud had completed a few days after sending Gizella the letter in which he had noted Ferenczi's fixation to the mother and the sister. Freud, it would appear, had Ferenczi's predicament and his desires very much in mind. That, we may conclude, is how he worked: with the everyday materials that came his way from the couch and his postbag. Psychoanalysis was built from the real, if not necessarily from the true.

Incest, we should remember, is the psychoanalytic theme par excellence. And the case of Ferenczi, Gizella, and Elma, highlighted now by the case of the young uncle's incest, should remind us of the ethical consequences of the particular focus on incest that Freud and his Oedipus complex required. Freud's attitude to the ethical dilemmas of life, such as incest and murder, was, in the best sense of that word, amoral: the naturalism of his "scientific" or "positivistic"—some would say Nietzschean—attitude was unequivocal in this respect. The superego with its ubiquitously noxious effects was a fundamental discovery of his psychoanalytic science.[138]

To illustrate the peculiarly amoral attitude of Freud to the question of incest, there is no better place to start than with Freud's reply to Marie Bonaparte, when, in the 1930s, she was considering having sexual relations with her adult son, Peter—who incidentally had recently decided to have an analysis with Rudolf Loewenstein, one of his mother's lovers, precisely because of his sexual jealousy of the analyst/lover in question. In 1932, Peter said to his mother: "If I were to spend a night with you, it might cure me";[139] Marie, always a champion of the therapeutic powers of eros, was tempted, both

83

erotically and out of maternal solicitude. Freud's advice, when she asked him, was that the question of incest was rather like the prohibition on cannibalism: there are "no grounds whatever against eating human flesh instead of animal flesh. Still most of us would find it quite impossible . . . Incest is not so remote, and indeed happens often enough . . . In individual exceptional cases incest would even to-day be harmless . . . [however] the trespass [might be] followed by feelings of guilt against which one is quite helpless."[140] This lack of foundation for the fundamental prohibitions which are synonymous with civilization means that the acts and impulses that are prohibited may vary enormously from one historical moment to another, and from person to person: "It is possible that cultural developments lie ahead of us in which the satisfaction of yet other wishes, which are entirely permissible to-day, will appear just as unacceptable as cannibalism does now."[141]

Marie Bonaparte was undoubtedly one of the more sexually extravagant of the Freud circle, what with her numerous lovers and the three surgical interventions on her clitoris to which she submitted in the hope of curing her frigidity.[142] With her, we see the possibility of the therapeutic value of incest considered as a serious question; and the judgment as to its expediency does not involve, either for Freud or for her, ethical considerations. And here I should note that Bonaparte's situation, that of a mother considering sexual relations with her adult son, is the primary sense of incest for psychoanalysts, as it was for the anthropologists who discussed—and still discuss— the universality of the incest taboo. The conception of incest as a crime modeled on the rape of children, rather than one modeled on conspiracy or collective blasphemy, is foreign to the early analysts. After all, the Oedipus complex is named after an adult perpetrator of the crime. The Oedipal desires of the child are to be understood on the model of adult desires; from the Oedipal child's point of view there is fundamentally no difference between adults and children. It is only adults who introduce the primordial distinction between the world of the adult and that of children, between the world of danger and purity, the profane and the sacred, manipulators and victims.[143]

––––––––––

It is a common enough view of psychoanalysis to see it as the epiphany of professional contractual relations. I myself argued this in my book *The Seductions of Psychoanalysis*. Ideally, the patient and the analyst enter into a contractual relationship, one in which the freedom of the patient from coercion by relatives and loved ones upon whom he or she is dependent is a necessary condition of a successful analysis. Freud had specifically seen Loe Kann's freeing of her sense of obligation to Ernest Jones, her common law husband, as a condition for the progress of her analysis; at the height of a crisis in her relations to Jones, her husband, and Freud, her analyst, the latter wrote to the former:

> There is a change in her position against you *as well as against me*. She considers herself free as long as treatment lasts, and according to the rules of psychoanalysis she has the right to do so. *I am glad she took up this position herself or I would have been obliged to force her into it.* I could not go on in the role of your friend as long as I am to act as her physician. I had to forget everything except this last. Now it has come natural to me, you know I am not working for you but for her delivery to the exclusion of every other aim.[144]

There is, as we have seen, a hint of this view in Freud's attitude to Elma, when he described how "she behaves very self-sufficiently and actually refuses help. She is now herself . . . She no longer plays the part of the good patient at all."[145] And he went on to add, thus indicating that his ideal patient, the one that mobilized his own strong countertransference, was the *indifferent* patient: "I believe it went so well only because she was so utterly indifferent to me. Now I value her more, naturally, and want to keep a close watch on the danger that is connected with that."[146] A few years later, Freud advertised, somewhat fancifully, his own demand that the patient be financially and emotionally independent: "In the years before the war . . . I followed a rule of not taking on a patient for treatment unless he was *sui juris*, not dependent on anyone else in the essential relations of his life."[147] The chief danger was always the relative: "In psycho-analytic treatments the intervention of relatives is a positive danger . . . they cannot be induced to keep at a distance from the whole business."[148]

The ideal of the economically independent patient, together with the assimilation of psychoanalysis to the public world of contractual relations, is part and parcel of the individualism that Freud, heir of the Enlightenment liberals and the English tradition of utilitarianism, never departed from. Yet Ernest Gellner was quite correct to point to the barrenness of the associationist psychology of rational calculation of self-interest to which Enlightenment individualism gave rise, to which Freud's emphasis on instinctuality and inner complexity was a riposte.[149] Even on its own terms, though, and before Freud, a rational psychology—or an economics—of egoistic self-interest could be undermined by a call on the higher ideals of religion, morality, and duty. Psychoanalysis removed this source of opposition, thus freeing up the individualist vision of the honest man: "To become candid about his egoism, to defy the admonitions that had made him feel secretive and ashamed of his self-interest, the honest man has needed a science exhibiting the pathology of moral aspiration."[150] It is the psychoanalyst, then, who will now represent the call of the public, against the network of covert ties and hypocrisies embedded everywhere, but most firmly in the individual's family. The psychoanalyst can hope to lever the patient into the honesty that heralds a cure only if she or he is detached from all those ties in which the dishonesty and hypocrisy of neurosis have become embedded.

It is quite evident from everything we know about Freud's practice that this independent patient was an ideal type, perhaps even his own idealization, never realized in practice. In fact, what his practice indicates is the messy "incestuous" character of his patients' relationships both inside and outside analysis. Particularly when he was dealing with followers and disciples—and who could draw a line with certainty between patients and followers?—the elaborate webs of their personal lives were often mapped onto convoluted and incestuous analytic transferences.

With Ferenczi, both in 1911 and in the 1920s, we see the logical extension of this state of affairs: switching at will between analytic and amorous modes, using love to advance analysis, and, when love came up against difficulties, using analysis to advance love. Freud may have postulated that psychoanalysis only works with independent, free agents, but in reality his patients were often bound into incestuous networks.

Conceptions of marriage may have been changing, so that the modern view of marriage as a contract between two independent agents had gained some hold; but the reality, particularly in Jewish circles, was one of much more tightly constructed webs of relationship. We can infer, I think, that the young man in question in Freud's paper on telepathy was Jewish, since marriages between uncle and niece are not incestuous in Jewish law.[151] We can also profitably recall that Freud's own father and half-brother had suggested to him when he was a young man that he should marry his own niece, Pauline; it was the enmeshing of the memories of this plan with Freud's early love for Gizella Fluss and her mother that was analyzed in his paper "Screen Memories." Incestuous unions in a sense that is somewhere between the metaphorical and the literal senses were frequent in Jewish circles in the late nineteenth century; indeed, Jews, freshly emerging from the ghettos, were often reviled for their incestuous marriages and the inbreeding that led to their frequent neuroses.[152]

Freud himself drew attention to the much more sweeping definition of incest to be found in Catholic Austria when he noted, in *Totem and Taboo*, that the Catholic church "extended the ancient prohibition against marriage between brothers and sisters to marriage between cousins and even to marriage between those who were merely spiritual relatives [godfathers, godmothers, and godchildren]."[153] Freud's own sexual desires had certainly taken his children's godmothers as their object.[154]

We do not even have to subscribe to the theory that sexual desire only arises when the relationship is transgressive in some sense; the networks of professional affiliation and family ties were firmly intertwined in Freud's typical Jewish circle. Not only had he considered marrying his half-niece, but, because Martha Bernays' brother Eli had married Sigmund Freud's sister Anna, Sigmund had actually married his sister's husband's sister. His own, distinctly pre-psychoanalytic conception of the benevolent intermingling of the professional and the familial had made Sándor Ferenczi into a very suitable potential husband for his eldest daughter, Mathilde, when they first met in the summer of 1908.

Even the triangle of Ferenczi-Elma-Gizella had the path laid for it by the network of which it was a part. Ferenczi was on occasion well aware of the mother-daughter fantasy structure, as his Freudian slip of early 1909 indicated: "I spoke [in my lecture] about Möbius's view that men have a longer active sex life, and got to speaking about cases where the man marries the daughter of his former lover. But instead of saying that such an action was justified, I said 'unjustified.' The conversation that I recently had with you will explain this parapraxis."[155] If this slip arose because of a fantasy, it was one for which the reality of "incestuous" relationships had more than adequately prepared the way. Ferenczi, after all, was involved with a married woman who was his brother's mother-in-law, and it had probably occurred to him that if his brother could marry Magda, why could he not marry Elma? Indeed, just as Sabina Spielrein, Jung's first analytic patient, his lover and pupil, first entered into his correspondence with Freud in the anonymous guise of case history, before being transformed into a figure embodying marital and professional crisis for him, so Ferenczi's very first mention in writing to Freud in 1909 of Gizella Pálos, who had been his lover since 1900,[156] was in the following curious formula: "my younger brother's present mother-in-law."[157] It is to the theory of the mother-in-law that I now turn.

————

Freud, it should now be remembered, did not only spend his time analyzing other people's incestuous networks; he also wrote theoretical tracts concerning incest. The Oedipus complex is a theory of the impossibility of escaping the effects of our earliest incestuous attachments: it is a theory both of the ubiquity and importance of those impulses and of the foundational status of incestuous impulses for all the later avatars of desire. The Oedipus complex was, by 1911–1912, the period of Ferenczi's crisis with Elma and Gizella, two years old[158] and decidedly coming into its own. In the summer of 1911, Freud set to work to explore the anthropological aspect of incest, keeping this new interest secret from Jung, who was working in a similar area, and in large part from his other disciples. Throughout late 1911, when the flow of letters from Ferenczi dried up as he became more and more involved with Elma, his most absorbing analytic patient, Freud slogged away at the topic of the origin of the incest taboo. The first essay of what was to become the four essays constituting *Totem and Taboo*, entitled "The Horror of Incest," was finished sometime in the weeks around Christmas of 1911. It is a short essay, and its uncharacteristic academic ponderousness amply justifies Freud's judgment of the whole book, delivered the day after finishing its writing in May 1913: "Whoever wants to kiss the princess who sleeps inside will certainly have to work through a few thorn hedges of literature and papers."[159] This first essay displays very little, seemingly, of psychoanalytic interest, consisting simply of a survey of the anthropological literature on the institution of totemism. The important problem that Freud extracts from this literature is the rule of exogamy: "a law against persons of the same totem having sexual relations with one another and consequently against their marrying."[160] The essay is devoted to the exploration of the character of this prohibition; it is only at the end of its seventeen pages that we suddenly come out of the thicket of ethnographic thorns—lengthy quotations from Frazer, Durkheim, Westermarck, and others—and discover the passages that Freud drew Ferenczi's attention to as being "interesting."[161] The topic that allows Freud to leave behind him the anthropological writers and turn to psychoanalytic knowledge of the civilized races is indeed the sleeping beauty of his essay—the mother-in-law.

Sir James Frazer had written: "The awe and dread with which the untutored savage contemplates his mother-in-law are amongst the most familiar facts of anthropology."[162] Freud takes it as a given of everyone's experience that "something in the psychological relation of a mother-in-law to a son-in-law breeds hostility between them and makes it hard for them to live together." In the discussion that he adds to Frazer's starting point, Freud is interestingly even-handed in the attention he pays to the quite separate sources for the woman's response to her son-in-law and for the man's response to his beloved's mother.

> On the man's side there is . . . an unwillingness to allow anything to interfere with the illusory overvaluation bred of his sexual feelings. The figure of his mother-in-law usually causes such an interference, for she has many features which remind him of her daughter and yet lacks all the charms of youth, beauty and spiritual freshness which endear his wife to him.[163]

The woman's view is entirely different:

> A woman whose psychosexual needs should find satisfaction in her marriage and her family life is often threatened with the danger of being left unsatisfied, because her marriage relation has come to a premature end and because of the uneventfulness of her emotional life. A mother, as she grows older, saves herself from this by putting herself in her children's place, by identifying herself with them . . . A mother's sympathetic identification with her daughter can

easily go so far that she herself falls in love with the man her daughter loves . . . And very often the unkind, sadistic components of her love are directed on to the son-in-law in order that the forbidden, affectionate ones may be the more severely suppressed.

But Freud once again turns back to the son-in-law:

Because of the barrier that exists against incest, his love is deflected from the two figures on whom his affection was centred in his childhood [his mother and his sister] on to an outside object that is modelled upon them. The place of his own and his sister's mother is taken by his mother-in-law. He has an impulse to fall back upon his original choice, though everything in him fights against it . . . A streak of irritability and malevolence that is apt to be present in the medley of his feelings leads us to suspect that she does in fact offer him a temptation to incest; and this is confirmed by the not uncommon event of a man openly falling in love with the woman who is later to be his mother-in-law before transferring his love to her daughter.[164]

This is the only passage concerning the mother-in-law to be found in Freud's complete works. It can hardly be a coincidence that this discussion was almost certainly written over Christmas of 1911, just when Freud was being asked to deal with the delicate relations of Ferenczi, his lover, and her daughter. Sándor Ferenczi and Gizella Pálos are the living basis for this portrait of the mother-in-law in civilized communities, resonating in Freud's text with stories from far-flung primitive tribes. As Ferenczi himself noted about Freud's way of working, when he was keen to disparage him in the early 1930s: "his brilliant ideas were usually based on only a single case, like illuminations as it were, which dazzled and amazed."[165] Ferenczi and Gizella may have been the privileged instance—it may well have been they who inadvertently sat for Freud so that he could create this portrait drawn from life. They are, however, as we have seen, not the only figures on whom it is based. It is also a portrait of

Sigmund Freud and Frau Fluss, and of Sigmund Freud, Emmeline Bernays, and her two daughters, Martha and Minna.

———

It is possible to read this chapter as showing how a number of Freud's works got written, among them, the description of the young man and the *demi-mondaine* and the three pages from *Totem and Taboo* discussing the mother-in-law—showing some of the materials, the evidence, on which those three pages are based, and showing why they are appended, as a sparkling jewel, to a somewhat dry essay entitled "The Horror of Incest" which consists largely of dutiful synopses of ethnographic studies of primitive peoples. It is the transgressive intimacies, the network of incest of civilized peoples, of psychoanalysts and their nearest and dearest, that constitute the vivid evidential base of those pages. Freud is quite clearly never anything other than a participant-observer in these networks, making sense out of what no one would sensibly want to conceive of as theory-independent observations. The figure of the mother-in-law emerges from the warp and weft of incestuous networks. She is, of course, only one version of the Oedipus complex as Freud conceived it, and she is also part of other, more theoretical, themes in Freud's work. But even if one puts to one side the claim that the Oedipus complex is the universal crossroads that all subjects encounter in their childhoods, one can see the force of asserting that all these incestuous networks are manifestations of the Oedipus complex. The Oedipus complex—and one of its manifestations, the ubiquitously taboo figure of the mother-in-law—is the simplifying, and therefore explanatory, principle for all the incestuous networks I have been exploring. We could, as Wladimir Granoff has suggested, clear up certain confusions by renaming it the Freud complex;[166] we could also bind it, in a spirit of explanatory humility, to the immediate world of Freud and his many circles. But I think there may be some virtue in being open-minded on this score, since we can also consider the incestuous networks I have traced as being another term for the cultural unconscious.

———

What is the bleakest view that one might take of Freud's actions in the long-drawn-out—the lifelong—episode of Ferenczi, Gizella, and Elma? One might accuse him of being hampered by the limitations of a provincial imagination and of hypocrisy (on two counts: with respect to analysis, and with respect to his own actions). Freud was ultimately blind to the effects of his own actions, whether as a friend or an analyst. But the blindness attached to the limitations of the imagination—a surprising lapse in urbanity and sophistication. In 1911, he had advised Ferenczi against marrying Elma, but at the same time warned Gizella to prepare herself for inevitable abandonment by her lover in favor of the youth and the promise of fertility of her daughter. By 1917 he had changed his tune: he confessed to Gizella that he had tried every trick in the book to engineer Ferenczi into marrying her, and every trick had failed. He always judged her to be a woman "still worth all the gold."[167] Like Ferenczi, Freud never wavered in his estimation of Gizella; but unlike Ferenczi, Freud never wavered in his view that the estimableness and preciousness of Gizella made her the only possible choice as marriage partner. More to the point, perhaps, he *assumed* that Gizella wished to marry Ferenczi and that the only satisfactory outcome of Ferenczi's attachment to Gizella was marriage.

The Elma episode of 1911–1912 was a turning-point for Ferenczi and Gizella. If Ferenczi slumped into a period of bodily ailments and deep indecision, Gizella emerged quickly from her feeling of wounded abandonment into unswerving advocacy of the course of action that Freud had counseled Ferenczi against: marriage to Elma. Freud appeared determined to make an "honest woman" of Gizella and, through his silences and his insistence on the centrality for Ferenczi of a marriage-decision, repudiated her solution—a stable, long-term triangle. Ferenczi's marriage to Elma would give him what he wanted (youth, fertility, sexual renewal); would give Gizella some of what she wanted (to keep his intimacy and friendship, to keep her daughter); and might be the solution to Elma's difficult marriage choices. Both Freud and Ferenczi repeatedly accused her of promoting the cause of her daughter as amends for her wounded, vengeful feelings toward Elma.[168] Yet neither seemed to consider seriously the possibility that, from her point of view, marrying Ferenczi to her daughter would be a convenient solution *for Gizella*.

Over the years of indecision before and during the First World War, Ferenczi procrastinated because he thought he could find someone more satisfying than Gizella: someone who would give him sexual fulfillment and paternity. The reasons for Gizella's procrastination never concerned them quite so much, so any discussion of her motives must be speculative. But she may well have been satisfied with the present state of affairs—with her thirty-year-long marriage to Géza Pálos and her lengthy affair with Ferenczi. There is not a single word of complaint or criticism throughout these letters about her husband. And the solution she had found to the problem of marriage—a stable and satisfying sexual relationship with her young, intellectually stimulating lover—was far from being unconventional. To Gizella, it looked as if this "solution to the marriage problem,"[169] as Freud called it in 1936, also offered her a solution to the "daughter problem." Freud's portrait of the mother-in-law, which, I have argued, was at the same time his portrait of Gizella, may have emphasized the excessive identification with her daughter and the liberation of the "unkind, sadistic components of her love," but these typical unconscious forces are not ones that would disallow actions arising from them, or qualify them as neurotic. All in all, Freud—and, when he was dutifully following Freud's analytic advice, Ferenczi as well—seemed little inclined to take seriously Gizella's solutions, whether as unconscious motives or as realistic proposals, or both. But Ferenczi and almost certainly Gizella had understood from the start that marriage to Elma would not in any sense preclude amorous relations between the mother and the son-in-law; in October 1913, Ferenczi had mentioned that during the brief period when he was engaged to Elma he had been "temporarily impotent with Frau G.,"[170] implying that he had had every intention of continuing his sexual relationship with Gizella during his engagement to her daughter, but the executive organ had decided against. And hadn't Ferenczi written to Freud, just two weeks after Elma's analysis in Vienna had started, to inform him how he was working "to ensure for myself Frau G.'s love also in the event of my marrying Elma. It is painful to me to see her unhappy, and I obviously wish that she should share in our joy"?[171]

Why was this? Put baldly, Freud saw Ferenczi's predicament as requiring a decision between two mutually exclusive objects: either/or. He even noted that Ferenczi's indecision was true indecision: "It is not even a no; he just doesn't want to change anything, do anything."[172] Ferenczi's indecision was tantamount to a refusal to accept that it was a question of either/or: he wished to say no neither to Gizella nor to Elma. He wanted, as the saying goes, to have his cake and eat it too. In this he found an ally, as ever, in Gizella. But not in Freud.

In the period from 1914 onward, and particularly after the termination of Ferenczi's analysis in 1916, Freud grew increasingly impatient with Ferenczi's perpetual indecision over his personal life. Past a certain point, he just wanted Ferenczi to get on with it, whatever it was. In this respect, he may have failed to read Ferenczi's overall character accurately. The long story of Ferenczi's experimentation with psychoanalytic technique—from deliberately frustrating proscriptions to supportive mutuality, encompassing every position in between and beyond—testifies to the fluidity and restlessly imaginative relations he established with patients. His indecision about his marriage to Gizella should be seen as all of a piece with these other manifestations of his mobile and roving character. What the conventional and decisive Freud might see as procrastination and indecision would in other lights be revealed as negative capability, "when man is capable of being in uncertainties, mysteries, doubts, without any irritable reaching after fact and reason." Perhaps Ferenczi enacted Keats's suggestion: "The only means of strengthening one's intellect is to make up one's mind about nothing—to let the mind be a thoroughfare for all thoughts."[173] If Ferenczi had made a shibboleth of truth, which had no great hold on Freud, then Freud had made a shibboleth of decisiveness. What determined Ferenczi finally to act decisively in the matter of Gizella, and led to his extraordinary—and successful—plan of asking Freud to propose to her on his behalf, was a passage he had just read in Freud's newly published *Introductory Lectures:* "Dealing with a conflict by forming symptoms is after all an automatic process which cannot prove adequate to meeting the demands of life, and in which the subject has abandoned the use of his best and highest powers. If there were a choice, it would be preferable to go down in an honourable struggle with fate."[174]

Ferenczi was finally won over by Freud's portrait of the compromising and dithering neurotic who evades—who refuses to choose— the struggle for what he desires. There is a further irony here, since Ferenczi had probably forgotten a very similar passage from Freud's Nuremburg Congress address of April 1910, which is the closest Freud ever came to espousing the radical transformative vision of psychoanalysis that Ferenczi had been urging on him in the months preceding the Congress: "What will [neurotics] have to do if their flight into illness is barred by the indiscreet revelations of psycho-analysis? They will have to be honest, confess to the instincts at work in them, face the conflict, fight for what they want, or go without it; and the tolerance of society, which is bound to ensue as a result of psycho-analytic enlightenment, will help them in their task."[175]

Neither should we overlook a certain hypocrisy in Freud's delicate position vis-à-vis his friend. He could not maintain, when it came down to it, the fiction of giving analysis in place of the advice that both Ferenczi and Gizella sought from him. In the year of 1913, when Freud himself was struggling with the only depression his daughter Anna ever saw him slide into, the direct result of his "King Lear complex" provoked by the marriage of his two elder daughters, he unwittingly made quite plain his desire for Ferenczi to marry Gizella, not Elma, just as he himself would resign himself to settling for his wife rather than his daughter. What irony, then, that Ferenczi should marry Gizella shortly after Freud began his analysis of Anna Freud,[176] the daughter he would thus bind to him so strongly for the rest of his—and her—life! Freud took both mother and daughter to himself, precisely the option he worked hard and cunningly to deprive Ferenczi of.

In the end, though, we should not forget the different interpretations that Ferenczi and Freud placed upon the ethical and pragmatic implications of psychoanalysis. To put it once again crudely, for Freud honesty and truthfulness were the technical means by which psychoanalysis achieved its ends—they had primarily pragmatic value. For Ferenczi, as we have seen, the honesty and truthfulness that the practice of psychoanalysis required overflowed into the more general requirement and ethic of social honesty. What tied him to Gizella, in the end, was his compulsion to be honest, and her admirable qualities of understanding of his truth—this Gizella, at the end of his life, still longed for an analyst "who will be concerned above all with truth."[177]

Like the ideal analysand, Ferenczi fell in love with those to whom he told the truth—Gizella and Freud. It was this coincidence of the powers of truth and love that convinced him of the epoch-making character of psychoanalysis. Ferenczi, unlike Freud, retained what he called his "fanatical belief in the efficacy of depth-psychology"[178] to the end of his life. His faith in psychoanalysis, embodying the highest morality that flows from its dedication to truth, allowed him to push its practice to the limits: "If one has a certain confidence in one's own ability to be impressed ultimately only by the truth, then one may resolve to risk the sacrifice, seemingly so horrifying, of putting oneself in the care and control of a madman."[179] Ferenczi believed that psychoanalysis would make one better, ethically superior. To put the matter at its most paradoxical, Freud believed that psychoanalysis might help to make people worse, less subject to the tyranny of morality. For Freud, morality was self-evident[180] and therefore needed no attention devoted to it beyond the destruction of the illusions we have about ourselves: "We tell ourselves that anyone who has succeeded in educating himself to truth about himself is permanently defended against the danger of immorality, even though his standard of morality may differ in some respect from that which is customary in society."[181]

As Adam Phillips sums it up, "Freud was saying: make the unconscious conscious because only then can you make intelligent ethical decisions . . . For Freud, psychoanalysis prepared one to make a morality for oneself . . . In this sense, Freud, despite his caution, was the revolutionary."[182] The first revolutionary step was to regard all morality that comes from outside the individual as a symptomatic formation, akin to religious rituals or beliefs. The second was to dispense with that condition which, since Kant, has been viewed as part of what we mean by morality: the condition of universalizability—"Act only on that maxim through which you can at the same time will that it should become a universal law."[183] As we have seen, Freud set his face against such universal laws, invoking their injustice: "It is one of the obvious social injustices that the standard of civilization should demand from everyone the same conduct of sexual life."[184] Morality comes from within, certainly not from without, from some moral order in the world or in society, and must arise from and in individual circumstance and disposition. The adjustment or calibration of other people's actions to one's own is a matter of convention, of convenience: "I cannot honestly see that any difficulties are created by patients' demands for ethical values; ethics are not based on an external world order but on the inescapable exigencies of human cohabitation."[185]

Freud, to be sure, recognized that morality applies to others as well as oneself, but only in the sense that it is inherent in the idea of any rule that it cover others. "Ethics are a kind of highway code for traffic among mankind"[186] was his pithiest formulation. But there is no imperative behind a highway code—or, to adopt a more modern analogy, behind a computer program—which gives the code or the procedure its privilege. Even Kant recognized, in his most Wittgensteinian mode, that there is no rule for applying a rule. Freud was skeptical about the feeling of obligation that Kant sought to embed in the very notion of morality, regarding it as no different from neurotic compulsion. Certainly the founding principles of civilization had no fundamentally ethical character: "The first requisite of civilization, therefore, is that of justice—that is, the assurance that a law once made will not be broken in favour of an individual. This implies nothing as to the ethical value of such a law."[187] Evenhandedness—justice, fairness—is a practical necessity, but is not an ethical value in itself. We have already seen in the previous chapter the extent to which Freud regarded such fundamental principles as justice and fairness as derivative of envy. Here it is appropriate to point out that Freud often enough underlined the fundamental *injustice* of being evenhanded. In the place of the feeling of moral obligation attaching to universal principles, Freud put greater freedom of choice as the source of moral, as opposed to compulsively "good," actions.

Philip Rieff has written most acutely of the skepticism of ethical aspiration implicit in Freud's work:

> He was a digger, not a builder, an archaeologist of the psyche. Digging at the foundations was the moral mission left to the psychologist after philosophy and religion had raised man too high. According to the Freudian counsel, man must not strain too far the limitations of his instinctual nature. Therefore, knowing, becoming conscious of these limits, is itself a primary ethical act. Consciousness, self-knowledge, interpretative revelation and decision, candor, talking things through—all presume a necessary reduction of ethical aspiration. Without this imperative, Freud's conception of therapy is meaningless. "A little more truthfulness,"[188] Freud recommends, instead of the painful old passion for goodness.[189]

Freud may have put veracity in the place of goodness, but there was no phobic fear of lying prompting this revalorization of honesty. More important, this valorization of honesty was purely formal, with no substantive content. Honesty can only ever be either formal and empty in character, or negative and dependent on that which it criticizes, correcting, through the negation of the negation, the toxic effects of the inhibitions, renunciations, and negations of the ethically driven subject.

This is why Freud's work lends itself, in the end, to interpretation as a project of pure technicity. If we look at Freud's views on issues which have become urgent, if not scandalous, in the recently refurbished sanctimoniousness of the liberal professions, such as the question of sexual relations between analyst and patient, we encounter a strictly nonethical and technical response. When considering the situation in which a female patient falls in love with her analyst, Freud did not repudiate the analyst's responding in kind on the basis of an ethic of sexual abstinence; all the analogies Freud introduced were designed to wean analysts away from thinking of sexual relations with patients in terms of the transgression of ethical norms: "The doctor . . . must not stage the scene of a dog-race in which the prize [the erotic satisfaction every patient hopes for from psychoanalytic treatment] was to be a garland of sausages but which some humorist spoiled by throwing a single sausage [the fine experience of an affair between analyst and patient] on the track."[190]

Or, when Freud counsels the analyst against believing that he can return the love of the patient and, using this love, still continue with the treatment:

The patient would achieve *her* aim, but he would never achieve *his*. What would happen to the doctor and the patient would only be what happened, according to the amusing anecdote, to the pastor and the insurance agent. The insurance agent, a free-thinker, lay at the point of death and his relatives insisted on bringing in a man of God to convert him before he died. The interview lasted so long that those who were waiting outside began to have hopes. At last the door of the sick-chamber opened. The free-thinker had not been converted; but the pastor went away insured.[191]

It takes such willfully light touches to displace the debate about sexual relations between patient and analyst onto the terrain where Freud believes it belongs: as primarily a pragmatic question, presenting no more moral implications to the analyst than the handling of explosive substances presents to the chemist. We might extend the chemical analogy to Freud's ethical views in general: ethics, that domain in which primitive notions of cleanliness and dirtiness come home to roost, might well be modeled on the principles governing the practice of chemists in keeping their test tubes clean.

There was to be, late in Ferenczi's life, an occasion for Freud to rehearse once again his essentially pragmatic conception of analytic practice. Through various sources, Freud heard rumors of Ferenczi's new experiments in analysis, of giving patients the affection they had been deprived of in childhood. These innovations, which went hand in hand with Ferenczi's concentration on the effects of real pathogenic traumas, were summed up in the report that "you kiss your patients and let them kiss you."[192] Freud assured Ferenczi that "I am assuredly not one of those who from prudishness or from consideration of bourgeois convention would condemn little erotic gratifications of this kind." The heart of his objection to the technique was a slippery-slope argument: "Why stop at a kiss?" if giving patients maternal affection is the curative factor in analysis. The conclusion for Freud was that giving affection is precisely that playing with explosive substances, rather than manipulating them under safe conditions, which the good chemist eschews. The analysis must be conducted under conditions of frustration for the patient— but not because the analyst is in need of restraint.

Just as in his 1915 paper on transference-love, Freud craftily adopted an admonitory tone which was both humorous and sarcastic: "Certainly one gets further when one adopts 'pawing' as well, which after all doesn't make a baby. And then bolder ones will come along who will go further to peeping and showing—and soon we shall have accepted in the technique of analysis the whole repertoire of demiviergerie and petting-parties, resulting in an enormous increase of interest in psycho-analysis among both analysts and patients." And he finished by referring Ferenczi back to his past professional elisions between sexuality and treatment: "according to my recollection a tendency to sexual play with patients was not completely alien to you in pre-analytic times, so that the new technique could well be linked to an old error." Freud—Ferenczi's analyst, Elma's analyst, party to all the twists and turns along the way before and since—was not engaging in moral condemnation; if he had been tempted to, it would have been somewhat late in the day for that. Rather, he was reminding Ferenczi that old dogs do often return to their old tricks.

Ferenczi's reply to this paternal admonition of his tender maternal technique was measured, containing a reminder to Freud that his barnacle-like insistence on one single technique meant that he had eschewed the experimentation that was the only school for learning in psychoanalysis: "'Sins of youth,' mistakes, once they have been overcome and analytically worked through, can even make one wiser and more prudent than people who have never experienced such storms . . . Now I believe that I am capable of creating a congenial atmosphere, free from passion, which is best suited to draw forth what has previously been concealed."[193] The dispute now turned around the possibility of creating an atmosphere that was "free from passion." When, Freud might well ask, was a kiss passionate or tender? The last paper Ferenczi wrote suggested a theoretical foundation for this distinction by discriminating between the adult's language of passion and the child's language of tenderness.[194] Here, finally, Ferenczi had put forward a theory which would justify the utopian theories of social transformation through psychoanalytic honesty of his early Freudian period: the child inhabits a world of tenderness, without lies, into which the adult introduces cruelty, guilt, and hypocrisy. But this theory of honesty was underpinned by its practice. Ferenczi's technique in the late 1920s and early 1930s had increasingly revolved around the dire effects of the hypocrisy of the analyst and the absolute requirement of the analyst's honesty.[195] His final paper produced the theoretical conception which capped this therapeutic necessity and thus fully expressed his social philosophy: the image of the world of the child in which there is neither passion nor lying. A world which is, therefore, honest without any possibility of being otherwise.

———

A final word concerning discretion and the transgression involved in writing about incest. Rebecca West once noted: "Just how difficult it is to write biography [we can add: and the history of psychoanalysis] can be reckoned by anybody who sits down and considers just how many people know the truth about his or her love affairs."[196] We know a small part about the love affairs of Ferenczi, Gizella, Elma, and Freud. No thanks are due to the guardians of the Freud estate for the little bit we do know. It is quite clear that the principal obstacle to the publication of the Freud-Ferenczi correspondence stemmed from Anna Freud's attempt to protect the reputations of the principal protagonists in the four-sided game of beds, couches, and writing desks that Freud and Ferenczi, Gizella and Elma played at for two decades.

From the very beginning of her work devoted to Freud's posthumous writings and correspondences—a labor that began within a few weeks of his death[197]—Anna Freud took the firm view that "we can always suppress what is too personal."[198] To be sure, such suppression would be done in the name not only of due propriety, but of love. From the start of the protracted negotiations over the publication of Freud and Ferenczi's correspondence, she made it clear to Gizella Ferenczi that only a *"partial use"*[199] would be made of them. Anna's tone here is consistent with all her other actions concerning Freud's letters: the rigorous protection of her father and his circle by the systematic expurgation of overly personal details. For Anna Freud, as for her father, love was a private matter and might well win out over the claims of historical or scientific truth. The Freuds never belonged to the school of open confessional, with its requirement of public exhibition for communal catharsis, however much psychoanalysis might have, by a curious twist of fate, fed such a historical development. Public life had its proprieties, just as the analytic chamber had its rules of confidentiality.

Until she died in 1949, Gizella was enthusiastic about the project to publish her late husband's correspondence with Freud. Elma, stepping into her mother's shoes as the negotiations dragged on through the 1950s, the 1960s, and up to her death in 1972, was equally keen. It is not clear, however, what their attitude was to a *complete* publication. It was Michael Balint, to whom Gizella delegated all responsibility for the Ferenczi estate, who began to have difficulties finding the correct editorial policy to follow. In 1966, after lengthy negotiations with Anna Freud, the two came to an agreement, but he still could not resolve the problem of what to reveal and what to conceal. He recognized that excerpting from the letters without mentioning Gizella or Elma would be, he wrote to Elma, "a falsification, or at least a *suppressio veri.*"[200] In 1968 Balint came up with a solution that has, given the question of incest and the strategies we have seen Freud employ when faced with the publication of such delicate material, a certain irony:

1. We give you [Elma] a pseudonym that would conceal your identity but not your existence.
2. We say that you were closely related to Gizella but do not reveal that you were her daughter.[201]

Elma approved this plan and approved the pseudonym "Sylvia."

The principle that Elma followed in giving her assent to publication of the letters was very different from those employed by the Freud family: not to publish, she wrote, "would be unethical and because historical truth does not allow one even to think of it."[202]

This motive was, of course, born of her high estimation, her idealization of Ferenczi and Freud, in the same way as Marie Bonaparte's desire in the 1940s to see a rapid publication of the complete Freud-Fliess correspondence—a view that was definitively overruled by the Freud family, particularly Martin and Anna Freud[203]—was born of her conviction of Freud's world-historical importance. For reasons which remain obscure—including the expense and difficulty of translating and publishing more than 1,200 letters and the preoccupation of Anna Freud, always in charge of any unpublished Freud papers, with other tasks such as the Freud-Jung correspondence—it took a further twenty-five years to publish the Freud-Ferenczi letters. And now they are published in full, without excision, suppression, or pseudonymity.

Given this history of publication, are we forced into a position wherein we must judge Elma, Balint, and Marie Bonaparte honest and the Freud camp, dominated by Anna, dishonest? Or are we here in the area where love and truth once again are each confined to their own element, so that, as in Freud's striking analogy, "the disputants can no more come to grips than, in the familiar simile, a polar bear and a whale"?[204]

Anna Freud, like her father, wrote no memoir: "I allow myself the privilege of taking it all with me."[205] Sigmund felt that the measured self-revelation which he had permitted himself in his writings stemmed from an exhibitionistic tendency which it was best to suppress beyond a certain point.[206] Elma's view of truth—like her stepfather's and sometime suitor's—entailed appearing naked in public. Ferenczi, we remember, fell in love with whomever he had told the truth. So, is the publication of the complete correspondence between Elma's lover and her analyst the definitive public exhibition of the incestuous network that kept her so tied to her mother and his lover, the final victory of the young woman whom Freud had described in early 1912 as follows: "She falls in love compulsively with doctors, i.e. with persons who see her naked, physically, and now mentally"?[207] Is this public display what she meant when she wrote to Michael Balint in 1952 that "she so wished to live to see the letters be published"?[208] Elma's imperative to reveal the truth and Anna's imperative to hold it back may both fall within the capacious register of love.

3

COLLECTOR, NATURALIST, SURREALIST

Even when one is no longer attached to things, it's still something to have been attached to them; because it was always for reasons which other people didn't grasp . . . Well, now that I'm a little too weary to live with other people, those old feelings, so personal and individual, that I had in the past, seem to me—it's the mania of all collectors—very precious. I open my heart to myself like a sort of showcase, and examine one by one all those love affairs of which the rest of the world can have known nothing. And of this collection to which I'm now even more attached than to my others, I say to myself, rather as Mazarin said of his books, but in fact without the least distress, that it will be very tiresome to have to leave it all.

Swann's Valediction,
Marcel Proust, *Remembrance of Things Past*

Imagine you are lying on Freud's couch. What can you see?

Directly above you on the wall to your left hangs a color print of the rock-cut temple at Abu Simbel in Egypt. To its left is an Egyptian mummy portrait, in tempera on wood, of a balding, middle-aged man wearing a white tunic decorated with two embroidered bands, dating from the Roman period, c. 250–300 A.D. Further along the wall, so that you can look at it if you raise your eyes from your feet and glance up and left, is a copy of a Roman frieze depicting the woman Gradiva, with her characteristic raised instep. On the wall facing you, above your feet, is a picture of Oedipus contemplating the question the Sphinx has put to him.

You are surrounded by objects from the ancient world. And the voice behind you tells you that these objects are a decaying reflection of equally ancient objects within you. Listen to what Freud records himself as having said to the patient known as the Rat Man:

> I then made some short observations upon *the psychological differences between the conscious and the unconscious,* and upon the fact that everything conscious was subject to a process of wearing-away, while what was unconscious was relatively unchangeable; and I illustrated my remarks by pointing to the antiques standing about in my room. They were, in fact, I said, only objects found in a tomb, and their burial had been their preservation: the destruction of Pompeii was only beginning now that it had been dug up.[1]

This characterization of the mind's contents as being like the objects in his collection of antiquities is given the virtuoso touch in a famous depiction of Rome, the city that Freud loved above all others:

> Let us, by a flight of imagination, suppose that Rome is not a human habitation but a psychical entity with a similarly long and copious past—an entity, that is to say, in which nothing that has once come into existence will have passed away and all the earlier phases of development continue to exist alongside the latest one. This would mean that in Rome the palaces of the Caesars and the Septizonium of Septimius Severus would still be rising to their old height on the Palatinate and that the castle of S. Angelo would still be carrying on its battlements the beautiful statues which graced it until the siege by the Goths, and so on. But more than this. In the place occupied by the Palazzo Caffarelli would once more stand—without the Palazzo having to be removed—the Temple of Jupiter Capitolinus; and this not only in its latest shape, as the Romans of the Empire saw it, but also in its earliest one, when it still showed Etruscan forms and was ornamented with terracotta antefixes. Where the Coliseum now stands we could at the same time admire Nero's vanished Golden House. On the Piazza of the Pantheon we should find not only the Pantheon of to-day, as it was

bequeathed to us by Hadrian, but, on the same site, the original edifice erected by Agrippa; indeed, the same piece of ground would be supporting the church of Santa Maria sopra Minerva and the ancient temple over which it was built.

This devoted evocation of history is imbued with the tender familiarity of the lover for all the parts and secret places of the loved one, a knowledge that is the fruit of long years of study and visiting. This Freud combines both the amorous passion of Don Giovanni for each and every woman and the satisfactions of Leporello, the cataloger of conquests.

But Freud's effort to bring all of history together in one picture is doomed to fail, as he himself immediately recognizes.

> There is clearly no point in spinning our phantasy any further, for it leads to things that are unimaginable and even absurd. If we want to represent historical sequence in spatial terms we can only do it by juxtaposition in space: the same space cannot have two different contents. Our attempt seems to be an idle game. It has only one justification. It shows us how far we are from mastering the characteristics of mental life by representing them in pictorial terms.[2]

Evoking, as if caressing in memory, one's familiarity with the history and topography of all the Romes, ancient, medieval, and modern, is only a prelude to the realization of how inadequate an analogy the archaeological, the antique analogy is. It is as if Freud collected all these objects, acquired all this knowledge of the classical past, only to find that it has all been "an idle game."

Freud's desire to be an archaeologist of the mind was a longstanding trait of his inner life. Stones talk to archaeologists, he asserted in 1896,[3] in one of his first psychoanalytic papers, and in exactly the same way, so do forgotten, buried memories talk to the psychoanalyst armed with the technique of free association—"the procedure of clearing away, layer by layer, the pathogenic psychical material, which we like to compare with the technique of excavating a buried city."[4] Perpetual student of the "prehistoric"—one of his favorite terms for the forgotten, infantile past of his patients—Freud the archaeologist of the mind was entirely committed to the archaeological analogy in looking upon the contents of the mind as so many objects to be uncovered, pieced together, dated, placed back in their original contexts, or treated as so many false leads planted by later grave-robbers. In 1896, one of his first models of the mind bore the unmistakable stamp of his enthusiasm for the prehistoric, couched in the evolutionary and philological dialect of his time:

> I am working on the assumption that our psychic mechanism has come into being by a process of stratification: the material present in the form of memory traces being subjected from time to time to a *rearrangement* in accordance with fresh circumstances—to a *retranscription* . . . the successive registrations represent the psychic achievement of successive epochs of life. At the boundary between two such epochs a translation of the psychic material must take place . . . If a later transcript is lacking, the excitation is dealt with in accordance with the psychological laws in force in the earlier psychic period . . . Thus an anachronism persists: in a particular province, *fueros* are still in force; we are in the presence of "survivals."[5]

And about the same time he wrote this, Freud began to collect antiquities.

By the time he died, in September 1939, Freud's collection was a considerable one: something over three thousand pieces, with hundreds of rings, scarabs, and statuettes. He kept them in the two rooms he worked in, making a distinct separation from the other family rooms, which were decorated in ordinary turn-of-the-century style, with heavy contemporary furniture and lots of family photographs.

This is a clear indication that his collection was both something private for him, to be kept separate from his familial existence, and that it was something bound up with his work, both as writer and analyst.

He started collecting sometime in the 1890s, and from the start most of the objects were sculptural. Having started with copies of Renaissance masterpieces, Freud quickly found the main theme of his collection: non-fragmentary pieces from Ancient Rome, Greece, and Egypt. In the 1920s he widened his compass somewhat to include Chinese pieces. The *Anschluss* of 1938 forced the Freuds to leave Vienna for London; Freud feared that his large collection of antiquities would be confiscated. With help from Princess Marie Bonaparte, from the official valuer of the Kunsthistorisches Museum, and others, he managed to take all of them with him—in contrast to his books, a large portion of which were, whether by necessity or because of their bulk, sold before departure.[6] Fearing the worst, Freud had entrusted one piece to Marie Bonaparte for her to smuggle out of the country in case the whole collection was confiscated: a 4-inch Roman copy of a fifth century B.C. Athena who sat in pride of place on his desk. As they were leaving Vienna, the family attempted to locate each piece of his formidable collection in its proper place. When the Freuds finally settled into their new house in Maresfield Gardens, Hampstead, the maid Paula Fichtl put the collection of antiquities back where each of them belonged, lining the walls and cabinets of the pair of large ground-floor rooms that became Freud's study and consulting-room.[7] As Freud wrote to his ex-analysand and friend, Jeanne Lampl de Groot: "All the Egyptians, Chinese and Greeks have arrived, have stood up to the journey with very little damage, and look more impressive here than in Berggasse. There is just one thing: a collection to which there are no new additions is really dead."[8] Freud himself died a few months later.

Freud's collection of antiquities had always been confined to his study and consulting-room, which had originally been, until 1907, on a different floor of Berggasse 19 from the family apartments, and which would always be a separate space from the family rooms. As Bettelheim noted:

> All these many, many objects were crowded into his treatment room and study; none of them spilled over into the many rooms next door which formed the family living quarters. What more definite statement could Freud have made that his collection was part and parcel of his psychoanalytic interests, and not at all of his life as paterfamilias? It is a contrast that seems to declare: "Unique though my life as the discoverer of the unconscious is, my life with my family is ordinary."[9]

The style of the family rooms was decidedly ordinary Viennese bourgeois of the end of the nineteenth century and was therefore in considerable contrast to the amassed figures of Egyptian, Greek, and Roman gods that lined the walls and swarmed over the desks and tables in Freud's professional space. When Stefan Zweig wrote a study of Freud, it rankled with Freud that he had not sufficiently appreciated this contrast between the private and the professional. Freud wrote to Zweig, noting how he had placed an "emphasis on the element of *petit-bourgeois* correctness in my person" and attempting to ameliorate this imputation as follows: "Despite my much vaunted frugality I have sacrificed a great deal for my collection of Greek, Roman and Egyptian antiquities, have actually read more archaeology than psychology, and that before the war and once after its end I felt compelled to spend every year at least several days or weeks in Rome, and so on."[10] One is reminded of the reaction of the French poet Comtesse Anna de Noailles on meeting Freud: "Surely," she exclaimed, "*he* never wrote his 'sexy' books. What a terrible man! I am sure he has never been unfaithful to his wife. It's quite abnormal and scandalous! [Freud ne trompe pas sa femme. C'est scandaleux! C'est anormal]."[11] To outsiders, the strict habits and familial dutifulness of Freud's life irremediably condemned him as a mediocre bourgeois professional, whereas Freud felt that his antiquities, his archaeology, and his psychoanalytic theories at least ameliorated, if not entirely exculpated him from, such a charge.

Freud's interest in his collection was, as we might expect, overdetermined. One feature is clear: his interest in his objects was historical rather than aesthetic, and partook of a late nineteenth century museum culture.[12] As Spector remarks: "Except for the bookcases, the interior resembles those old-fashioned provincial museums housing collections of local specimens, both geological and historical (collected for their cultural and historical rather than for their aesthetic value), such as one can see in parts of Austria even today."[13] Yet it was not a public collection—although I will modify this judgment somewhat later in this chapter—and was essentially for the personal enjoyment of its owner. Nor was it a systematic collection; it was acquired in a slow and steady fashion over some forty years, but each acquisition depended primarily on the virtues of the newly acquired piece, on its particular contingencies, rather than its place within a predestined order. As the quotation from Freud's letter to Lampl de Groot indicates, the vitality of his collection did not stem from its embodying some ideal of completeness or universality; its vitality depended on new acquisitions, and Freud continually rang the changes on the arrangement of all his pieces in his rooms. When he died, the collection stopped growing and turned into the curious entity it now is: a museum within a museum, a collection of antiquities within a museum devoted to the founder of psychoanalysis. His daughter Anna fostered the transformation from living collection into dead museum by preserving Freud's study, with his collection, intact and untouched for over four decades, while she continued to live in the rest of the house, which was decorated with less anxious attention to the preservation of the family's past—although it does house its fair share of turn-of-the-century Austrian stoves and stuffed armchairs, promiscuously rubbing shoulders with more modern, functional furniture. She probably imagined that her father regarded only his psychoanalytic work as worthy of such preservation; the maternally dominated side of the house deserved no such sepulchral devotions. While Anna was alive, the living museum of Freud's consulting-room was occasionally opened up and used for a seminar. Now, after her death, the Freud Museum is a properly functioning public space, with opening hours, a visitor's book, staff on duty, people running things backstage, and its quota of Youth Training Scheme attendants and trainees.

If the collection was only alive if it was being added to, it was also characteristic of Freud's attitude to his pieces that he was ready to surrender them, give them away, and swap them for others. For instance, an Egyptian mummy mask of the Roman period which eventually sat beside Freud's armchair behind the couch was acquired from one of his regular dealers who would bring objects for him to consider buying. Freud was quite taken with it, but found its cost prohibitive. Unwilling to let it go, he made a deal with the dealer, saying he would pay something like a third in cash, and the rest in antique rings from his collection. He showed the dealer the drawer in which the rings were, and asked him to choose the ones he would take that would make up the price. Such an easy come, easy go attitude to his pieces indicates that Freud's initial collecting impulse was not the systematic miser's refusal of differentiation but was more akin to the hobbyist's welcoming of the individuality of each acquired item in the collection. Freud had no difficulty in de-sacralizing—in de-accessioning, one might say—the gods in his collection.[14] Such an attitude was, it should also be said, entirely characteristic of Freud's generosity: not only did he support his own large family of six children, wife, and sister-in-law, but a steady flow of gifts, sometimes akin to grants, went out to a wider circle of young friends and the children of hard-up families. "My psychic constitution urgently requires the acquisition and the spending of money for my family as fulfillment of my father complex that I know so well,"[15] he wrote to a colleague during the First World War. This may well have been true, but the father complex also insisted that Freud spend money on an ever-widening circle of friends and disciples. And the father complex had an important say in the founding and development of his collection of antiques.

———————

Freud started acquiring artistic objects just after his father's death in October 1896, and almost explicitly in response to that event, since he found these objects a "source of exceptional renewal and comfort."[16] The majority of historians have agreed with Freud himself that this death was a major turning-point in his life and work, precipitating him into a neurotic crisis of self-doubt and obliging him to undertake his self-analysis. The eventual product of this period of self-doubt was the mature Freud and his masterpiece, *The Interpretation of Dreams*, finished in 1899. Looking back at that work in 1908, when he was writing the preface to its second edition, Freud declared that "it was, I found, a portion of my own self-analysis, my reaction to my father's death—that is to say, to the most important event, the most poignant loss, of a man's life."[17] Inaugurated by the father's death, only kept from death as long as it was growing, Freud's collection of antiquities elegantly demonstrates how a collection can symbolize the battle of life within death, of life being infiltrated by death, of a space cleared for the expression of this battle by the objects the collector has chosen as his personal representatives.

In what sense was Freud's collecting a response to this most poignant of all losses? In early 1895, he had offered an explanation of such behavior: "When an old maid keeps a dog or an old bachelor collects snuffboxes, the former is finding a substitute for her need for a companion in marriage and the latter for his need for—a multitude of conquests. Every collector is a substitute for a Don Juan Tenerio, and so too is the mountaineer, the sportsman, and such people. These are erotic equivalents."[18] The idea of cultural activity—keeping domestic animals, collecting snuffboxes—as a substitute for the libidinal tie to an idealized object is already implicit in this account. The absence of the phallic object, both for old maids and bachelors, is the source of their eccentric habits. Yet there is a difference between men and women, which Freud pursues: "Women know them too. Gynaecological treatment falls into this category. There are two kinds of women patients: one kind who are as loyal to their doctor as to their husband, and the other kind who change their doctors as often as their lovers. This normally operating mechanism of substitution is abused in obsessional ideas—once again for purposes of *defense.*"[19] The women collect doctors, symbolic substitutes for the lovers they refuse themselves, just as the men collect substitutes for the conquests they never, or no longer, have. Freud's own thesis about collectors will thus easily apply to himself: but for him, it is his father who is the Don Juan—the father whose three wives cast him somewhat in the light of a ladies' man[20]—and Freud's collecting is both a substitution for the father's conquests and an act of homage to the dead father he is tempted to idealize. Indeed, it is in Freud's consulting-room that we see take shape the collection that is the response to his father's death: not only the antiquities, but also the case histories of women, the legitimate scientific collection which is distinctively Freud's, the mark of his own, as opposed to his father's, or anyone else's, originality and sublimated "sexual megalomania."[21]

I have already noted how the location of Freud's collection of antiquities exclusively in his working-space signals its intimate connection with his psychoanalytic work. However, we should not let the impressive and visible weight of Freud's collection of antiquities, its sepulchral resonance with the museum, obscure the fact that this was not the only sort of collecting he engaged in. The case histories of patients were, to be sure, seemingly a conventional enough form of medical writing, in which he followed in the footsteps of teachers such as Charcot and the other clinical neurologists who influenced him, Hughlings Jackson for example. And in certain respects, Freud followed faithfully on the work of Richard von Krafft-Ebing, one of the founders of sexology, and the Professor of Psychiatry in Freud's Vienna, which consisted precisely in the pedantic form of the collecting and naming of sexual perversions—for example, sadism and masochism, the best known of his many categories.[22] As one of Krafft-Ebing's contemporary Viennese critics put it, he was "an untiring collector who has acquired the false reputation of an expert."[23] When it came to collecting and naming sexual perversions and characteristics, Freud was remarkably orthodox and unadventurous; his flair for original scientific collecting lay elsewhere.

Freud found his true métier as a scientific collector in the late 1890s, in a series of unprecedented collections he started at that time. The first collection was his set of cases: within each case, the work consisted in collecting "scenes," collecting "memories," and establishing the links between these discrete items and thus making overall sense of them. The second collection was of dream texts and their analyses, begun in 1895, but turned into a substantial segment of his working activity in the late 1890s. The third such collection followed shortly after, in June 1897: "I must confess that for some time past I have been putting together a collection of Jewish anecdotes of deep significance."[24] The latter two collections became intertwined—in one dream-analysis published in 1900, Freud noted: "The material out of which the dream was woven included at this point two of those facetious Jewish anecdotes which contain so much profound and often bitter worldly wisdom and which we so greatly enjoy quoting in our talk and letters."[25] And then there was a fourth collection, perhaps the most unusual, but one that was marginally less eccentric for a neurologist who necessarily paid great attention to the minute details of sensory and motor disturbances: slips of the tongue, misreadings, mistakes, misnomers, mislayings, misprints, faulty actions—all those failures of action which are signaled in German by the prefix Ver-.[26] Freud's first paper on these parapraxes, as they were eventually called in English, was published in 1898: the example he selected from his collection was an instance of forgetting he himself had suffered. The next year, in 1899, he published another paper, this time on his earliest childhood memory, noting that "before dealing with the psychological problems attaching to the earliest memories of childhood, it would of course be essential to make a collection of material by circularizing a fairly large number of normal adults and discovering what kind of recollections they are able to produce from these early years."[27]

Just before its publication, Freud described his "Egyptian dream-book,"[28] as he jocularly referred to *The Interpretation of Dreams*, in the following endearing way: "No other work of mine has been so completely my own, my own dung heap, my seedling and a *nova species mihi* on top of it."[29] With these three ways of characterizing his dream collection, he returned to the botanical interests of his youth, when he "was an enthusiastic walker and nature lover, and would roam the forest and woods near Vienna with his friends, bringing back rare plants and flower specimens."[30] In these crucial years, then, Freud opened up a whole set of related fields of phenomena, whose scientific study would require assiduous and painstaking collections: dreams, jokes, parapraxes, early memories. It is alongside these distinctively Freudian collections that we should place his contemporaneous collection of antiquities.

If the late 1890s was the most significant period in Freud's development of psychoanalysis, which was founded upon the idiosyncratic collections he established at that time, it was also, he later claimed, his period of splendid isolation, when his ties of collegial friendship were loosened, with the exception of his dependence on Wilhelm Fliess. When he did reestablish strong and many-sided relations with others, if he ever did, it was in a new mold, as he drew around him a steadily growing band of followers, disciples, and admirers. This movement of withdrawal and detachment from the world followed by a reattachment in a different modality is reminiscent of, maybe even formed the model for, his later theory of narcissism, and in particular its application to the processes underlying paranoia: "the process of repression proper consists in a detachment of the libido from people—and things—that were previously loved. It happens silently . . . What forces itself so noisily upon our attention is the process of recovery, which undoes the work of repression and brings back the libido again on to the people it had abandoned."[31] In the period when Freud was developing his thesis concerning the mechanism of paranoia and its relationship to narcissism, he offered an account of the paranoiac and the artistic creator in whose illness occurs "the detachment of the libido from the objects (a reverse course is taken by the collector who directs his surplus libido onto the inanimate objective: love of things)."[32] Whereas the paranoiac fails to reestablish libidinal relations, enlarging his own ego at their expense, the collector restores ties with the world—but only in the form of loved things, rather than loved people. He has found a balance between the newly pressing needs of narcissism and the requirements of the world. The collector thus rediscovers his narcissism in the charm of the objects, which each reflect back to him a portion of his lost libidinal objects.

The refrain of the charm of the object that is out of reach, contained and self-sufficient—either because of its own nature or perhaps because this object is dead, only the shadow of an object—is continued in Freud's famous portrait of the narcissistic woman: "Another person's narcissism has a great attraction for those who have renounced part of their own narcissism and are in search of object-love. The charm of a child lies to a great extent in his narcissism, his self-contentment and inaccessibility, just as does the charm of certain animals which seem not to concern themselves about us, such as cats and the large beasts of prey."[33] In his friend and follower Lou Andreas-Salomé, Freud had found the model for such a woman. And she had noted in her diary a telling story Freud told her, of a cat who would climb into his study every day through an open window and "inspect in passing the antique objects which he had placed for the time being on the floor. But when the cat proceeded to make known its archaeological satisfaction by purring and with its lithe grace did not cause the slightest damage, Freud's heart melted and he ordered milk for it. From then on the cat claimed its rights daily to take a place on the sofa, inspect the antiques, and get its bowl of milk." Freud may have now warmed to the cat, but "the cat paid him not a bit of attention and coldly turned its green eyes with their slanting pupils toward him as toward any other object."[34]

Baudrillard sees the object in a collection as "the perfect domestic animal,"[35] and there may be a grain of truth in the crude view that after his self-analysis Freud's "libidinal" relations turned toward narcissistic women—women he could admire and who would not threaten to overwhelm him—domestic animals, and the objects in his collections.[36] The collector may be using his collection to express relatively simply his attachment to his ideal objects: collectors talk to their collections, just as dog-owners talk to their dogs. When he had made a new acquisition, Freud would bring it into the dining room, place it on the table in front of him and commune with it in silence over lunch.

At first sight, there are two features of Freud's collection of antiquities which make it quite different from the collection of dreams and jokes. First, the antiquities are material objects, whereas dreams and jokes are purely verbal or mental phenomena. Second, the antiquities have a cultural sanction of respectability, whereas Freud was under no illusion that the accusation that dreams, jokes, and slips were phenomena of no cultural or psychological significance would be rebutted by either common sense or scientific authority. Consideration of both these seemingly divergent characteristics will help us understand more about how all of these collections functioned within Freud's psychoanalytic work.

The first distinction—that antiquities are material, whereas dreams are nonmaterial and mental—is where we started from, with Freud's attempt to draw an analogy between the historical topography of Rome and the simultaneous coexistence within the mind of psychic events from different epochs. Freud's conclusion, we should remind ourselves, was that the mind preserved its past better than the city of Rome ever could: "the destruction of Pompeii was only beginning now that it had been dug up."[37] In a curious way, the blurred, fragmentary, and inscrutable characteristics of so many of the objects in Freud's collection of antiquities—the scarabs, the funerary urns—serve to remind us that the material survivals from the past are less loquacious than the psychic survivals from infancy that Freud's psychoanalytic method could decipher with confidence. In Freud's world-view, when it came down to it, psychic reality was more real than material reality. Dreams were more stable objects than sepulchers.

H.D., the most eloquent of Freud's former patients, captured this vacillation between confidence in the reality of the psyche and the consolations offered by the reality of the material past in her description of her first meeting with Freud in his consulting-room:

> Automatically, I walk through the door. It closes. Sigmund Freud does not speak . . . I look around the room. A lover of Greek art, I am automatically taking stock of the room's contents. Pricelessly lovely objects are displayed here on the shelves to right, to left of me . . . no one had told me that this room was lined with treasures. I was to greet the Old Man of the Sea, but no one had told me of the treasures he had salvaged from the sea-depth . . . waiting and finding that I would not or could not speak, he uttered. What he said—and I thought a little sadly—was, "You are the only person who has ever come into this room and looked at the things in the room before looking at me."[38]

Yet this poet's enormous interest in his things did not prevent her from seeing very clearly the interplay between the mental and the material in his method:

> Thoughts were things, to be collected, collated, analysed, shelved or resolved. Fragmentary ideas, apparently unrelated, were often found to be part of a special layer or stratum of thought and memory, therefore to belong together; these were sometimes skilfully pieced together like the exquisite Greek tear-jars and iridescent glass bowls and vases that gleamed in the dusk from the

121

shelves of the cabinet that faced me where I stretched, propped up on the couch in the room in Berggasse 19, Wien IX. The dead were living in so far as they lived in memory or were recalled in dream.[39]

Their journeys into the past and future together—"a present that was in the past or a past that was in the future"[40]—allowed them to share objects. She had been to the Temple at Karnak that hung above the couch; they could both share in reminiscences of the flowers of Rome, he the gardenias he so loved to wear and she the almond blossoms. And H.D.'s recollection of her analysis points us back to the second of the superficial differences between a collection of antiquities and a collection of jokes.

The transience of a flower may commune with a second century A.D. Artemis through the beauty that they have in common. But flowers are not the only ephemera that are the objects of analysis: an analysis will look to farts as much as flowers for its truth. Freud became, in all seriousness, an archaeologist of farts:

> while, as they lie in the grass of our neglect,
>   so many long-forgotten objects
> revealed by his undiscouraged shining
>
> are returned to us and made precious again;
> games we had thought we must drop as we grew up,
>   little noises we dared not laugh at,
> faces we made when no one was looking.[41]

Freud is a collector of farts and grimaces, an archaeologist of rubbish *avant la lettre*, as well as a collector of the fading yet precious detritus of Western civilization. The public Freud, with his reputation for shocking, distasteful, and immoral claims about all human beings; the private Freud, with his well-ordered life and his bourgeois collection of culturally respectable art objects. These dichotomies are also familiar in the Janus-faced character of psychoanalytic aesthetics: How could the founder of the quintessentially modernist movement that is psychoanalysis have had such unimpeachably conservative taste in art?

The lack of an account of form in Freud's personal aesthetic has often been the answer that critics have given to the deficiencies of psychoanalytic aesthetics, and this criticism has often been illustrated by referring to his own confessions of inability to appreciate beauty in art in any other way than by analyzing and understanding it.[42] One thing is clear: for Freud, the only skill he felt he could bring to bear in any sphere was that of analysis. Synthesis, he would say, was a function of the ego, and the ego, as the enemy of the unconscious, would and should always take care of itself without the aid of the psychoanalyst. Hence the formal characteristics of art were something he would turn away from as essentially uninterpretable; he would turn instead to detail. It is in the preoccupation with detail that the radical innovations of psychoanalysis are to be found. Traces, signs, small things, overlooked singularities: the science of clues whose genealogy Carlo Ginzburg sketches for us in linking Holmes the detective, Freud the analyst, and Morelli the art historian.[43] Certainly the unsystematic character of Freud's collection is also an indication of his disinclination for the formal; his statues were precious as individuals, with histories and distinctive peculiarities. Freud's inclinations, even in science, were never toward counting; he never needed a Leporello to enumerate his conquests. No catalogue of his collection was ever compiled in his lifetime.[44]

To illustrate how everyday objects are transformed by Freud's principles of interpretation, and thus a new theory of objects (including collectibles) in general becomes possible, I want to examine a long footnote from the analysis of one of Freud's own dreams in *The Interpretation of Dreams*. The "Count Thun" dream included the following passage: *"It was as though thinking and experiencing were one and the same thing. He [an elderly gentleman] appeared to be blind, at all events with one eye, and I handed him a male glass urinal . . . Here the man's attitude and his micturating penis appeared in plastic*

form." In a long, complex, but by no means complete analysis of this
lengthy dream, Freud disclosed how when he was seven or eight, he
had urinated in his parents' bedroom and his father had reprimanded
him, saying: "The boy will come to nothing." As did so many of
Freud's dreams, this dream represented a reversal and a refutation
of the father's crushing of the boy: now it was his elderly father, the
man in the dream, who was urinating in front of the son—the father
had come to nothing (had died some months before). And it was the
son who had become "something"—in particular, he had made profound discoveries about the theory of hysteria.

Freud concluded a long and ill-organized footnote (to which he
had consigned a number of unassimilated associations that had come
up in the course of the lengthy dream analysis) with the following
explanation:

The phrase *"thinking and experiencing were one and the same thing"*
had a reference to the explanation of hysterical symptoms, and the
"male urinal" belonged in the same connection. I need not explain
to a Viennese the principle of the *"Gschnas."* It consists in constructing what appear to be rare and precious objects out of trivial
and preferably comic and worthless materials (for instance, in
making armour out of saucepans, wisps of straw and dinner
rolls)—a favourite pastime at bohemian parties here in Vienna. I
had observed that this is precisely what hysterical subjects do:
alongside what has really happened to them, they unconsciously
build up frightful or perverse imaginary events which they construct out of the most innocent and everyday material of their
experience. It is to these phantasies that their symptoms are in the
first instance attached and not to their recollections of real events,
whether serious or equally innocent. This revelation had helped
me over a number of difficulties and had given me particular
pleasure. What made it possible for me to refer to this by means
of the dream-element of the "male urinal" was as follows. I had
been told that at the latest *"Gschnas"*-night a poisoned chalice

belonging to Lucrezia Borgia had been exhibited; its central and principal constituent had been a *male urinal* of the type used in hospitals.[45]

The dreamer is thus offering his father a male urinal that is also a poisoned chalice: an Oedipal act, to be sure. But this "poisoned chalice" includes within itself its own inner principle of transformation: this rare object, Lucrezia Borgia's own chalice, an object any museum curator would give his eyeteeth for, is constructed "out of trivial and preferably comic and worthless materials (for instance, in making armour out of saucepans, wisps of straw and dinner rolls)" or male urinals. The Viennese principle of the *Gschnas* becomes the underlying principle for mental objects in general: what is rare and precious is constructed out of the worthless and trivial—and vice versa. And the dream itself becomes such a carnival, Freud's own *Gschnas*-night, in which worthless objects—the male urinal—are transformed into a celebration of filial triumph over the father.

This attention to the trivial detail of the life of everyday objects is typical of Freud's analysis of dreams. The mechanisms of displacement and condensation transform such everyday objects into veritable philosopher's stones; they become infinitely displaceable, perpetually unstable. In the lability of Freud's nighttime celebrations and the analyses that accompany them we encounter the typical modernist objects—the ready-made, the found object, the bit of detritus, the god as a shout in the street, the surrealist celebration of the transvaluation of all values. We are a long way from those musty archaeological objects infected with "chronic necrophilia," as an Italian futurist call to arms damned them. Yet the interpreter of dreams, the celebrant of the principle of the *Gschnas*, would never have dreamed of adding a Picabia or a Duchamp to his collection of antiquities. Where he outdid anything that Duchamp or the Dadaists would later achieve was in turning his collections of dreams, jokes, and slips into the serious stuff of science. Each dream, each slip,

125

each joke, each fart is a urinal that unconscious mechanisms transform into a grail worthy of inclusion in any museum of modern science.

Thus Freud's psychoanalysis did transform despised and neglected objects into precious things; it did bring ubiquitously covert objects of shame into a public world of objects. These collections of his started off as very individual and idiosyncratic examples of the genre: collections of jokes and dream texts must, without the benefit of hindsight, rank with stamp and bottle-top collecting as narrowly conceived and single-mindedly eccentric.

However, the antiquities that Freud also collected give the lie to one aspect of this view of him as an eccentric. These antiquities represent the first appearance of Freud's vision of his work as embodying essential elements of the cultural traditions to which he was self-consciously heir:[46] Winckelmann the archaeologist and Goethe the traveler, lover, and worshiper of Italy; Akhnaten the founder of monotheism, Moses the Egyptian; Aeschylus the teller of ancient family tragedies and Athena representative of justice, mercy, and wisdom. All these are embodied in the collection of objects, and it is their possession that realizes Freud's desire to be a universal and public citizen of this world, walking through the Museum of history and culture.[47] Collectors are often extremely private, especially when they collect such strange objects as dreams. In contrast, all of Freud's collections were permeated by a public and Enlightenment ideal—an ideal, however, always in tension with his less public taste for the eccentric. As Adam Phillips remarks, "The Enlightenment Freud wants to tell us what we have in common; the post-Freudian Freud, his collaborative antagonist, is the connoisseur of anomalies."[48]

The power of the public ideal informing Freud's collection can be gauged from his own skeptical analysis of it, when, like all other ideals, it was revealed as an illusion by the First World War. The idea of European civilization had been based on universal moral standards which made each participant in that civilization a citizen in a "new and wider fatherland," of both south and north, sea and mountain: "This new fatherland was a museum for him, too, filled with all the treasures which the artists of civilized humanity had in the successive centuries created and left behind . . . each of these citizens of the civilized world had created for himself a 'Parnassus' and a 'School of Athens' of his own."[49] Freud's collection of antiquities, and the very idea of psychoanalysis itself, as embodied in his collections of jokes and dream texts, constituted his own museum of these treasures come down to us from Parnassus. To paraphrase Marx's description of money as "general wealth in the form of a concise compendium, as opposed to its diffusion and fragmentation in the world of commodities,"[50] one could say that Freud's collection of antiquities was a concise compendium of his version of civilization, as opposed to its diffusion and fragmentation in the world of everyday life—a world that nonetheless could be measured and weighed in the scales of the analytic method. All this was lost in the descent into the barbarism of the war, with its blood, its complete disregard of law and ethical requirements, and its liberation of the hate and loathing with which all these universal citizens now mutually regarded one another: the war "tramples in blind fury on all that comes in its way, as though there were to be no future and no peace among men after it is over."[51]

––––––––

Freud's collecting thus always aspired to a public and social function, even when the civic context of the Great War undermined the untroubled sense of participation in "this common civilization." His private collection never became a furtive or private vice. The impulse to give friends and followers pieces out of the collection came to him often. Even though his collection was a private affair, it was not a hoard, not a sequestered treasure, jealously guarded. Baudrillard depicts this mode of relation to the hoarded object in the following way: "The reason why you don't lend your car, your pen, your woman is that these objects are, within jealousy, the narcissistic equivalent of the ego: if this object is lost, or is damaged, that's castration. You don't lend your phallus, that's the basic thing."[52] Freud's easy giving of precious antiques to his friends and disciples showed he was not afraid to lose the phallic element located in his collection. Perhaps this urge to generosity was like his public collection of dreams: insofar as he gave to these disciples various rings and statuettes, they became Freudians, part of his international movement, part of his political/scientific collection.

Freud's use of his collection indicates a further feature that contrasts with the mode of pure accumulation. His collection of antiquities was itself already public and fully integrated with the public functions of psychoanalysis: as symbol, as pedagogic device, as seductive gadget. The (private) impulse to acquire, derivative from one aspect of the father-complex, the desire to have all the women, was overshadowed and overtaken by another aspect of that same complex, the (public) impulse to spend, to dispense largesse to his family, followers, and readers. In this sense Freud's collections were a natural history of civilization, constructed in the same spirit of self-serving public service that other nineteenth-century scientific collectors envisaged. In Britain in the mid-nineteenth century, one or two individuals would act as centralized exchanges, correspondence network organizers, for collections of objects, such as butterflies, flowers, orchids, seafish.[53] Participants would send in specimens collected locally and would receive in return, via the central communication system, excess specimens from collectors in other parts of the country. In order to acquire, one had to give. And the scientific fruit or product of this market was the map of the flora and fauna of the British Isles. Freud's collections functioned in a similar way. Potential followers instinctively knew that an item for the collection, whether of dreams, jokes, or antiquities, was the appropriate gift for Professor Freud: the later editions of both *The Interpretation of Dreams* and *The Psychopathology of Everyday Life* are greatly expanded versions, filled out with these additional contributions to his scientific collections. The product of this centralized system of dream-specimen collection would be the cartography, the completed natural history of dreams.

Following Susan Stewart's fine analysis in her book *On Longing*, we can see that Freud's objects (both antiques and texts) served the functions both of evoking the past, of entering into the nostalgic dimension of the souvenir, and of effacing the past, of building a new, timeless world of the collection. Freud's collections embodied at the same time the principle of the souvenir and of the collection, that is, both the aesthetic of origin and presence, of restoration and provenance, and the aesthetic of collection, accumulation, and exchange, with its indefinite seriality. His objects were souvenirs precisely because they did confer authenticity on the past and served the primary function of remembering—they were postcards from the past; they were souvenirs in the sense that they involved adventure and the danger and risk of discovery: think of Freud's identification with Heinrich Schliemann, the risk-loving entrepreneurial discoverer of the souvenir of all of Western culture, or of his identification with the conquistadors. Freud's objects were also souvenirs in that that they infected him and his patients with the scenes they depicted, just as Stewart describes the souvenir magically bringing us back to the scene of its origin.

In a scrapbook, Stewart argues, "the whole dissolves into parts, each of which refers metonymically to a context of origin or acquisition . . . In contrast, each element within the collection is representative and works in combination toward the creation of a new whole that is the context of the collection itself. The spatial whole of the collection supersedes the individual narratives that 'lie behind it.'"[54] One might think that, inasmuch as Freud's collections were committed to the rediscovery of the past, they were more like a scrapbook than a museum gallery. But they were also items in a collection that denied history, that found a nonhistorical principle of ordering and classification: the theory of desire, libido, and the drives, the inner logic of the passions—the ultimate time of the collection is the atemporality of the unconscious.

Yet the model of the dream consistently subverts the model of permanence offered by the ancient statues in their cases, standing guard over desk and couch. Freud's analysis of the collection of screen memories revealed how memories are tendentious, how their function as witnesses is a false function, a false form of remembering instead of desiring. Where the souvenir exhorts memory, Freud's collections also exhort forgetting, the forgetting that will do away with repression, which is an inexpedient form of remembering. Freud's collections encourage us finally to forget the effects of the murder of Akhnaten and Moses, of Clytemnestra and Laius. But whereas Winckelmann's pilgrimage to Rome, repeated so faithfully by Freud his epigone, would eventually lead to the "tyranny of Greece over Germany," so well captured by Freud's collection of antiques and palpable in museum collections throughout the world, the aim of Freud's other collecting activities, in his psychoanalytic practice, was to render palpable so as to dissipate the tyranny of each individual's forgotten past. You enter the analyst's consulting-room, and you bring a collection whose internal structure is then made visible as inherently tyrannical. And Freud's collectibles, whether Athena or an absurd dream, are not only derisory remnants of past cultures, but also objects beyond price, standing simultaneously outside monetary exchange systems and ready to enter into them. The dream will be revealed to be both what is most singular, eccentric, and peculiar to you, and also as what is most ineluctably your heritage, your place in the exchange systems that presided over your birth and destiny and your value to others.

Freud offered his patients two different models of remembering and forgetting:[55] remembering as a means of disinterring the past so as to destroy it and finally release it into oblivion, and remembering as a means of preservation, a lucky chance amidst the processes through which the past inexorably vanishes. In the language of the oldest instincts, there is forgetting as spitting out, as rendering utterly alien, an absolute form of forgetting; and then there is forgetting as digesting, incorporating, in which one remembers by becoming the

130

thing remembered.[56] Freud's collection of antiques was used to tack between these two senses of remembering. The objects retrieved from the wreckage of Pompeii were only glimpses of a past irretrievably lost, although Freud and others like him—connoisseurs, antiquarians, museum curators—made every effort to preserve these objects, as they inevitably crumbled into dust. They remind us that psychoanalysis is a cure through the kind of remembering that makes forgetting possible.

But couldn't this process of preservation, Freud's patients asked him, be in the end as destructive as the forgetting from which the torment of their neurotic symptoms arose? Might it not be more dangerous to dig up these forgotten objects than to let the sleeping dogs of Pompeii lie? No, Freud assured them: remembering would never result in their being overwhelmed by the evil impulses and desires from the past. The desire to be rid of the present tormenting ideas would always mean that a victory over the past was assured. Digging up Pompeii, Freud implied, did not risk causing another eruption of Vesuvius.

Yet this answer is fundamentally disingenuous; the transference was the permanent reminder of the vitality of the volcanic forces slumbering in the patient's symptomatic forgetfulness. "In view of the kind of matter we work with, it will never be possible to avoid little laboratory explosions,"[57] he wrote to Jung when the erotic passions of both analyst and analysand were clearly getting out of hand; it is the word "laboratory" that is consolatory here—the reassurance that the psychoanalysis is only an experiment, not real life. And that the dark forces that are released in the course of psychoanalysis can be left behind, forgotten forever, when one leaves the couch. Yet the ambiguity, the ambivalence about forgetting and the permanence of the cultural achievement of remembering is left behind, with the "exquisite Greek tear-jars and iridescent glass bowls and vases that gleamed in the dusk from the shelves of the cabinet."

Freud's collection was undoubtedly his treasure. There is a curious irony in that the London Freud Museum's function is totally divided by this fact. Freud's collection only became a museum collection once it became part of a museum of memorabilia, of souvenirs. The creation of the Freud Museum simultaneously brought into being a museum within a museum: a museum of precious ancient objects, within an ordinary house in Hampstead where a great man died. The Sigmund Freud Haus at Berggasse 19 in Vienna illustrates this clearly by contrast. In 1975, the time of my first visit, it was an apartment with bare walls, no furniture, and a few glass cases with manuscripts and other minor memorabilia. It was dominated visually by photographs, blown up to life size, of how it once had been, photographs that stood in for all the objects that had been removed to London when the Freuds escaped from the Nazis. It had a derisible atmosphere, perhaps one deliberately induced to remind visitors of yet one more loss that the war had visited on Vienna; but it still prompted the thought that a museum of fake souvenirs is a fake museum—a screen museum, the Freudian might say. In London, however, we find a meticulously conserved milieu: the real furniture, the books, the little objects useful in everyday life and useless anywhere else, Freud's couch, his pen, the photographs of his dogs—yes, in his old age, after his cancer operations, he even began to collect dogs. And to remind us that this is truly the world of souvenirs, locked away in a cupboard upstairs there are his dentures and the dreadful prosthesis that served him for an upper jaw in his later years, visited and scrutinized by Professors of Dentistry and Cancer, writing histories of Freud's illness, operations, and death, or histories of early twentieth century treatments of the particular carcinoma Freud had been forced to live with. Yet within this perfect souvenir-world is a "living" collection of antiques, ready to tour the world as Freud's collection, ready to be loaned to other museums for exhibitions on Umbrian bronzes, or early terracotta statuettes.

————

H.D. knew better than anyone what sort of collector Freud was. Once he had settled into his house in Hampstead in November 1938, she anonymously sought out and sent him those flowers that she alone knew were his favorites: gardenias, which reminded him of being in Rome. On the accompanying card, she scribbled: "To greet the return of the Gods." This meant, in their private language: the settling in of his collection of antiques. Freud wrote her the following note:

> Dear H.D.,
>
> I got to-day some flowers. By chance or intention they are my favourite flowers, those I most admire. Some words "to greet the return of the Gods" (other people read: Goods). No name. I suspect you to be responsible for the gift. If I have guessed right don't answer but accept my hearty thanks for so charming a gesture. In any case,
>
> affectionately yours,
> Sigm. Freud[58]

Freud's favorite flowers were the quintessential gift that this intimately attuned patient of his could give him. And she and he had already remarked upon the closeness in English between the words "Gods" and "Goods." Goods meant to them what is exchanged, and also what is highest, most ethical, and aesthetically pure. And this anonymous gift then provoked an elegant thank-you that pretended to preserve her anonymity: because Freud asks her not to reply if she is the giver. In other words, he will never know for sure whether she was the giver or not. But in assuming it, and in thanking her, he continues the exchange that the play on words between Gods and Goods opened up. For Freud, if for no one else, the treasures were continuous with the everyday life of analysis, were potentially exchangeable as gifts or for money; they were something more than goods, but not quite gods. They did not strive for a timelessness beyond the world of goods. In 1938, in Vienna, Freud did not utter one cry of despair or complaint at the prospect of losing his whole collection. It never occurred to him that he might die with his treasure rather than part from it. It was not a *priceless* collection in the sense of being beyond financial calculation—which makes of the economic the only possible measure of value—but priceless in the sense that it did not matter very much whether a monetary value was attached to it or not. Yet again, Freud would have appreciated Marx's description of money as "the god among commodities . . . it represents the divine existence of commodities, while they represent its earthly form."[59] But he also knew that if certain objects, certain "commodities," become gods, they can only do so by retaining their dynamic relationship to more earthly objects. Without the presence of measure and exchange, Marx wrote, "accumulating [treasure] is nothing more than the accumulation of gold and silver, not of money."[60] We might apply this dictum to Freud in the following way: without the dynamic relationship between his collection of antiquities and his psychoanalytic work, the antiquities would simply have been a collection of old objects, things of neither historical nor personal value, displaying what Simmel called that "most remarkable mania for accumulation, a trait that often leads people to compare [such collectors] to hamsters."[61]

The amicably intimate word play between "gods" and "goods" by Freud and his gifted patient reminds us of one further dimension of Freud's collecting activities: the manner in which the collections mediated between the Jewish and non-Jewish cultural heritage. By definition, or rather by biblical edict, Freud's gods could not be Jewish gods. No Jew can make a collection of material objects without knowing that these are profanities, false gods, marks of the alien cultures outside the mental and physical space granted to the Chosen People. Quite self-consciously, in 1897 Freud started a collection of Jewish anecdotes, almost as a deliberate counterpart to his collection of pagan and Gentile antiquities; there certainly could be no collection of Jewish antiquities. The Jew and his goods—this is the cultural image which neither H.D. nor Freud could, in 1938, readily forget; instead H.D. welcomed the arrival of the Jew and his gods. Freud did not pass up the opportunity to underline the ambiguous function of his collection of pagan and Gentile art, the symbol of his participation in the non-Jewish universal history of Enlightenment. And his refusal to forget allows us to underline, finally, that his collection of jokes, alongside the equally textual, some have said Talmudic,[62] collections of dreams and slips, allowed yet one more assimilation of the Jewish culture of the immaterial word.

Many men who have devoted their lives to making money have ended up wishing for the form of immortality that a public collection of priceless goods confers. Freud was neither a man who devoted his life to making money nor someone whose artistic collection would earn him immortality. But he may well have had the desire for immortality that the act of collecting so often embodies—and it turns out that Freud's collection of dreams is in fact his guarantee of immortality. For some, like the mythical figure who buys the only extant second copy of a first edition he already possesses in order to burn it, recognizing the necessary incompleteness of every collection is the kiss of death to their fantasy of mastery; for others, to complete a collection is the end of a life's work, so they continually postpone acquiring that "final" object. Many different collectors, wealthy or not, find in their collections a means of jousting with death. Yet Freud and the Annenbergs, the Mellons, the Thyssens of our age might share something in common: the desire to free a space in which money, while not excluded, does not rule. We know that psychoanalysis obeys the law of the market. And it is possible that regulating dreams according to that market may pull them away entirely from their function as souvenirs toward their function as items in a collection. Yet Freud wished to establish dreams, jokes, symptoms, and their material symbol, his collection of antiquities, as emblematic of a shared and universal humanity, neither economic, nor quite aesthetic or ethical. For many of the rich men mentioned above, collecting functions as a nostalgic vestige of a pre-abstract, pre-monetary relation to the object. The collection is an attempt to restore such a nonarbitrary, nonaccidental relation, although the means by which this is achieved, through money, defeats precisely this aim. Yet the objects, the items in the collection represent this hope through their not being money, through their being objects organized in a classification that is not that of number and abstract exchange, whether the principle of unification and distribution is that of Impressionist paintings, Egyptian scarabs, stamps, or women. Each of these collections represents an attempt at withdrawal from the public discourse of the market, and an attempt to find a local shelter from that discourse in the scent of the harem, whose charm is always that of intimacy restrained by seriality, and seriality infused with intimacy.[63]

Freud's collection certainly partakes of this ideal, yet it appeals to science—whether archaeology or psychology—as the ground of this ideal. This does not mean that discovering the particular eccentricities of a collection—whether it be the sensual avarice of Don Juan or the ascetic moderation and imperial completeness of Darwin's collection of barnacles—reveals the ideal as hollow or self-deceiving. Rather, it shows us the genealogy of the scientific or analytic ideal. Clearing the space, the space of analysis, for dreams and jokes was for Freud first and foremost a scientific task: his collection was to rank alongside that of Linnaeus or of Darwin. And it may well be the spirit of "scientific" acquisition pervading Freud's collections that will continue to dissuade us from aligning Freud more closely with ethical naturalists such as Montaigne and Nietzsche, as we are often tempted to do, than with those empirical scientists who always remained his models. In the end, his collection of antiquities was clearly more commonplace, despite its personal and private character, than his public collections of cases, dreams, and jokes.

There was one dream that, throughout his adult life, Freud said resisted all of his attempts at analysis.

He was standing before the gates of a beer garden, supported in some way by statues, but he could not get in and had to turn back. Freud told the princess that actually he had once visited Padua with his brother and had been unable to enter the grottos behind a very similar gateway. Years later, when he returned to Padua, he had recognized the place as the one in his dream, and this time he had managed to see the grottos. Now, he added, every time he found himself unable to unriddle an enigma, he would dream this dream again.[64]

The superficially wish-fulfilling meaning of the dream appears clear, whatever the enigma of its depths: Freud would dream of the locked gates because he had, by a fortunate accident, eventually gained access to the grottoes guarded by the statues. The wish was surely that a similar fortunate accident would once again grant him such access. Being granted access to a place that we have visited before, but do not recognize in our dreams: this is the scene of the uncanny, as Freud himself analyzed it in his paper on that theme. And the place that we have visited before but will not allow ourselves to recognize on this second visit is the mother's womb. There is a clear resonance with the only dream, a nightmare, that Freud recorded from his own childhood: "I saw *my beloved mother, with a peculiarly peaceful, sleeping expression on her features, being carried into the room by two (or three) people with birds' beaks and laid upon the bed.* I awoke in tears and screaming, and interrupted my parents' sleep."[65] The figures with bird beaks were recognized by Freud as taken from a book his family owned, the Philippson Bible, pictures of gods from an ancient Egyptian funerary relief. The dream, he decided, fulfilled the wish that he might make his mother his own.

Every problem that Freud confronted, then, took on the same character: a riddle of the Egyptian Sphinx that this new Oedipus must answer, whose solution would allow him to take possession of the mysterious space over which, like the gods in his collection arrayed silently on his desk, the statues stood guard. Every piece or item in each of his collections thus represented a paternal figure standing guard over the mysterious feminine. And every successful act of analysis of them represented an Oedipal victory. Perhaps Freud regarded this dream as resisting analysis because it hinted that successful analysis was only a matter of good luck, just as every collector's most precious piece comes from a chance encounter.

4

DREAM READERS

Romeo: I dreamt a dream tonight.
Mercutio: And so did I.
Romeo: Well, what was yours?
Mercutio: That dreamers often lie.
Romeo: In bed asleep while they do dream things true.
Mercutio: O, then I see Queen Mab hath been with you.

Shakespeare, Romeo and Juliet, I.4.49–54

Don't you find it very touching to read how a great person [Cervantes], himself an idealist, makes fun of his ideals? Before we were so fortunate as to apprehend the deep truths in our love we were all noble knights passing through the world caught in a dream, misinterpreting the simplest things, magnifying commonplaces into something noble and rare, and thereby cutting a sad figure. Therefore we men always read with respect about what we once were and in part still remain.

Freud to Martha Bernays, August 1883

International scientific movements as we know them started with the railways, from which Charles Darwin made a fortune and about which Sigmund Freud had a phobia. How do these movements begin, gather momentum, and grow into networks of activity, discovery, and practice? The first heroic age presents us with ready models: Quételet and the international statistical movements from the 1830s to 1860s; Pasteur and bacteriology, in the 1860s to 1890s; Darwin and the theory of evolution in the 1860s and 1870s; hypnotism in the 1880s and 1890s.[1] Very roughly, we can expect to see emerge, not necessarily in the same temporal order: a charismatic leader or leaders (Pasteur; Charcot); a core set of doctrines and pamphleteering documents defining the ideas and practices which determine the conditions for membership of the movement (the Normal distribution; the bacterium and its management; the idea of suggestibility); belligerent exponents and organizers (Huxley; Pearson; Bernheim); a small group of devoted followers and disciples (the X club; the Nancy group); a rudimentary organization (Office of the Registrar-General; Sections of the British Association for the Advancement of Science); a system for the preservation, handing on, emendation, expansion, and consolidation of the work of the practitioners (the well-placed enthusiast engineered into a new professional post; the co-opting of resources for the establishment of new institutions, such as bacteriological laboratories, dominated by the members of the movement).

The history of the international psychoanalytic movement can be told in such a way as to conform tidily to this model. The charismatic leader, Freud, set out the core theories and practices: infantile sexuality, dream interpretation, free association. A small group of disciples gathered around him from 1902 on, including more than its fair share of belligerent exponents (Stekel, Jung, Jones); a rudimentary organization was established with the branch societies—the Vienna, Berlin, Zurich Psychoanalytic Societies—and the umbrella international association, from 1910 onward. By the 1920s a system for training professional practitioners and for disseminating psychoanalytic ideas was established: the Berlin Policlinic, the Vienna Institute, the London Institute of Psycho-analysis. Alongside these public institutions a small, secret society of close followers of Freud was set up—the ring-bearers—whose fidelity to Freud's person and his conception of orthodoxy was not dissimilar to the private machinations of Huxley's X-club.[2]

Is this a sufficiently comprehensive account of the development of psychoanalysis? On balance, I think not. Two crucial features need to be added. The first is the distinctive system of training analysts, which subjects them to the same procedure as patients—undergoing an analysis themselves. The second is the fact that Freud was not only a doctor and a scientist, but also a writer of immense distinction. Not only that: the founding text of psychoanalysis, its pamphlet and recipe-book all in one, is also an autobiographical document. It is Jacques Derrida who has asked most succinctly the question I want to explore in this chapter: "how can an autobiographical writing, in the abyss of an unterminated self-analysis, give birth to a world-wide institution?"[3] The "autobiographical writing" in question is *The Interpretation of Dreams*. The institution is the international psycho-analytic movement, a professional body governing the practice of psychoanalysis, based on the work of Freud.

Like Derrida, I think it is justified to call *The Interpretation of Dreams* "autobiographical writing." Like Derrida, I think it is fair to regard the book as the centerpiece of Freud's self-analysis. This was also Freud's view. In the preface to the second edition of 1909 he wrote: "For this book has a further subjective significance for me personally—a significance which I only grasped after I had com-pleted it. It was, I found, a portion of my own self-analysis, my reaction to my father's death—that is to say, to the most important event, the most poignant loss, of a man's life."[4] How did this auto-biographical writing which Freud allowed himself after his father's death, both in triumph and in homage, produce an international movement?

Many psychoanalytic commentators, including Freud himself, have a twofold and contradictory view of the autobiographical ele-ment in the dream book. As Freud wrote in the preface to the second edition, immediately after confessing to his readers that the book they hold in their hand is the author's reaction to the most important event in his life: "Having discovered that this was so, I felt unable to obliterate the traces of the experience. To my readers, however, it will be a matter of indifference upon what material they learn to value and interpret dreams."[5] This book, Freud claims, however autobiographical it may be, is still a work of science: the personal dimension of the dreams and their analyses can be discounted without loss of substance.

The second reaction, the exact obverse of the posture of indifference that Freud insists a reader should adopt in reading the book, recognizes that the book is, precisely because it is a "portion of my own self-analysis," exemplary and originary of psychoanalysis itself: the first self-analysis in history, and the exemplar of all analyses. This was Ernest Jones's judgment on Freud's self-analysis: "his most heroic feat—a psycho-analysis of his own unconscious . . . the uniqueness of the feat remains. Once done it is done for ever. For no one again can be the first to explore those depths."[6]

Two other analysts, Anzieu and Grinstein, have devoted much research and writing to this momentous event, so intimately tied up with the writing and publication of *The Interpretation of Dreams*.[7] Freud's self-analysis is here treated as exemplary of all analyses, and this makes *The Interpretation of Dreams* the *Principia* of psychoanalysis: *fons et origo* of all that came later—in theory, in practice, and institutionally.[8]

There are those who find this moment of "Let there be . . . analysis!" too divine and unique a point of origin, and seek to domesticate Freud's self-analysis. True, their view admits, Freud founded psychoanalysis through this first analysis, but the very theory of that psychoanalysis he established demonstrates that this act of foundation was impossible. True self-analysis, it is often argued, and even more often implied, is impossible: psychoanalysis as a practice utterly disdains the possibility of self-analysis being in any sense comparable to the depth of understanding and transformation achieved through analysis by an other, by an analyst. To cope with this contradiction, many psychoanalytic commentators postulate that Freud did not engage in his own analysis entirely alone. The two most obvious candidates for the historically privileged office of Freud's analyst are Wilhelm Fliess, and "Freud's patients," taken collectively as acting in some sense in concert.

Freud certainly regarded himself as a patient being treated by someone. In August 1897, while on holiday, he wrote to Fliess: "The chief patient I am preoccupied with is myself . . . The analysis is more difficult than any other. It is, in fact, what paralyses my psychic strength for describing and communicating what I have won so far. Still, I believe it must be done and is a necessary intermediate stage in my work."[9] Two and a half months later, he wrote: "All of what I experienced with my patients, as a third [party] I find again here—days when I drag myself about dejected because I have understood nothing of the dream, of the fantasy, of the mood of the day; and then again days when a flash of lightning illuminates the interrelations and lets me understand the past as a preparation for the present."[10]

It is not only the psychoanalytic orthodoxy that argued for the impossibility of self-analysis. Freud was quick to inform Fliess of this fact: "My self-analysis remains interrupted. I have realized why I can analyze myself only with the help of knowledge obtained objectively (like an outsider). True self-analysis is impossible; otherwise there would be no (neurotic) illness. Since I am still contending with some kind of puzzle in my patients, this is bound to hold me up in my self-analysis as well."[11] It is remarks like these, in which Freud places himself on a par with his patients and treats in a dialectical fashion his knowledge of them and a strangely subjectless other's knowledge of himself from the outside, that has tempted some commentators to see, in a proto-Ferenczi-like spirit, Freud's work of the 1890s as a form of mutual analysis. How are we to read these forthright exclamations at the necessity of Freud's analysis and of its impossibility without an "Other"? Surely the force of these comments leads us to deduce that Fliess was that Other, and it was through his fantasied relationship to his friend in Berlin, supplemented by their occasional meetings, all mediated by Freud's writing to his "sole audience," that Freud's analysis was achieved? The distinctive feature of the Fliessian option is that Freud's analysis was, as he himself described in *The Interpretation of Dreams*, in part based upon his methodical *writing down* of his dreams,[12] whose analysis he then sends to the Other in Berlin.

However, if we scrutinize Freud's letters to Fliess over the period 1897–1898, we observe a number of different forms of writing merging into one another: there are letters brimming with advances in clinical and theoretical ideas; there are the confessional letters about his dreams and his childhood. Then, in December 1897, Freud starts to correspond in a new genre, his "Dreckology" or Shitology, papers which have not survived—"the Dr., in which I now deposit my novelties."[13] By early 1898, the Dreckology passes over into, or is finally superseded by, the dream-book: "I am sending you today a long, finished issue of the DR, which I will perhaps ask you to return soon because of the beautiful dream example . . . My self-analysis is at rest in favor of the dream book."[14] Two weeks later, the Shitology has explicitly become the dream book: "I have finished a whole section of the dream book, the best-composed one, to be sure, and am curious about what else will occur to me. Otherwise, no scientific novelties; the DR have been interrupted, since I no longer write them for you."[15]

We do not possess the Dreckology; nor are the beautiful dream examples that Freud regularly passed to Fliess included in the Fliess papers bought by Marie Bonaparte, via an intermediary, from Fliess's widow in late 1936. The reason is simple and obvious: Freud asked Fliess to return the dreams and the Dreckology, and he then included them in the dream book. In this way, Fliess, the first reader of Freud's dreams and theories, is the exemplar for the psychoanalytic reader in general. Given those instances, and there are some, where we possess two versions, the letter and the version published in the book, it is probable that Freud changed very little in shifting these dream examples, written seemingly for Fliess's eyes only, onto the more public stage of *The Interpretation of Dreams*.

So, if we envisage that Fliess was, as first reader, Freud's analyst, we are invited to depict the first readers of *The Interpretation of Dreams* themselves as partaking in this analytic function of Fliess's.

Lacan was the first to formulate this argument in his discussion of the dream of Irma's injection:

> Freud all by himself, analysing his dream, tried to find in it, proceeding as an occultist might, the secret designation of the point where as a matter of fact the solution to the mystery of the subject and the world lies. But he isn't all by himself. Once he communicates the secret of this Luciferian mystery to us, Freud is not confronted with this dream by himself. Just as the dream is addressed to the analyst in an analysis, Freud in his dream is already addressing himself to us.[16]

Thus, Freud's readers stand in the position of analysts to Freud. What does this analytic bond between reader and dreaming-writing tell us about the analytic function itself? How do, and how did, readers respond to becoming Freud's analyst?

In exploring this question, one must guard against assuming that Freud was in some sense naive—that he might have been innocent of the effect of his own writing. Alongside the seeming mastery that the position of reader brings with it—the freedom that the very structure of writing accords to each reader to do what he or she will with the text—the author in question, Freud, was well aware of the possible preconceptions, even prerequisites, a reader might bring to or with which he might combat his writing. So Freud took great pains to place his readers, from Fliess to Forrester, exactly where he wanted them.

Fliess was not only Freud's first reader; he was also his first censor. Indeed the very idea of the censorship, so important in Freud's theory of the dream, seems to develop hand in hand with Fliess's interventions, at Freud's invitation, in the composition of the dream book. The first hint of the idea of censorship is Freud's description in December 1897 of the graphic and textual Russian censorship: "Have you ever seen a foreign newspaper which passed Russian censorship at the frontier? Words, whole clauses and sentences are blacked out so that the rest becomes unintelligible. A *Russian censorship* of that kind comes about in psychoses and produces the apparently meaningless *deliria*."[17] The first draft of the dream book, which had started with analyses of dreams sent to Fliess, then took on a more definite shape in the early spring of 1898 in the wake of this clear conception of the censorship, soon to play such an important role as a component of the dream theory. By May 1898, Freud was writing at high speed, sending two chapters to Fliess in less than three weeks, with Fliess now firmly in place as the author's, if not the dreamer's, omnipotent censor: "I shall change whatever you want and gratefully accept contributions. I am so immensely glad that you are giving me the gift of the Other, a critic and reader—and one of your quality at that. I cannot write entirely without an audience, but do not at all mind writing only for you."[18]

At the congress Freud and Fliess held in early June, for which Freud had "nothing but the dream, the dream,"[19] Fliess decisively exerted his influence by censoring from the manuscript of the dream-book the one and only completely analyzed dream of Freud's:

> I am reasonable enough to recognize that I need your critical help, because in this instance I myself have lost the feeling of shame required of an author. So the dream is condemned. Now that the sentence has been passed, however, I would like to shed a tear over it and confess that I regret it and that I have no hopes of finding a better one as a substitute. As you know, a beautiful dream and no indiscretion—do not coincide.[20]

This act of censorship by Fliess had an immediate effect on Freud: he spent four more weeks completing what turned out to be an unsatisfactory version of the final chapter of the book—and then stopped writing. He was "mourning the lost dream,"[21] and still doing so in October 1898. By December 1898 he had decided to brave the dream literature; in May 1899 he was still dithering, but suddenly later that month he set to work with eagerness and renewed confidence, rebelling against his censor. A substantially revised structure of the book emerged:[22] "The dream is suddenly taking shape, without any special motivation, but this time I am sure of it. I have decided that I cannot use any of the disguises, nor can I afford to give up anything because I am not rich enough to keep my finest and probably my only lasting discovery to myself."[23] Freud wrote fluently and with great confidence over the summer. He sent the first section to the printer at the end of June. Throughout the summer, as Freud produced chapter after chapter, he sent them and the proofs alternately to the printer and to the censor: "You will have several more occasions to red-pencil similar instances of superfluous subjectivity. Your looking through the proofs is indeed a tremendous reassurance to me."[24]

Why did Freud need reassuring? He himself felt he had "lost the feeling of shame required of an author" and had thus lost control of the dialectic of revealing and concealing that formed one of the principal axes of the dream book's plot. Initially, in the years 1895–1897, he had revealed himself to Fliess and acted as his own censor; now, in writing his dream book, he was revealing himself—without shame—to his public and asking Fliess to be his censor. The dialectic of revealing and concealing that so preoccupied Freud had thus been played initially with Fliess first as object—of reverence, of sustenance, later and implicitly, of criticism and contempt—and then as censor.

The dialectic then began to disseminate itself into Freud's entourage. He enjoyed the prospect of Breuer being "appalled" by the "abundant indiscretions,"[25] just as he had confessed to Fliess his enjoyment at "the thought of all the 'head shaking' over the indiscretions and audacities it contains."[26] By the time of the book's completion, with a hint of defiant, I-told-you-so pride, he had come to expect that all his friends would, like Oscar Rie, express the "most serious misgivings"[27] over publication. The first response to publication elicited more of the same—the position he had adopted as author went hand in hand with the feeling that he was offending the world: "The book has just been sent out. The first tangible reaction was the termination of the friendship of a dear friend, who felt hurt by the mention of her husband in the *non vixit* dream."[28] The dear friend was Sophie Schwab-Paneth, godmother of one of his daughters, widow of a friend and colleague whose reputation Freud had sacrificed in one of his own ambition dreams which culminated in the thought "after all, I reflected, was not having children our only path to immortality?"[29] I will return to this remark to explain how such a thought, seemingly innocuous, could appear to a perceptive reader as an insult.

The question of indiscretion and dissimulation emphatically did not end with the final publication of the book. Thirty years later, André Breton accused Freud of having, like a "prudent bourgeois," deliberately withheld the sexual motives in the analyses of his own dreams while displaying such motives in the dreams of others. Freud replied:

> I believe that if I have not analysed my own dreams as extensively as those of others, the cause is only rarely timidity with regard to the sexual. The fact is, much more frequently, that it would have required me regularly to discover the secret source of the whole series of dreams in my relations to my father, recently deceased. I maintain that I was in the right to set limits to the inevitable exhibition (as well of an infantile tendency since surmounted).[30]

It is the infantile tendency to exhibitionism that Freud appears to denounce as underlying his virtuoso performance of self-disclosure in *The Interpretation of Dreams*. And Freud's exhibitionistic tendencies, that is, his desire to write a book based on his dreams, may have been the very first set of those desires implicated in his relationship to Fliess to fall victim to the censorship, in July 1897, when he had not as yet named it: "I still do not know what has been happening in me. Something from the deepest depths of my own neurosis set itself against any advance in the understanding of the neuroses, and you have somehow been involved in it. For my writing paralysis seems to me designed to inhibit our communication."[31]

Three paragraphs later in the same letter, Freud points to the area of his dream life with which this inhibition is connected: "There is an interesting dream of wandering about among strangers, totally or half undressed and with feelings of shame and anxiety. Oddly enough, it is the rule that people do not notice it—for which we must thank wish fulfillment. This dream material, which goes back to exhibiting childhood, has been misunderstood and worked over didactically in a well-known fairy tale. (The king's imaginary clothes—'Talisman.') The ego habitually misinterprets other dreams in the same way."[32] Two months earlier, he had had another dream about being naked: "I was going up a staircase with very few clothes on. I was moving, as the dream explicitly emphasized, with great agility. (My heart—reassurance!) Suddenly I noticed, however, that a woman was coming after me, and thereupon set in the sensation, so common in dreams, of being glued to the spot, of being paralyzed. The accompanying feeling was not anxiety but erotic excitement. So you see how the sensation of paralysis characteristic of sleep was used for the fulfillment of an exhibitionistic wish."[33]

These themes—of the inhibition in writing to Fliess, connected with exhibiting himself in writing about dreams, of the meaning of dreams of being naked—enact the subjective maneuvering that Freud is engaged in as he prepares to write about his dreams to Fliess, and thus to the reader. The feeling of inhibition in dreams, of being rooted to the spot, Freud will eventually theorize as the most clear-cut intervention of the censorship, of the censorship in its most "naked" form: saying "No!", "the censorship demands that it shall be stopped."[34] "Not being able to do something" is a way of expressing a contradiction, "so that my earlier statement that dreams cannot express a 'no' requires correction."[35] We are at the heart of the structure of Freud's rhetoric of censorship and disclosure; and, interestingly enough, we are at the heart of Freud's account of childhood, the Paradise in which we are always naked and never feel shame. Just following the theme of dreams of being naked in the final version of the dream book, we come upon the typical dream of the death of those we love, where Freud discloses the universal desires of children to possess one parent and do away with the other. And, chronologically, in his own discovery of these "Oedipal" impulses, it was his own analysis of the dream of being partly undressed and glued to the spot under the gaze of an old woman that paved the way for his discovery of the old nurse of his childhood and his sexual desires for her.[36] Derrida has very astutely drawn attention to the fact that the fairy tale "The Emperor's New Clothes," with which Freud illustrates his account of dreams of nakedness, of exhibitionism, is, in its logic of revealing and concealing, of being naked but surrounded by (invisible) clothes, exactly the allegory of the veiling and unveiling of truth with which Freud struggles and which he attempts to master.[37] And, to round off this intertwining of truth, nakedness, disclosure, and censorship, what could be more appropriate than the fact that Freud's modern critics, his enemies in the Freud Wars, can find no story more allegorically fitting for their labors than that of the Emperor's New Clothes, in which Freud is cast as the Emperor, the fawning followers are the people duped and seduced into admiring his attire (his theories), and the Freudian critics, who see clearly what is plain for all to see, if only they look, adopt the position of the small child who points out that the Emperor has no clothes?

Surely it would have been possible for Freud to use the dreams of others, principally his patients, as the material upon which his dream-book was based? The substance of the preface to the first edition of the book explains why he had not:

The only dreams open to my choice were my own and those of my patients undergoing psycho-analytic treatment. But I was precluded from using the latter material by the fact that in its case the dream-processes were subject to an undesirable complication owing to the added presence of neurotic features. But if I was to report my own dreams, it inevitably followed that I should have to reveal to the public gaze more of the intimacies of my mental life than I liked, or than is normally necessary for any writer who is a man of science and not a poet. Such was the painful but unavoidable necessity; and I have submitted to it rather than totally abandon the possibility of giving the evidence for my psychological findings. Naturally, however, I have been unable to resist the temptation of taking the edge off some of my indiscretions by omissions and substitutions. But whenever this happened, the value of my instances has been very definitely diminished.[38]

Freud is thus, despite himself, bowing to necessity. He goes on to plead for clemency from his reader for his indiscretions: "I can only express a hope that readers of this book will put themselves in my difficult situation and treat me with indulgence, and further, that anyone who finds any sort of reference to himself in my dreams may be willing to grant me the right of freedom of thought—in my dream-life, if nowhere else."[39] Thus, from the very first page, Freud cunningly engages the reader in a sinuous dialectic: the dreamer—reluctantly and despite himself—reveals himself and simultaneously challenges the reader to be curious and critical, prurient and censorious. The indiscreet dreamer (Freud) and the censorious critic (Fliess) are immediately propelled on stage as the principal actors in the book itself.

At the opening of Chapter 2, the crucial moment prefacing Freud's entry as the principal protagonist of his own book, his recalcitrance is again emphasized, as is the necessity of putting himself at the mercy of the reader. This time the demand on the reader is expressed even more forcefully:

Thus it comes about that I am led to my own dreams, which offer a copious and convenient material, derived from an approximately normal person and relating to multifarious occasions of daily life. No doubt I shall be met by doubts of the trustworthiness of "self-analyses" of this kind; and I shall be told that they leave the door open to arbitrary conclusions. In my judgement the situation is in fact more favourable in the case of *self*-observation than in that of other people; at all events we may make the experiment and see how far self-analysis takes us with the interpretation of dreams. But I have other difficulties to overcome, which lie within myself. There is some natural hesitation about revealing so many intimate facts about one's mental life; nor can there be any guarantee against misinterpretation by strangers.[40]

And the powerful theatrical effect which will, finally, justify this self-exposure is now revealed:

Nun muß ich aber den Leser bitten, für eine ganze Weile meine Interessen zu den seinigen zu machen und sich mit mir in die kleinsten Einzelheiten meines Lebens zu versenken, denn solche Übertragung fordert gebieterisch das Interesse für die versteckte Bedeutung der Träume.[41]

And now I must ask the reader to make my interests his own for quite a while, and to plunge, along with me, into the minutest details of my life; for a transference of this kind is peremptorily demanded by our interest in the hidden meaning of dreams.[42]

Here, finally, is the bait—and the hook—by which the reader becomes interested in, fascinated by, engaged, contracted, pledged to Freud's book. The reader is kindly requested to make Freud's interests his own,[43] to transfer onto the dreamer portrayed in the book. The structure of Freud's sentence acknowledges that the reader must give up something in this process—his own interests—so as to then take on something else: Freud's own interests. How far should the reader go in this process?

Freud lets his reader know that he is well aware that indiscretions have an intrinsic interest, but he is confident that this somewhat disreputable curiosity will be transformed into something more worthy: "it is safe to assume that my readers too will very soon find their

initial interest in the indiscretions which I am bound to make replaced by an absorbing immersion in the psychological problems
upon which they throw light."[44] There is an ambiguity, however, in
the evocation of these "psychological problems" which will draw the
reader's attentions away from Freud's personal indiscretions. He does
not specify that these are *general* psychological problems. Rather, the
suggestion is—here as well as in the preface to the second edition
quoted earlier—that they are *specific* problems. Freud implies that
the reader will follow his example and soon become absorbed in his
own dreams. In other words, the reader will pass rapidly through the
stage of curiosity over Freud's indiscretions to emerge a Freudian.[45]
But what if he remains caught at the stage of prurient curiosity, if
he remains caught at the stage of transference onto Freud? He may
then emerge as another kind of Freudian, one who is identified, to
all intents and purposes, with the protagonists of Freud's dreams.

We have seen how Freud's "Other" functioned as object of indiscretion, then also as censor, then again as the invited participant in
transference onto Freud's interests and inner life. Having agreed to
accompany Freud on his "imaginary walk,"[46] having been led along
the "concealed pass" of the specimen dream of Chapter 2, the
famous dream of Irma's injection,[47] "all at once" the reader, arm in
arm with Freud, contemplates the next step: "When, after passing
through a narrow defile, we suddenly emerge upon a piece of high
ground, where the path divides and the finest prospects open up on
every side, we pause for a moment and consider in which direction
we shall first turn our steps. Such is the case with us, now that we
have surmounted the first interpretation of a dream."[48]

The trope of the walk through the country is a classic one both
in the Christian literature concerning the spiritual quest for truth
and in the secularized genre of confession and autobiography that
supplanted it from Rousseau on. Freud and the reader may now
engage in the journey Freud envisages: part spiritual quest, part
autobiography, part account of a "sudden discovery"—a momentous
event in the development of science. It is this mixture of genres that

has so intrigued many of Freud's readers—"scientific treatise, intimate diary, confession, key to dreams, fantasy journey, initiatory
quest, essay on the human condition, and what is more, a vast
allegorical fresco of the unconscious."[49] But at every moment on the
journey, the promised goal also recedes; as Alexander Welsh notes,
"concealment provides the drama of the dream book." Throughout
the book, Freud plays a game of hide and seek with the reader. He
seems to disclose his innermost secrets; yet, just as regularly, he
peremptorily, though with apparent reluctance, closes the door on
the reader. Freud entices the reader on, but just as clearly brings him
up short: "I can assure my readers that the ultimate meaning of the
dream [of the Botanical monograph], which I have not disclosed, is
intimately related to the subject of the childhood scene."[50]

In *On Dreams*, the simplified guide to the larger dream-book,
Freud writes:

> I might draw closer together the threads in the material revealed
> by the analysis, and I might then show that they converge upon a
> single nodal point, but considerations of a personal and not of a
> scientific nature prevent my doing so in public. I should be obliged
> to betray many things which had better remain my secret, for on
> my way to discovering the solution of the dream all kinds of things
> were revealed which I was unwilling to admit even to myself. Why
> then, it will be asked, have I not chosen some other dream, whose
> analysis is better suited for reporting, so that I could produce more
> convincing evidence of the meaning and connectedness of the
> material uncovered by analysis? The answer is that *every* dream
> with which I might try to deal would lead to things equally hard
> to report and would impose an equal discretion upon me.[51]

As far as the reader is concerned, it seems that the censorship will
always win. Yet the whole strategy of dream-analysis is an imple-
mentation of techniques of circumventing the censorship. This dialectic, of the secret wish striving for expression and the censorship
ensuring its suppression, is played out between dreamer and reader.

But the roles are continually being reversed. Sometimes the reader is asked to identify with the wish, only to find Freud acting as censor. At other times, the reader is expected to repudiate the dream. So, for example, when Freud discusses the censorship of affect in dreams, he chooses to give an account of a short dream in which he urinated away from the edge of an open-air lavatory "small heaps of faeces of all sizes and degrees of freshness." He then rushes to point out that this dream "will fill every reader with disgust."[52] Or take the footnote in which Freud refers to the skeptical response of Wilhelm Fliess, and immediately invites subsequent readers to identify with this response:

> The first reader and critic of this book—and his successors are likely to follow his example—protested that "the dreamer seems to be too ingenious and amusing." This is quite true so long as it refers only to the dreamer; it would only be an objection if it were to be extended to the dream-interpreter. In waking reality I have little claim to be regarded as a wit. If my dreams seem amusing, that is not on my account, but on account of the peculiar psychological conditions under which dreams are constructed; and the fact is intimately connected with the theory of the jokes and the comic. Dreams become ingenious and amusing because the direct and easiest pathway to the expression of their thoughts is barred: they are forced into being so. The reader can convince himself that my patients' dreams seem at least as full of jokes and puns as my own, or even fuller.[53]

This passage not only links subsequent readers in a chain with the first reader; it is also typical of the way in which Freud preempts the reader's response to the book, its dreamers, and their dream interpretations. It invites the reader not only to inspect the patients' dreams, but also to inspect his own—"actual experience would teach them better," Freud remarks later in the book.[54] "Am I," the reader is invited to ask, "as witty a dreamer as Freud? Perhaps the lack of puns and jokes in my interpretations of them is a sign that I have not as yet found their full interpretation?" We know with what determination Freud rose to the challenge of Fliess the skeptical censor: he wrote a whole book, *Jokes and Their Relation to the Unconscious,* to "refute," or at least lay to rest, the implicit charge of the over-ingenuity of the dream-interpreter.

The alacrity with which Freud defended himself against Fliess's criticisms[55]—including his other principal criticism of anxiety dreams—is displayed throughout the book. Indeed, as in that other work of skillfully crafted, semi-autobiographical scientific advocacy, Darwin's *On the Origin of Species,* Freud's first priority was to elicit and then meet his reader's skeptical responses to a bold theory. Freud forestalls the reader's criticisms by voicing them on his behalf; once again, the "censor" and the "repressed" change places.

The strategy is quite deliberate and informs the entire plan, even its principal thesis. Why, we might ask, did Freud put forward, as the result of the interpretation of one single dream of his own, the thesis that "when the work of interpretation has been completed, we perceive that a dream is the fulfilment of a wish"?[56] Precisely, we might answer, in order to elicit the skeptical response of the reader. Let us consider the structure of Freud's argument in terms of the sequence of chapters, so as to examine this strategy of his.

The principal thesis of wish-fulfillment is stated at the close of Chapter 2. Chapter 3 considers a number of dreams in order to render plausible the thesis that this is the universal characteristic of dreams. The dreams considered are straightforwardly confirmatory—dreams that are reasonably transparent fulfillments connected with bodily needs, together with a collection of children's dreams. As a whole, their tone is engaging. So too is the tone of the dreams of convenience: the medical student who oversleeps and dreams he is already in the hospital, the newly married woman who dreams she is having her period so as to postpone having to accept the reality of her first pregnancy. But these dreams are not sufficient to establish the thesis. Freud, a keen student of Mill's, would have known that the simple enumeration of confirmatory instances is never sufficient to establish a universal generalization, let alone render it plausible. And Freud, as an even keener student of the art of persuasion, knows full well that he cannot lull his critic for long with these charming examples. Nor does he wish to: he *needs* the skeptical critic, his reader, to become embroiled with the next step in his argument.

So, after the few pages spent showing the reader the lulling vistas opened up by the wish-fulfillment theory, Freud begins Chapter 4, "Distortion in Dreams," with a very different welcome for the reader: "If I proceed to put forward the assertion that the meaning of *every* dream is the fulfilment of a wish, that is to say that there cannot be any dreams but wishful dreams, I feel certain in advance that I shall meet with the most categorical contradiction."[57] You, the reader, are *certain* to deny me! Freud tells us. There then follows a long paragraph in quotation marks in which this critic, everyreader, voices his categorical contradiction. Even when the "natural" voice of Freud finally emerges from outside the quotation marks, it confesses that "anxiety-dreams make it impossible to assert as a general proposition . . . that dreams are wish-fulfilments; indeed they seem to stamp any such proposition as an absurdity."[58]

But Freud has not lost his battle; far from it, he has simply opened up the terrain on which he will win over this skeptical critic. All he has to do is to make a distinction, here for the first time in the book, between the *manifest* and the *latent* content of the dream. The reader's critical objection is left high and dry. He is left tilting at the windmill of the manifest content, while Freud can consolidate his discoveries by bringing to light the mysteries of the latent content.

With the distinction between latent and manifest, Freud repeats the founding act of splitting that initiated the writing of his dream book: between dream and interpretation, between writer and censor, between discretion and exposure. With the idea of "latency," Freud both shores up and specifies the object of the act of interpretation: the interpreter is seeking what is latent, not what is manifest. And Freud also introduces the hint of secrecy which is to be such a seductive feature of the reader's progress through the book. Like

Sigmund Freud, who dreamed of erecting a plaque at Bellevue, where "the secret of dreams revealed itself"[59] to him, each reader will go in search of the secret, not only of the dream, but also, through the "transference" peremptorily demanded of him, of Sigmund Freud, and through him, of his own inner dream-life.

The idea of the latent is then explored through the analysis of another of Freud's dreams, a dream whose fundamental feature was the dreamer's struggle to *dissimulate from himself* his contemptuous judgment of a friend as a simpleton—thus alluding to the contemptuous reader who judges Freud to be a simpleton. Disguise in dreams—the very principle of latency—thus amounts to a defensive distortion, entirely analogous to the dissimulation practiced in everyday social life by a person in the presence of someone with power over him. Freud rubs the point home: "when I interpret my dreams for my readers I am obliged to adopt similar distortions."[60] That is, in the face of the all-powerful and censorious reader, Freud pointedly indicates, he adopts a disguise. Here we come upon that fundamental posture of the Freudian in relation to the world so aptly described by Paul Ricoeur: "as a man of desires I go forth in disguise."[61] But the very act of disguise and dissimulation has two sides: I dissimulate for the others, but I find a way of making the secret available for your eyes only. "The stricter the censorship, the more far-reaching will be the disguise and the more ingenious too may be the means employed for putting the reader on the scent of the true meaning."[62] The reader switches, from paragraph to paragraph, from being the censor from whom the truth must be hidden to being Freud's complicit partner in the secret truths of the adept. What is bad news for one party to the power struggle, for instance the censoring governmental agency, will be good news for the insurrectionists plotting in disguise. In this way, the anxiety dream of those in power is identical with the wish-fulfillment of those under their thumb.[63]

But the truly skeptical reader is still waiting for a reply; he will not be taken in by the pleasures of collusive complicity. It is to silence this skeptic that Freud introduces a third party—the clever, wily, witty, and skeptical patient, who in the course of Freud's psychoanalytic interpretations subjects him to "a remorseless criticism, certainly no less severe than I have to expect from the members of my own profession. And my patients invariably contradict my assertion that all dreams are fulfilments of wishes."[64]

So, for the first time in the dream book, the patient occupies center stage. And he—or rather she, since Freud's most sympathetically and thus critically intelligent patients seem to have been women—does so principally as critic. "'How do you fit that in with your theory?'"[65] is their insistent refrain. The "cleverest of all my dreamers"[66] dreamed of spending her holiday near her hated mother-in-law:

> The dream showed that I was wrong [about the nature of dreams]. *Thus it was her wish that I might be wrong, and her dream showed that wish fulfilled.* But her wish that I might be wrong . . . related in fact to . . . [my inference that] at a particular period of her life something must have occurred that was of importance in determining her illness. She had disputed this, since she had no recollection of it; but soon afterwards it had turned out that I was right. Thus her wish that I might be wrong, which was transformed into her dream of spending her holidays with her mother-in-law, corresponded to a well-justified wish that the events of which she was then becoming aware for the first time might never have occurred.[67]

This is the model for Freud's answer to his critic's categorical contradiction: every such contradiction is not only a refutation of his theory, but embodies the *wish* that he might be wrong. In this way every possible criticism of the theory is undercut.

In 1909 and then in 1911, Freud supplemented his account of these dreams that prove him wrong by calling them "counter-wish dreams [*Gegenwünschträume*]": these are the dreams elicited by a person's first contact with psychoanalysis—thus explaining why he places them so strategically, immediately after the statement and confirmation of the wish-fulfillment hypothesis, as the first dreams of someone other than himself:

I can count almost certainly on provoking one of them after I have explained my theory that dreams are fulfilments of wishes to a patient for the first time . . . or to people who have heard me lecturing . . . Indeed, it is expected that the same thing will happen to some of the readers of the present book; they will be quite ready to have one of their wishes frustrated in a dream if only their wish that I may be wrong can be fulfilled.[68]

What is so important about this strategic argument of Freud's is that it finally places the reader in the position of the *patient* dreaming refutations of Freud's theory. The patient is always a counter-wisher (in resistance); the reader is invited to adopt this position as well.

We might call the patient's and the critic's protest against the logic of "Heads I win, tails you lose" the principle of bloody-mindedness. But that is precisely what Freud is pointing to as a fundamental property of human relations: the critic, the censor, the counter-wish—which in 1915 he called, somewhat misleadingly, the "instinctive tendency to fend off intellectual novelties."[69]

The layman asks: "Where is the wish-fulfilment?" And instantly, having heard that dreams are supposed to be wish-fulfilments, and in the very act of asking the question, he answers it with a rejection.[70]

And with this move, Freud introduced a thesis that has provoked the ire of his critics ever since: one can never disagree with Freud without being a mere resister to truth. Is this an empirical finding, along the lines of a survey that revealed that all Cretans are liars? Or is Freud's seemingly genial distrust of surfaces simply a result of learning Pascal's lesson—"nous ne sommes que mensonge, duplicité, contrariété, et nous cachons et nous déguisons à nous-mêmes"[71]— and his inversion of La Rochefoucauld's observation that, "however much we distrust the sincerity of those with whom we speak, we always believe that they are more truthful with us than with others"?[72] Is Freud's strict application of the hermeneutics of suspicion a determination never to be taken in by the sincerity of others?

Certainly Freud points toward the function of negativity and nothingness as found in post-Hegelian philosophy—in Heidegger and Sartre—where it is intimately linked to the capacity for human freedom. Yet he wishes to disarm, to take the sting out of the "categorical contradiction" that he has provoked—provoked deliberately, it might seem, precisely for this purpose.

This provocation of absolute opposition—the staging of the confrontation between interpreter and skeptic—demonstrates the willed and deliberate character of Freud's strategy. On one side of this confrontation, there is the reader, easily provoked into bloody-minded refusal of Freud's arguments and interpretations.[73] On the other side, fully prepared, there is not only the wily interpreter, but also the wily dreamer. Just as the reader is, in the very act of bloody-minded opposition, conforming to Freud's strategy, so had Freud's dream life become entirely subordinate to the requirements of writing the dream book. In May 1897, he had

> dreamed of overaffectionate feelings for Mathilde, only she was called Hella; and afterward I again saw "Hella" before me, printed in heavy type. Solution: Hella is the name of an American niece whose picture we have been sent.
>
> Mathilde could be called Hella because she recently shed bitter tears over the defeats of the Greeks. She is enthralled by the mythology of ancient Hellas and naturally regards all Hellenes as heroes. The dream of course shows the fulfillment of my wish to catch a *Pater* as the originator of neurosis and thus puts an end to my ever-recurring doubts.[74]

Here Freud's wish to pin down the father expressed itself as a self-inculpation: he was dreaming a confirmation of his seduction theory to order.[75] He wishes to see more clearly, *heller*. A year later, when Fliess censored the complete interpretation of his big dream and Freud mourned its irreplaceable loss, he immediately reasserted his authority over his dream-life and asked: "Let me know at least which topic it was to which you took exception and where you feared an attack by a malicious critic . . . So that I can omit what you designate in a substitute dream, because I can have dreams like that to order."[76] Dreaming to order—a dream life subordinate to the requirements of writing—then became the persistent theme of Freud's burst of creativity of 1899:

> One day I had been trying to discover what might be the meaning of the feelings of being inhibited, of being glued to the spot, of not being able to get something done, and so on, which occur so often in dreams and are so closely akin to feelings of anxiety. That night I had the following dream [of climbing the stairs and suddenly feeling ashamed, inhibited and rooted to the spot].[77]

And, at the height of the final spurt of writing the dream book, Freud's dreams are nothing but commentaries—enigmatic enough at times—on his own writing:

> My own dreams have now become absurdly complicated. Recently I was told that on the occasion of Aunt Minna's birthday Annerl said, "On birthdays I am mostly a little bit good." Thereupon I dreamed the familiar school dream in which I am in *sexta* [sixth grade] and say to myself, "In this sort of dream one is mostly in sixth grade." The only possible solution: Annerl is my *sexta* [sixth] child! Brr . . .[78]

The willfulness of Freud the theoretician of the dream, whose dreams become nothing but theory, is thus the match of the willful reader, whose first impulse on reading Freud's book, on hearing him speak, will be to dream a refutation of him. They make a right pair, it would seem. Indeed, that is the strategy of Freud's writing: they *are* a right pair.

We have seen how the reader of Freud's text is invited to make Freud's interests his own, to transfer entirely; we have seen how the roles of desirer and censor are apportioned out between the author and the reader, as they easily exchange roles; we have seen how the reader is expected, on the model of all Freud's interlocutors, to repudiate forcefully Freud's theories and in consequence to be drawn ever more tightly into the embrace of his theory, of an identification with him. Typical—but salutary—was the response of Freud's first serious reader after publication, a philosopher, Heinrich Gomperz, son of a patron and patient of Freud's, who approached Freud in late November 1899 and started studying the method of dream interpretation with him: "My philosopher, Harry G., is very amusing. Supposedly he believes nothing whatsoever, but has all sorts of beautiful and witty ideas . . . His dreams constantly quote my dreams, which he then forgets, and so forth."[79]

There are two diametrically opposed ways of characterizing this process of identification and transference. The first sees the *autobiographical* dreamer and writer as the central protagonist of the dream book, and thus views the reader's involvement with "Freud" as a form of personal and intimate seduction, in which the reader and author perform Freud's perfectly choreographed dance of disclosure and withdrawal. In reviewing Freud's *An Autobiographical Study*, Hanns Sachs captured this fascinating autobiographical aspect of the dream-book:

> Some of Freud's works, especially the *Interpretation of Dreams* reveal the true substance of his personality, and not his *Autobiography* . . . Thus he had to make use of a language of his own invention, of puzzles and allusions, wherever he thought it better to cover up again for strange eyes what had been revealed; for a reader who attempts to bring to light what is hidden of his person and to join together what has been torn apart intentionally, the book can easily become a maze.[80]

This maze is more properly Freud's web, spun to capture the reader, to render him Freudian through an identification with and a driven pursuit of the person of Freud. This strategy of Freud's accounts

162

for the personal and intimate details of the dream book, so absent from more officially autobiographical texts of Freud's, for the simple reason that this is not autobiography for its own sake, but for the pedagogical and analytic purpose of making readers into Freudians.

Being a Freudian has, I am stressing, a number of senses. It can mean subscribing to Freudian doctrines and theories. And this is the second way of characterizing the process that the reader of the dream book undergoes: confirming or being convinced of the *scientific* (as opposed to autobiographical) truth of the theories advanced in the book. Freud's scientific strategy in this respect is resolutely universalistic: the propositions he advances are only important insofar as they have the form, "All X's are Y's"—all dreams are wish-fulfillments. Freud's was never a statistical sensibility, despite the rise of statistical thinking, particularly in the burgeoning human sciences of the late nineteenth and early twentieth centuries.[81] The only statistics quoted in *The Interpretation of Dreams*—that 57.2 percent of dreams are "disagreeable" and only 28.6 percent positively "pleasant"— Freud had put into the mouth of the first skeptical critic of the hypothesis of wish-fulfillment; they are not taken seriously. A statistical law could not be serious science for Freud. His conception of "serious science" was, however, audacious in one respect: he took as an axiom that if one could find meaning in *one* dream then it was methodologically justified to treat *all* dreams as meaningful. Similarly, he was convinced that the law that all dreams are wish-fulfillments could be adequately defended. But it never occurred to him to consider whether there might be different types of dreams specific to different subjects: that he might be a wish-fulfilling-type, whereas another person might be an anxiety-type. Freud assumed that one dreamer stood for all dreamers, just as contemporary physicists might assume that one substance subject to gravity stood for all substances, or biologists that one sample of hemoglobin stood for all samples. In this Freud is utterly unlike those biometricians or statisticians whose object of study was the very diversity of characteristics of a field of phenomena.

One could say that Freud was behaving like modern physicists when they accept without question—and without qualms—that the CERN laboratory is the sole place on earth capable of yielding significant results about the next level down of subatomic events. It is the sole place on earth that is capable of measuring, and of measuring itself against, the universe. To Freud, the dreams of "an approximately normal person," as he described himself, were without question a sufficient basis upon which to build a universal theory of all dreams, for all dreamers.[82]

This is Freud's scientific assumption, which would be contested by critics; Ernest Jones reported one such set of criticisms to Freud, after a meeting of the American Psychological Association that he attended in late 1909:

> The part of my paper ["Freud's theory of dreams"] that aroused most opposition was, curiously enough, my statement that the *Traumgedanke[n]* were always egocentric. One wild female flourished two dreams at me that were "entirely altruistic," and declared there was nothing selfish in her, even in her subconscious. Another one said you had no right to generalise that all dreams were egocentric because you hadn't analysed all dreams; it wasn't scientific. What was true of Austrians might not be true of Americans! I said that experience had shown that a man died if he was immersed in deep water for ten minutes. Was one not justified in generalising this statement before proving it on all men and in all seas? Another psychologist said he had been using your psychoanalysis in the study of the aesthetics of humour and found that the results of the analysis depended on the temperature of the room. As you have shamefully neglected to publish records of the varying temperature of your consulting-room, your conclusions are all worthless.[83]

To Freud and his disciples, the idea that an American's dreams might obey different laws from those of a Jewish Viennese doctor's was preposterous—not only because it asserted in a smug and self-serving

164

fashion that Americans were ethically higher than the Viennese, but principally because it imagined that an American Freud would not be exemplary of all humanity. The autobiographical Freud could only be exemplary for all dreamers and all readers if this axiom of universality held. It is as if Freud extended the principle he had enunciated to his fiancée in 1882: "I always find it uncanny when I can't understand someone in terms of myself."[84] The psychoanalytic axiom becomes: "Understanding of myself is both necessary and sufficient to understanding someone, anyone. And you, dear reader, do likewise, by understanding me—which becomes understanding you as if you were me."

Before we turn to look at the success of Freud's strategies, as measured by the actual responses of reviewers and disciples in the early years of this century, we can gauge his own sense of the actual reader of *The Interpretation of Dreams* from the extraordinary preface, written in 1909, to the second edition:

> If within ten years of the publication of this book (which is very far from being an easy one to read) a second edition is called for, this is not due to the interest taken in it by the professional circles to whom my original preface was addressed. My psychiatric colleagues seem to have taken no trouble to overcome the initial bewilderment created by my new approach to dreams. The professional philosophers have become accustomed to polishing off the problems of dream-life (which they treat as a mere appendix to conscious states) in a few sentences—and usually in the same ones; and they have evidently failed to notice that we have something here from which a number of inferences can be drawn that are bound to transform our psychological theories. The attitude adopted by reviewers in the scientific periodicals could only lead one to suppose that my work was doomed to be sunk into complete silence; while the small group of gallant supporters, who practise medical psycho-analysis under my guidance and who follow my example in interpreting dreams and make use of their interpretations in treating neurotics, would never have exhausted the first

edition of the book. Thus it is that I feel indebted to a wider circle of educated and curious-minded readers, whose interest had led me to take up once more after nine years this difficult, but in many respects fundamental, work.[85]

Setting to one side the portrait of a misunderstood and somewhat embittered author that this preface paints, Freud makes it clear that *The Interpretation of Dreams* has not been, and by implication will not be, read and understood by "the professional circles to whom my original preface was addressed," "my psychiatric colleagues," "the professional philosophers," and the "reviewers"; nor—and this should make us wonder somewhat—do the "gallant supporters" count. Who does count as the readership of Freud's dream book? Only "a wider circle of educated and curious-minded readers," the common reader, counts as constituting the appreciative and approved readership of his book. Irrespective of whether they are critics or followers, the professionals—whom we might redescribe as "those in positions of interpretative power"—do not count; only the dreamers, the potential patients, the potential auto-analysts, the potential Freudians count. In case the reader had not bothered to read the preface to the second edition, Freud makes the point again in a passage added to the end of Chapter 1: "It [my work] has, of course, received least attention from those who are engaged in what is described as 'research' into dreams, and who have thus provided a shining example of the repugnance to learning anything new which is characteristic of men of science. In the ironical words of Anatole France, *'les savants ne sont pas curieux.'*"[86]

The reviewers, the *savants*, were not entirely hostile to the book, nor were they few in number, as Freud often implied. Certain adopted the "American" position: this holds for Freud, maybe, but not for me ("his theories compel our full agreement, provided we are not expected to subject every dream to his schematics").[87] Many found Freud "ingenious" and "stimulating." Only one, Max Burckhard, set out to refute Freud's theories by analyzing his own dreams in public—and it was possibly this strategy that infuriated Freud, who called it a "stupid review . . . hardly flattering, uncommonly devoid of understanding."[88] But, we might well ask Freud, wasn't this precisely what he expected of readers? Burckhard reacts in exactly the way that the patients who make their entrance in Chapter 4 reacted: he presented a "counter-wish dream," and teasingly imagined what Freud would say in reply.

Burckhard's dream derived from one Christmas of his student days, when a romance began to blossom between him and a girl he spied sitting sewing at her window across the courtyard from him. The sighs and glances exchanged eventually led to a clandestine meeting, at which the young man discovered the pretty girl was hard of hearing. On New Year's Day, he dreamed an anxiety dream in which she and a man invaded his room through the open window, only to be chased back by his chaperoning uncle; as they retreated, both lost their grip. First the man and then the girl fell to their deaths. When he awoke from the dream, the dreamer nailed a blanket over his window, so he would never see the girl again. "May I ask where the wish fulfillment is in my dream?" Burckhard asks.

> I suppose Dr. Freud would have me say that I was disgusted when I learned that she was hard of hearing, even if I didn't articulate it consciously. I was then ready to get rid of her somehow, and my dream fulfilled the wish. This is the way, you must know, in which Dr. Freud artfully suggests various wishes to his patients so that he can then toss their dreams on the same pile with other "wish-fulfillment dreams."[89]

No other reviewer tried to fight Freud on the field of dream-interpretation, and it is easy to see why. Freud's strategies of meeting such criticism make it too easy to see how Burckhard had swallowed the bait. As Freud wrote to Fliess about Burckhard's review, "even Oscar Rie thinks that these are the sorts of objections one raises *before* one has read the book."[90] Burckhard had come half way to meet Freud, venturing onto the terrain of dream-interpretation, not knowing that once one gives Freud a toe, he takes the whole leg. Who, any reader of the dream-book would ask Burckhard, introduced the idea that he was disgusted by the beautiful deaf girl? Certainly not Freud. And might he not consider that he was not so much disgusted by her as disgusted by himself, for killing off someone—in his dream, in his heart—just because she was deaf? The form of his skeptical response, in which he attributes to Freud rather than himself the idea that he was disgusted, implies that he is certain that at least someone is disgusted with him. Such obvious rejoinders are already laid out by Burckhard himself, but in the form of a negation. Freud was annoyed that the dialectic of author and reader had been entered into and yet so obviously misunderstood. In later works, such as his discussion of the difference between an "idea" and a "wish" in the Rat Man's case history, Freud had shown how to engage in a discussion that maneuvered around such objections:

> Thereupon the idea had come to him that she would be kind to him if some misfortune were to befall him; and as an instance of such a misfortune his father's death had forced itself upon his mind. He had at once rejected the idea with energy. And even now he could not admit the possibility that what had arisen in this way could have been a "wish"; it had clearly been no more than a "train of thought."
>
> —By way of objection I asked him why, if it had not been a wish, he had repudiated it.
>
> —Merely, he replied, on account of the content of the idea, the notion that his father might die.
>
> —I remarked that he was treating the phrase as though it were one that involved *lèse-majesté:* it was well known, of course, that it was equally punishable to say "The Emperor is an ass" or to disguise the forbidden words by saying "If any one says, etc., . . . then he will have me to reckon with." . . .
>
> —He was shaken, but did not abandon his objection. I therefore broke off the argument.[91]

168

In his self-imposed splendid isolation, Freud greeted nearly all reviews of his dream book with short-tempered grumpiness over their stupidity; what grated upon him the most was their failure to recognize that he had already met all their objections in the book itself, and that their carping at wish-fulfillments or at the egoistic character of all dreams betrayed a lesser intelligence than the "patients" who already criticized Freud in the book itself. "You've understood nothing—go and read it again!" was his implicit rebuke of his lukewarm reviewers. His followers were to adopt similar tones with critics; in 1911 Jones recounted one Freudian's response to unenlightened professional colleagues:

> The Congress in Munich was unutterably stupid and tedious except for a few jokes that enlivened the discussions. Tromner last year read a paper on sleep, and Seif said he would give him one piece of advice—to read the *Traumdeutung*. This year he read a silly paper on dreams, and frequently quoted the *Traumdeutung*. Seif said he was glad to find he had taken his advice about reading the *Traumdeutung* and that he would now give him another piece— to read it again.[92]

Ignorance of the *Traumdeutung* was treated by Freud's followers as a sure index of stupidity and resistance.[93] Inversely, the sure sign of being a follower was willingness to bring additional material to support the theory of dreams, and Freud dispensed acknowledgments to his growing band of followers by including their material in later editions of the book. Stekel contributed much material on symbolism and was largely responsible for the only major structural change in the book in later editions, when a new section on Symbolism was added to Chapter 6 on the Dream-Work.[94] Ferenczi's contributions on symbolism and the question of the translatability of dreams (in particular, questions concerning linguistic usage in Hungarian and German in relation to dream-elements) were included, as were Jones's remarks about Hamlet, the relation of dreams to madness, and additional individual dream interpretations. Two papers by Rank on myth and creative writing were included in the editions from 1914 to 1922, and he contributed expanded bibliographies to these editions. The most substantive new theoretical contribution, which Freud included in the 1911 edition, came in the form of the "functional phenomena" described and analyzed by Herbert Silberer—and even he, a good Freudian, introduced the phenomena by analyzing Freud's own dreams.[95]

The response of the followers to Freud's dreams reveals how successful Freud's specification of the reader-function had been. The simplest of these responses was permanent identification. Each follower would reread, as if to learn by heart, the original text and its later editions—for example, Jones, writing to Freud in July 1914: "I shall look forward to the *Traumdeutung*. I have not read it since the last edition appeared, which is a long interval for me."[96] Jones could good-humoredly spot a fellow-disciple's identification in the form of a parapraxis in his learning of English when on a visit to London in 1914: "There is only one mistake in English that I cannot cure [Sachs] of—he obstinately confounds the genders (Starfish. Tr. D. identification!)"[97] Jones knowingly concludes that Sachs refuses to correct his grammatical error by identifying with a passage in *The Interpretation of Dreams* where Freud recounts how he, on a visit to England as a young man, referred to a starfish as "he," thus "bringing in sex where it did not belong."[98] Sachs, Jones implies, clings to his grammatical error in order to be like the Freud who confused "he" and "it"; like Freud, perhaps, he wants to continue to bring in sex where it does not belong. Ferenczi's letter to Freud of 1910 makes a strong case for the necessity of this identification, and thereby reveals its strength:

> Whether you want to be or not, you are one of the great master teachers of mankind, and you must allow your readers to approach you, at least intellectually, in a personal relationship as well . . . I am convinced that I am not the only one who, in important

decisions, in self-criticism, etc., always asks and has asked himself the question: How would *Freud* relate to this? . . . So I am and have been much, much more intimately acquainted and conversant with you than you could have imagined.[99]

Even the haughty Ernest Jones could give Freud marks on the publication of his *Autobiographical Study* because he thus recognized the necessity of his making further personal revelations: "I am glad you realise that . . . your mental development cannot be isolated from psycho-analysis as a whole and that you have been willing to repeat the sacrifice of your own privacy already undertaken in the *Traumdeutung*."[100]

Ferenczi was most acutely sensitive to the possibility of deciphering in *The Interpretation of Dreams* the signs of Freud's ambivalent relations to his readers and followers, and to what this might mean for the follower who identified too strongly with Freud. Freud had described how, after what he felt to be a poor lecture, his solitude had been invaded by an admiring member of the audience, who "began to flatter me: telling me how much he had learnt from me, how he looked at everything now with fresh eyes . . ., that I was a very great man. My mood fitted ill with this paean of praise; I fought against my feeling of disgust, went home early to escape from him."[101] Patently mindful of perpetually appearing in the guise of this unwanted flatterer, Ferenczi reminded Freud of this passage:

I know that the many years in which you have been misunderstood have very strongly diminished your receptivity to admiration, recognition, etc. (see in connection to that the passage in the Interpretation of Dreams where you so morosely disdain the effusive admiration of a pupil [in the coffee house]—but you must gradually accustom yourself to the fact that times have improved, and that, without the danger of later disappointment, you can rely upon having enhanced the lives and occupations of a very large number of people who were previously striving in vain for recognition. It is my unshakeable conviction, however, that these adherents are but the predecessors of all humanity.[102]

As Erik Erikson noted in 1962, when discussing Freud's "Dora" case history, trainee psychoanalysts of his generation knew the dream book and the case histories by heart.[103] Heinz Kohut gave a somewhat different inflection to his account of psychoanalytic training when he talked of the deep identification that arose in him because of his use of the dream book when becoming an analyst.[104]

This repeated evidence of the identification of Freud's followers with his person, through their reading of *The Interpretation of Dreams*, thus shades over into the next phase I have disentangled: the use of Freud and his dreams as common property, the property of all mankind—but, for starters, of his professional followers. Nor could these followers escape this next phase: the temptation to analyze further the dreams of *The Interpretation of Dreams*—what Welsh calls "the way Freudians love to one-up Freud."[105] In January 1908, a few months after their first meeting, Karl Abraham wrote to Freud: "I should like to know whether the incomplete interpretation of 'Irma's injection' dream . . . is intentional. I find that trimethylamin leads to the most important part, to sexual allusions which become more distinct in the last lines. After all, everything points to the suspicion of syphilitic infection in the patient."[106] Freud knew how to reply, adopting a distinctly corrective tone, but volunteering further "associations" for this wild, but entirely predictable, analytic interpretation of his would-be disciple's: "Syphilis is *not* the subject-matter . . . Sexual megalomania is hidden behind it, the three women, Mathilde, Sophie and Anna are my daughters' three god-mothers, and I have them all! There would be one simple therapy for widowhood, of course. All sorts of intimate things, naturally!"[107]

With judicious timing, but never more than sparingly, Freud would share self-analytic insights with his disciples, often using elements from *The Interpretation of Dreams* as a common code, in the process devising a covert test of his followers' immersion in his dreams with all their personal references. At the time of his final conflict with

Jung, when Freud, Jung, and the other psychoanalytic leaders were gathered in Munich for organizational discussions, Freud had fainted for the second time in Jung's presence. Explaining this "lapsus" to Jones, Freud wrote:

> There must be some psychic element in this attack which besides was largely fundamented on fatigue, bad sleep and smoking, for I cannot forget that 6 and 4 years ago I have suffered from very similar though not so intense symptoms in the *same* room of the Parkhotel; in every case I had to leave the table. I saw Munich first when I visited Fliess during his illness (you remember: "Propyläeen" in the *Traumdeutung*)[108] and this town seems to have acquired a strong connection with my relation to this man. There is some piece of unruly homosexual feeling at the root of the matter.[109]

Not only were the followers tempted to conduct reanalysis of the *Traumdeutung;* so was Freud. And when it came to that new class of blood sport, fights between Freud and his estranged disciples, for instance in late 1912, the *Traumdeutung* was the first weapon to come to Jung's hand: "May I draw your attention to the fact that you open *The Interpretation of Dreams* with the mournful admission of your own neurosis—the dream of Irma's injection—identification with the neurotic in need of treatment. Very significant."[110] As might be expected, even before his open break, Jung had already presented the greatest challenge to Freud's authorial authority over the *Traumdeutung*. In 1911, when Freud asked if Jung had "any points you would like me to consider for the addenda?"[111] to a new edition, the reply reminded Freud how sharply he, Jung, had "drilled my seminar students in the most rigorous Freudian usage," as a result of which he and his students found certain passages "objectionable in terms of *Freudian* dream interpretation."[112] Jung's letter continued:

> I also miss a specific reference to the fact that the essential (personal) meaning of the dream (e.g. Irma, uncle, monograph, etc.) has *not* been given. I insist on my students learning to understand

dreams in terms of the dynamics of libido; consequently we sorely miss the personally painful element in your own dreams. Perhaps this could be remedied by your supporting the Irma dream with a typical analysis of a patient's dream, where the ultimate real motives are *ruthlessly* disclosed . . . In my seminars we always concentrate for weeks on *The Interpretation of Dreams,* and I have always found that inadequate interpretation of the main dream-examples leads to misunderstandings and, in general, makes it difficult for the students to follow the argument since he cannot conceive the nature of the conflicts that are the regular source of dreams. (For instance, in the monograph dream the crucial topic of the conversation with Dr Königstein, which is absolutely essential if the dream is to be understood properly, is missing.) Naturally one cannot strip oneself naked, but perhaps a model would serve the purpose.[113]

Freud's reply was conciliatory but firm. As with all other attempts to demand more of his privacy than he was prepared to give, he politely declined, while throwing the pressing inquirer a small, extra smidgen for his personal delectation:

You have very acutely noticed that my incomplete elucidation of my own dreams leaves a gap in the over-all explanation of dreams, but here again you have put your finger on the motivation—which was unavoidable. I simply cannot expose any more of my nakedness to the reader . . . In none do I bring out all the elements that can be expected of a dream, because they are my personal dreams . . . (In the dream about the monograph, the crucial conversation with Königstein dealt with the very topic we touched on in Munich. Cf. the Egyptian statue allegedly costing 10,000 kronen. When I was a young man my father chided me for spending money on books, which at the time were my higher passion. As you see, all this is not for the common people.) So even if the critic and the seminar are perfectly right, the author cannot do anything about it. The book proves the principles of dream interpretation by its own nature, so to speak, through its own deficiencies.[114]

And this, surely, is the point: that the complicated structure, the play of self-exposure and discretion—what Freud here nicely calls the book's "deficiencies"—are what allow the reader to be seduced by its autobiographical and personal elements while at the same time being persuaded by the scientific claims, the universality, of the book.

Freud was unquestionably an ambitious man. One of the high points of interpretive virtuosity in the book, what he himself called "my central accomplishment in interpretation,"[115] was his interpretation of the *non vixit* dream, in which he accused his friends of wishing other men dead to further their own ambitions. "As he was ambitious, I slew him" is one of the themes. Freud once again plays hide and seek with his reader, withholding a full interpretation because that would mean "sacrificing to my ambition people whom I greatly value."[116] But Freud did not have the self-control to withhold a more complete interpretation from his reader, which he disclosed some sixty pages after his first interpretation: he sacrificed his own friends to his ambition—by making *public* his own ambition in the form of a successful interpretation of his dreams. Freud's dream-thoughts, preoccupied with the early death of his own brother, with the loss of his childhood playmate, asserted: "no one is irreplaceable."[117] As he finished writing this section of the book, he even flaunted his satisfaction to Fliess: "In the *non vixit* dream I am delighted to have outlived you; isn't it terrible to suggest something like this—that is, to have to make it explicit to everyone who understands?"[118] As we have already seen, one of the very first readers of the book, his friend's widow, a woman whom Freud would have liked to have as a patient but never did, offered Freud as explicit an interpretation as any analyst could have offered of this dream: she terminated a longstanding friendship with Freud—thus enacting the refutation of his dream-thought. "If you think no one is irreplaceable you will have to do without *my* friendship." By publishing the dream Freud let it be known that he cared more for readers than for friends: his wish was for immortality, no matter what the consequences.

Yet this ambition is sublimated in the final paragraph of his interpretation where he asks the rhetorical question, which corresponds to the fundamental wish of the dream: "After all, I reflected, was not having children our only path to immortality?"[119] It is his children, in the end, who represent the most complete and fullest satisfaction of his ambition.[120] That's what *he* says, the occasional reader might reply. With this sentence, Freud surreptitiously draws back from stating his true dream wish—the unquenched ambition for immortality—and fobs off the reader with this piece of eternal wisdom. And it is in the very act of so doing that he translates his ambition into reality: it will be the reader—not his children—who will be his guarantee of immortality. So it might have been more apposite for the final epigraph to the finest piece of dream-interpretation in Freud's book, a monument to ambition if ever there was one, to have been the following, somewhat adapted version: "Is not having readers my only path to immortality?"

Freud's friendship with Fliess did not last long beyond the completion of *The Interpretation of Dreams*. Their last "congress," in August 1900, ended in a quarrel, patched up but never undone. As Freud got involved in writing *The Psychopathology of Everyday Life* throughout late 1900 and early 1901, Fliess was not asked to be his reader. In the summer of 1901, Freud took the side of another of his first readers, Oscar Rie, against that of Fliess, closing ranks with the Viennese, even Breuer, against Wilhelm. And something that Fliess had either said in their row the previous year, or, more likely, written in a critical letter now rankled deeply with Freud:

You take sides against me and tell me that "the reader of thoughts merely reads his own thoughts in[to] other people," which renders all my efforts valueless. If that is what you think of me, just throw my "Everyday Life" unread into the wastepaper basket. It is full of references to you—manifest ones, for which you supplied the material, and concealed ones, for which the motivation goes back to you . . . you can take it as a testimonial to the role you have played for me up to now. Having announced it in this way, I feel

I can send you the essay when it comes into my hands without further words.[121]

It is entirely appropriate that Freud's First Reader should be the first to make this fundamental criticism of the Reader of Thoughts; yet there is a deep ambiguity in it. Did Fliess mean that Freud placed his own thoughts in people and then found them there, not knowing—or preferring not to know—that it was he who had put them there in the first place? Or did Fliess mean that Freud could only see what his own thoughts allowed him to see, and that he could thus only see what Freud and other people had in common? The entire ambiguity rests on the difference between "reading his own thoughts into" or "reading his own thoughts in" other people—a difference not evident in the German—the difference between projection and identification. "Reading his own thoughts in" corresponds closely to the exemplarity that Freud assumed his own dreams would inevitably display, and thus to the strategy I have outlined whereby dreamer, patient, and reader are articulated closely together. In the autumn of their friendship, the First Reader Fliess was refusing to comply—was feeling the effects of having been that First Reader.

Freud was not finished with this First Reader; in September 1901 he pressed his point and indicated which reading he gave of the accusation of being a thought reader:

> For whom do I still write? If as soon as an interpretation of mine makes you uncomfortable, you are ready to agree that the "reader of thoughts" perceives nothing in the other [*am anderen*], but merely projects his own thoughts, you really are no longer my audience either and must regard my entire method of working as being just as worthless as the others do.[122]

Freud acted on this loss:

> When I came back from [my first visit to Rome] . . . I withdrew my last work from publication [*Dora*] because just a little earlier I

had lost my last audience in you. Nestroy, looking through a peephole before a benefit performance and seeing only two people in the house is said to have exclaimed: "The one 'audience' I know; he has a complimentary ticket. Whether the other 'audience' has one too, I do not know."

Freud had thus, it appears, split the Reader function into two: one was now superfluous, to the point where the text prepared without it could, without danger or loss, be thrown unread into the wastepaper basket—this is the other he is certain has a complimentary ticket. The other function had become singularized and absolutely necessary—*Dora* would not appear because Fliess was no longer there to read it. The uncertainty of not knowing if this other had a complimentary ticket could not be sustained. Freud would not perform in this uncertainty.

This lapse of Fliess's function as reader should not be treated entirely as if it were an internal struggle of projections and identifications. Freud was to publish less in the period 1901–1905 than at any other time since the end of the 1880s: it is the one fallow patch in his whole writing career. And because there are no writings, and no sustained correspondence of any intimacy, we as a result know less about this period than any other period of Freud's adult life. Our knowledge of the unfolding of Freud's life and of the autobiographical writing that is the same thing as the worldwide psychoanalytic institution is only restored in the years after 1906, when replacements—Jung, Ferenczi, Jones, Abraham—unknowingly allow themselves to fulfill Fliess's function as correspondent, as reader. The continuum that runs from intimate correspondent, then to follower and member of the international psychoanalytic movement, is one both of whose ends are occupied by the Reader: at one end, Fliess as irreplaceable Other, at the other, the "wider circle of educated and curious-minded readers," always positioned on the outer limits of the psychoanalytic movement, always defining that limit. And, in a splendid irony of history so common in the history of psychoanalysis, which is such a family affair, Fliess's son Robert would become a psychoanalyst best known for his edited collection of psychoanalytic papers, *The Psychoanalytic Reader,* a book whose title commemorates his father's function in psychoanalysis even if its contents are a more conventional celebration of the professional and scientific hierarchy of Freud's closest followers. *The Psychoanalytic Reader* was published in 1950, the same year as his father's correspondence with Freud would have been published, along with Freud's, if only Freud had not destroyed—or mislaid—all of Wilhelm's letters. Put simply, it is the contention of this chapter that the censored edition of Freud's letters to Fliess published in German in that same year, *The Origins of Psychoanalysis: Letters to Wilhelm Fliess, Drafts and Notes, 1887–1902*—an edition on whose title page Robert Fliess's name is conspicuous by its absence—would have been more appropriately entitled *The Psychoanalytic Reader.*

Are readers in the late twentieth century in a different position from Freud's reviewers, followers, or apostates? It has been my claim that the reader specified by Freud for *The Interpretation of Dreams* has three different characteristics: he is Freud's analyst; he is required to be Freudian by the structure and rhetorical maneuvers of the text; and he is required to adopt the position of the common reader. Remember Freud's emphatic remarks about his readership in the preface to the second edition of *The Interpretation of Dreams,* where he set to one side both ignorant opponents and enthusiastic followers as constituting his readership. The strategy of the dream book requires one to partake in the experience of analysis in both positions: as interpreter (which shades over into the almost irresistible urge to one-up Freud)[123] and as dreamer. The position of dreamer divides straightforwardly into three. Insofar as the reader identifies, at his explicit invitation, with Freud, making his interests his own, he becomes the subject of those dreams of his that he analyzes. Insofar as the reader adopts the position of the intelligent and skeptical patient and critic, a position that Freud's strategy of argument makes very tempting, he becomes that outsider who resists, so necessary to and common a part of psychoanalytic cultures—psychoanalysis requires its enemies in order to be psychoanalysis. Insofar as the reader takes Freud at his word, and tries out his techniques on his own dreams, he becomes the common reader who is now part of a common culture that takes Freudian interpretation as a given. As Freud himself wrote, in a loosely didactic moment: "And here I will mention a number of further, somewhat disconnected, points on the subject of interpreting dreams, which may perhaps help to give readers their bearings should they feel inclined to check my statements by subsequent work upon their own dreams."[124]

This analysis of the reader-function helps us to see two clearly different senses in which one might be "a Freudian." The Freudian that *The Interpretation of Dreams* produces is a reader who knows how to interpret—or, at the very least, who knows what it is like to interpret—and, necessarily, by imaginative transference, knows what it is like to have his dreams interpreted. The reader of *The Interpretation of Dreams* is not first and foremost a Freudian in the sense of *believing*—either for quasi-religious or quasi-scientific reasons—in Freud's theories, or in the sense of being professionally *qualified* to practice psychoanalysis. In contrast with the more professionally disciplined—closed-shop—views of his disciples and colleagues, Freud maintained that self-analysis, and in particular analysis of one's own dreams, was the principal means for becoming an analyst: "The interpretation of dreams is in fact the royal road to a knowledge of the unconscious; it is the securest foundation of psycho-analysis and the field in which every worker must acquire his convictions and seek his training. If I am asked how one can become a psycho-analyst, I reply: 'By studying one's own dreams.'" So wrote Freud in 1909, for the first grand public of psychoanalysis, in Worcester, Massachusetts. And, as ever, whenever the question of the interpretation of dreams came up, the figure of the censor and critic was always present, to be addressed in the very next sentence: "Every opponent of psycho-analysis hitherto has, with a nice discrimination, either evaded any consideration of *The Interpretation of Dreams*, or has sought to skirt over it with the most superficial objections."[125]

At the very least, we can assert that Freud thought that anyone who shied away from self-analysis, from the analysis of his dreams, no matter how extensive and orthodox his relations with an analyst were, did not qualify to be called "Freudian." "Anyone who fails to produce results in a self-analysis of this kind may at once give up any idea of being able to treat patients by analysis."[126] The touchstone of psychoanalysis and of the opposition to it would always remain the interpretation of dreams: "I have acquired a habit of gauging the measure of a psychologist's understanding by his attitude to dream-interpretation; and I have observed with satisfaction that most of the opponents of psycho-analysis avoid this field altogether or else display remarkable clumsiness if they attempt to deal with it."[127]

Freud retained his sympathy for the lone dream-analyst. Rebuking Jones in 1924 for wishing to dismiss a maverick writer on psycho-analysis, Pickworth Farrow, with a hasty diagnosis of dementia prae-cox, Freud told Jones how, unknown to Jones, the man had been let down by the incompetence of two London analysts and had embarked on a self-analysis.[128] Freud felt sufficiently kindly toward Farrow to write a preface for his self-analytic writings, where he implicitly admonished analysts like Jones who thought the heroic era of self-analysis was thankfully over, replaced with an efficiently policed, hierarchical system of professionally run analyses:

> The author of this paper is known to me as a man of strong and independent intelligence. Probably through being somewhat self-willed he failed to get on good terms with two analysts with whom he made the attempt. He thereupon proceeded to make a systematic application of the procedure of self-analysis which I myself employed in the past for the analysis of my own dreams. His findings deserve attention precisely on account of the peculiar character of his personality and of his technique.[129]

The implication is clear: a reader of *The Interpretation of Dreams* may be entirely at odds with the institutions of psychoanalysis, but as long as he plants himself firmly on the privileged terrain of self-analysis, dreams, he will very likely turn out a better Freudian than others.

It is true that psychoanalytic training institutions still require Freud—often introductory, intermediary, and advanced—as an essential element of their courses. But it is not this that makes the psychoanalytic movement distinctive—or even Freudian—although it is a peculiar enough professional practice.[130] It is at this point that I return to my initial question, concerning the character of the international psychoanalytic movement. The true Freudians, the backbone of the psychoanalytic movement, are Freud's readers, not the psychoanalysts. No amount of policing of institutions can stem the "wild analysis" that is unleashed by Freud's writing-effects, among which the constitution of the reader is one of the principal achievements.

Freud is consistently one of the best-selling authors of mass paperback nonfiction in the Western world today. Reading Freud is not a supplement to another source of psychoanalytic knowledge. It is an obligatory passage point for entry into psychoanalysis: one first becomes a Freudian through reading.[131] It is this fact that differentiates psychoanalysis from other international scientific, cultural, or political movements—even from the Darwinian movement, despite the clear similarities between *The Origin of Species* and *The Interpretation of Dreams*.[132] It is this fact that makes the presence of Freud in humanities departments—departments that specialize in reading techniques—so often entirely appropriate, a true reflection of the character of Freud's invention. Insofar as practitioners of psychoanalysis model their institutions and practices on those common to bacteriology, statistics, or hypnosis, they inevitably distrust these other Freudians. But in their distrust and their attempts at policing the boundaries between the qualified experts and the rest, they render themselves blind to the full measure of Freud's achievement.

The "educated and curious-minded" who have just read Freud for the first time will often express reactions which range from quite explicit gratitude and love for the feeling of being recognized, albeit by a figure who adopts the position of a parent or educator, to explosive rage that does not usually prevent them from picking up once again the book they repeatedly throw down. Perhaps this is the best indication of Freud's achievement in inventing the transferential machine we know as *The Interpretation of Dreams*.

5

"A WHOLE CLIMATE OF OPINION"

if often he was wrong and, at times, absurd,
to us he is no more a person
now but a whole climate of opinion

under whom we conduct our different lives:
Like weather he can only hinder or help

W. H. Auden, "In Memoriam Sigmund Freud"

If Auden's diagnosis is still accurate, writing the history of psycho-analysis is rather like writing the history of the weather in the twentieth century: its presence is so constant and all-pervasive that escaping its influence is out of the question. And precisely because of its inescapable character, it cannot be isolated from the various and myriad striking events which can be singled out more straight-forwardly as part of the histories of science, of medicalization, of great ideas, of cultural movements, of modernisation, of all the other movements to which it might apparently belong. Freud, it seems, is rather like electric lighting—the twentieth century is unthinkable without it, but not many histories of this century pause to evoke the customary and natural darkness of all previous generations dispelled forever by light bulbs, car headlights, flashing neon tubes, and the nighttime flicker of the cinema and TV screens. There is, of course, a history of electricity in which names such as Maxwell and Edison figure prominently; but theirs is not the only history of electricity, nor is it the most important history. Likewise, there are histories of psychoanalysis where it belongs alongside radiotherapy and hypnosis, alongside energetics and the advent of causal medicine, alongside brain anatomy and the history of linguistics, alongside Durkheimian sociology and intelligence testing; but these assembled together do not make up the most important history.

Whether or not one assents to Auden's portrait of Freud as the weathervane of the twentieth century, the tone of his tribute unmistakably captures a striking feature of the historiography of psychoanalysis: its personal tone. Auden's poem depicts Freud's death as first and foremost his own personal loss. Of all the histories of psychoanalysis, the first was, in one sense of the term, undoubtedly the most unabashedly and explicitly personal: Sigmund Freud's "On the History of the Psycho-analytic Movement." This work contained some of Freud's most astringent criticism and intolerant ostracism. It is a personal vendetta conducted in the Olympian impersonal voice that only autobiography, that completely unanswerable genre, can adopt. The history of psychoanalysis, Freud implies, is inextricably the history of refusals, resistances, and the necessary regroupings of the orthodox. What is more, his scathing attacks on the renegades and heretics were not only an attempt to preempt the judgment of history; they were also intimately entwined with a reordering of psychoanalytic concepts. Out of Freud's diatribe against Jung would develop the concept of narcissism and the necessity to revise his first dualist theory of drives; out of his diatribe against Adler would develop the musings on the essential nature of femininity that came to fruition in some of his best-known and most notorious papers, those written under the sign of penis envy.[1] Controversies were perennially not only occasions for rewriting the history of psychoanalysis, as the expelled—Rank, Ferenczi (almost)—retrospectively had their earlier work removed or downgraded, but also, and *necessarily* so, occasions for major conceptual clarification. It is not for nothing that the history of psychoanalysis appears to be synonymous with the history of its splits, schisms, and dissidents.

185

However, Freud did not have to wait until he had dissenting followers for the process of rewriting the history of psychoanalysis to take place. From the outset, the interpretations upon which psychoanalysis was founded were reinterpretations of the treatments of patients, of the significance of nonsensical past events, of the validity of childhood memories. Inasmuch as psychoanalytic writing embodies a specific theory about the relation of the present to the past, Freud's scientific style preempts the rational reconstruction of the historical development of his concepts. To understand the concept of repression, one follows his account of its genesis out of the experience of the resistance of patients. And to give an account of the "resistance" of patients, one must follow Freud in recounting the history of doctor-patient relationships at the end of the nineteenth century, including therein the ideal of the transparency and absolute authority of the relationship between hypnotist and subject in hypnosis.[2] The rational reconstruction of concepts and the personal narrative of Freud's experience as a therapist, indeed as a sexed being, are entwined. Freud "discovered" that he could not analyze himself without knowledge of his patients, nor could he analyze his patients without knowledge of himself; the historian is placed in the position of having to treat psychoanalytic concepts both as strictly personal documents and as governed by the architectonic of a theoretical system.

Three classic studies of the history of psychoanalysis illustrate the intertwining of the personal, the contextual, and the conceptual, despite their idiosyncratically fastidious conceptions of the historian's task: Jones's biography of Freud; Ellenberger's study of the development of dynamic psychiatry, in particular the systems of Freud, Janet, Jung, and Adler, in the nineteenth and early twentieth centuries;[3] and Jean Laplanche and J.-B. Pontalis's conceptual dictionary of psychoanalytic concepts.[4]

Jones attempted to write a traditional neo-Victorian life-and-work of his subject, and went as far as to divide Volumes 2 and 3 into separate sections dealing with the "Life" and the "Work." However, even Jones found it impracticable to separate the Life and the Work in Volume 1, which deals with "the young Freud" from his birth to the publication of *The Interpretation of Dreams* at the age of 43. Jones established what has since become the psychoanalytically orthodox version of this early history: the intimate connection between Freud's inner personal life and the outer work of theory building, medical practice, and publishing. The self-analysis—as he described it—of the late 1890s became the historical linchpin for biographers and historians of science alike. "Once done it is done forever": this was Jones's view of the self-analysis that revealed a New World as definitively and epoch-transformingly as the voyage of Christopher Columbus. This view is that of the first-generation disciple of his Master. And psychoanalysts themselves—most eminently and illuminatingly Wladimir Granoff[5]—have questioned first whether an account that is quite such a naked transference, such a naked apology for both disciple and master, can stand as history, let alone as psychoanalytically sophisticated history, and second whether any other account is feasible.

Many of those who have followed the biographical path since Jones have enthusiastically pursued the goal of rendering a life of Freud that is also the key to the conceptual development of psychoanalysis, not only because of a psychoanalytic *parti pris* in favor of seeking the causes of the outer trappings of life in the inner vicissitudes of personal history, but also because of a nervous eschewal, often going as far as an energetic repudiation, of psychoanalytic visions of a life in favor of more traditional biographical approaches. Even those, such as Ola Andersson and Henri Ellenberger, whose works in the 1960s had provided firm foundations for the early intellectual history of Freud's work in the 1890s, found in previously unpublished documents concerning early patients of Breuer's and Freud's—Bertha Pappenheim and Fanny Moser—material for a revisionist account of this early history.[6] Biographical history could now compete with case history, as well as with Freud's accounts of psychological mechanisms. Since these works of the 1960s, Fichtner, Hirschmüller, and others have worked along similar lines, making available a new level of detail and mastery of previously inaccessible sources.[7]

The edge of iconoclasm in these new and detailed historical studies was to be expected: history from below, as the contemporaneous social history proclaimed itself, was self-consciously an attempt to revise and unsettle the stories told by those with an interest in a stable version of the past. The iconoclasm is explicit in the work of Swales.[8] In particular, Swales has demonstrated that controversial and always interesting results are to be had from combining techniques of close reading that both mimic and repudiate those of Freud's with high-class sleuthing: delving in the archives and hotel registers of fin-de-siècle Austro-Hungary, interviewing and coaxing the memories of the descendants of forgotten or previously unknown historical participants in Freud's early work. It is Swales more than anyone else who has struck a chord in Freud studies to which there is an immediate response on the part of the general reader—who is intensely aware that psychoanalysis reveals hidden truths and that, if they are hidden, these truths of psychoanalysis must surely be worth hearing: Did Freud have an affair with his sister-in-law, arrange for her to have a secret abortion, and then use these skeletons in his closet as the foundations upon which to build a theory about skeletons in the closet?[9] Did Freud owe so much to his one-time friend Fliess that, rather than admit his debt, he planned to murder him?[10] Once we know exactly where and when Freud masturbated in an Alpine meadow, Swales implies, we will be less tempted to take seriously his theories of the importance of masturbation fantasies and their relation to childhood.

These iconoclastic studies, invaluable for the evidence they have produced and the dramatically new picture they paint of the milieux in which psychoanalysis arose, are as psychoanalytically *parti pris* as Jones, Schur, Eissler, and other psychoanalytically orthodox historians. Like the analysts at work on the self-deluding memories of their patients, the iconoclasts often aim to deprive psychoanalysis of firm foundations by demonstrating the tendentiousness of its own history.

In a very different vein the contextualists, of whom Ellenberger is the doyen, also are at odds with the history the psychoanalysts tell.

Once one establishes, as Ellenberger and others have attempted to, that psychoanalysis is only one among many similar projects, both in space—the synchronic Europe-wide invention of dynamic psychiatry, of psychotherapies, of discourses on sexuality—and in time—the reinvention of the secret therapeutic mysteries and sects of the Pythagoreans, the Mesmerists and popular hypnotists and healers—then its claim to its unique position can no longer be upheld. Not only that: other contextualist arguments—such as Schorske's and McGrath's[11]—paint psychoanalysis as only comprehensible within the wider context of the pressure-cooker of *fin-de-siècle* Vienna: psychoanalysis, like so much else in the declining years of the Hapsburg empire, was a nonpolitical means for achieving the frustrated political and class aims of the first generation of the new bourgeoisie. In more recent years, a new twist has been given to the politically sensitive question that ran like a red thread through the early dealings of Freud with his disciples and on into the Nazi era that transformed the demographics of psychoanalysis: is psychoanalysis a Jewish science? Whereas Schorske emphasized the frustrations of the Viennese liberal bourgeoisie, more recent cultural historians emphasize the fact that this liberal bourgeoisie was overwhelmingly Jewish: the Jews became the numerically preponderant group in the cultural renaissance of Vienna, despite making up only 10 percent of the overall population. More than half of the doctors and lawyers in Vienna in 1890 were Jewish. Steven Beller drives the point home as follows:

> [Freud] was born a merchant's son in the Bohemian crownlands; 85 per cent of the Viennese *Gymnasiasten* with this background were Jewish. At his school . . . 97 per cent of merchants' sons were Jewish, and of those pupils born in the Bohemian crownlands, 73 per cent were Jewish . . . He chose to do medicine at university; 78 per cent of the "liberal bourgeois" sector—into which Freud

had, of course, been born—among *Maturanten* who opted to study medicine were Jewish. A staggering 93 per cent—76 Jews as opposed to only 5 non-Jews—of the merchants' sons in the *Gymnasien* sample who chose medicine were Jewish. He went on to become a practising physician . . . Jews comprised 65 per cent of all former *Gymnasiasten* from a liberal bourgeois background who went on to be doctors and lawyers . . . Freud, at least, could hardly have been anything else but Jewish, in the Viennese context.[12]

Such studies of the delicate position of these Jews in the liberal professions have also found in the autobiographical odyssey of *The Interpretation of Dreams* the model for a search for a new identity for those Jews in flight from their truncated Jewish identities; it "could provide a rallying point for both Jews and non-Jews who rebelled against the prevailing tendency to assign social identities on the basis of religious affiliation."[13]

But if the specificity of psychoanalysis, if not its originality, is to be sought here in Vienna, such arguments increase the urgency of the question: can the enduring fascination of psychoanalysis—of Freud's grandiose autobiography—in inter-war America, in post-war France, in late twentieth century South America also be found in the obligation on the newly educated urban professional classes to undertake the Great Modernist Trek in search of a secular identity?

Thus there is a historiographic tension between the need to find an explanation for the emergence of psychoanalysis in Vienna (rather than somewhere else) and the need for a historical characterization of psychoanalysis that will also explain its rapid dissemination and acceptance in Western culture in the early years of this century. Curiously enough, this problem of the universality of the appeal of a theory and a movement whose specific and unique historical origins are pinpointed more and more accurately is the structural duplicate of an even deeper historiographic problem: the question of Freud's originality. Looking forward from Freud's Vienna, we see psychoanalysis disseminating out to other cultures and institutions; looking backward from Vienna's Freud, we see a myriad of diverse progenitors and precursors.

As I have already implied, iconoclasm makes itself felt, in the history of psychoanalysis as in so many other areas in the history of science, in the attempt to demonstrate the commonplace character, even ubiquity, of a scientist's most distinctive claims. The unconscious, it is argued, is a product of Romantic thought, if not earlier;[14] infantile sexuality had been recognized as common, even by doctors, for decades, if not centuries, before Freud.[15] But, it is riposted, Freud's originality did not stem from his discovery of these "facts," just as Newton's did not stem from his "discovering" gravity, but in his systematizing of them, in the manner in which he transformed and undercut earlier conceptions of sexuality and the mind.[16] The history of Freud's precursors has been and will inevitably be a burgeoning and sizable part of the historiography of psychoanalysis. However, the significance of each precursor diminishes the more names are added to the list: each precursor transforms Freud's significance from that of being a discoverer (who is then shown not to be one by the precursor-hunting historian), to that of being the conduit for the heterogeneous cultural resources of his—and our?—times.

If the French tradition of epistemology was to produce the *Vocabulaire* of Laplanche and Pontalis, which I shall discuss shortly, the most representative, and revealing, product of the equivalent Anglo-American tradition of history of science was Frank Sulloway's *Freud: Biologist of the Mind.* If the French tradition errs by ignoring context in favor of conceptual analysis, Sulloway attempted to reduce conceptual development to intellectual context: in his case, to exactly that intellectual context to which a historian of science whose training had been in the familiar territories of the physical and biological sciences would appeal. According to Sulloway, psychoanalysis was an offshoot of the biological sciences of the nineteenth century that had never freed itself from the parent plant. Ignoring the fact that, just to count crude heads for a moment, there are 75 instances of Freud quoting Goethe in the *Standard Edition*, 74 quotes from Shakespeare, and only 21 mentions of Darwin, Sulloway proposed that psycho-analysis was a crypto-biology, a sort of sociobiology *avant la lettre;* and, most triumphantly, he used the gaps in the evidence for this view as proof of a cover-up, proof of the sustained effort (to what end?) of Freud and his disciples at promoting the myth that psycho-analysis is not an art of interpretation and a science of mental life, but a self-deluding conceptual system intended to answer biological problems. Rereading Sulloway's rewriting of history, one cannot but feel that the iconoclasm of the biographical detectives had become intertwined in an unfortunate manner with the somewhat self-contradictory conviction that no psychology is worthy of the name unless it is really a biology (as with the sociobiology of the 1970s). Certainly, the closure of historical development that his argument concerning Freud being mired in the neo-Lamarckian biology of fin-de-siècle Vienna produces does not help us understand how psychoanalysis as an endemic practice and as a cultural system ever came into being.

At the opposite pole to the contextualist histories we find the third of my classic studies in the history of psychoanalysis, which at first blush does not appear to be history: Laplanche and Pontalis's *Vocabulaire de la Psychanalyse,* first published in French in 1967. Organized as a lexicon or manual of conceptual terms, it is focused primarily on the conceptual development of Freud's terminology, although certain terms from later analysts, notably Lacan and Klein, are given a place. In the process of teasing out the subtleties of the changes in these concepts, the authors give the most thought-provoking and textually accurate of the internal histories of the science of psychoanalysis, so that every student of Freud's writing is indebted to them and will be for many years. However, to call their work "history" raises interesting questions, not only about the rela-tion between the "internal" and the "external" histories of science— as historians of science have, in something of a mood of resignation, become used to calling one of the oldest and most important debates in their field—but about the nature of psychoanalytic knowledge itself and its relation to the discipline's history.

While this in no sense detracts from Laplanche's and Pontalis's independence and originality, the very possibility of their project of a conceptual dictionary of Freudian terms is to be found in the conditions of psychoanalysis in postwar France. The very idea of a conceptual dictionary of such subtlety and sophistication could only be attempted and brought to fruition in a psychoanalytic environment which was open to alliances less with medicine than with the "human sciences": the dictionary could thus be constructed employing the techniques of the historian of philosophy and the French tradition of the epistemology of the sciences (a very different tradition from the philosophy of the sciences in postwar Anglo-American intellectual life, where history of science was a burgeoning discipline in its own right, always more contextualist and eager to distance itself from the overly formal account of the sciences associated with Viennese logical positivism and the falsificationism of Karl Popper). This atmosphere of philosophical sophistication and enthusiasm for close and accurate commentary on the Freudian *textes* (as the French, and later the English-speaking commentators, would call them) was provided by the "return to Freud" of Jacques Lacan, with its mistrust of the medicalization of psychoanalysis in favor of alliances with the proto-structuralism of the "conjectural sciences": ethnology, linguistics, and cybernetics.

If Jones's official biography of Freud was written in part by the disciple wishing to cast his own life—as early follower and bearer of the psychoanalytic Good News to England, as mainstay of the International Psychoanalytic Association for some forty years— together with that of the Master, in the heroic mode, and in part to establish an abundantly researched official history to pit against the tendentious popularizations; if Ellenberger's history was that of an eclectic psychiatrist wishing to rescue his discipline from narrow-minded commitment to any one system of dynamic psychiatry; then Laplanche and Pontalis were attempting to establish the historical

193

baseline for a discipline that has a very curious and distinctive relation to its own history. The works of Jones and Ellenberger both illustrate how the "history" of psychoanalysis is inextricably bound up with a conception of what psychoanalysis is *and should be;* the work of Laplanche and Pontalis demonstrates how a specific conception of what psychoanalysis is and should be is built upon a definitive and historically defensible reading of Freud.

It was almost certainly the example of Lacan's return to Freud and the sophisticated exegetical enterprises associated with the energetic dissemination of psychoanalysis in France in the 1950s and 1960s, of which Laplanche and Pontalis's work was among the most distinguished, together with the burgeoning quasi-analytic textual procedures of Jacques Derrida, that led Michel Foucault in 1968 to write his essay "What Is an Author?" Almost in the style of an analytic philosopher, Foucault clarified the various usages of the term "author," which range from the tautological—well captured by Aldous Huxley's bon mot: *"The Odyssey* was written by Homer or by some one with the same name"—through the material sense ("the author asserts her moral right") to the more interestingly transdiscursive senses. Names such as Dickens or Darwin are transdiscursive not only because they have oeuvres associated with them, so that the name "Darwin" evokes not only *The Origin of Species* but also *The Descent of Man,* but also because they are associated with texts and social movements that go beyond "mere" or tautological authorship, or even possession of a "corpus": there is a Darwinian revolution, there is Dickensian London. Authors of founding religious texts— such as Mohammed or Joseph Smith—have an equally transdiscursive function, in part because of their ambiguous relationship to their "coauthors," in part because their texts become "canonical"—unquestionably imbued with a truth whose extraction requires exegesis and commentary. In addition to such transdiscursive authors, Foucault concentrates on the novel breed of nineteenth-century writers who gave rise to "discursive practices"; these authors "produced not only their own work, but the possibility and the rules of the formation of other texts."[17] Freud and Marx are the best examples: their work is not just the first in a series, but is distinctly separated off as unique and foundational in relation to all other texts that followed. In this respect, so Foucault argues, Freud's work is different from the works of other authors in the history of science.

Although one may doubt whether the history of science displays no other founding authors of the ilk of Marx and Freud—one could point to the relation of British mathematical natural philosophy in the eighteenth century to Newton, or to certain fundamentalist Darwinians of the last two decades—the distinctiveness of psychoanalytic communities with respect to Freud is unquestionable. The preservation and teaching of the theories of Sigmund Freud are often enough enshrined in the statutes of psychoanalytic societies and institutes; every student of psychoanalysis spends some years mastering Introductory, Intermediate, and Advanced Freud. Here, mastering means what it might mean in a practical art such as painting, or building a computer: being able to put oneself in the position of Freud and enact the interpretations or the conceptual developments oneself.

At the very same time, the student must undertake a training analysis and must perform, and have performed upon him or her, what Freud performed upon himself: the act of analysis. The training analysis is closely linked to a more specific feature of Freud's psychoanalytic writing: its autobiographical character. This personal tone, the fact that every reader, certainly every early follower, is obliged to establish a personal relationship with the theory, means that histories of psychoanalysis often read as if they are accounts of Freud's autobiography—as if they are biographies of Freud and his extended analytic family.[18] And hence the history of psychoanalysis for the period following Freud's death appears to lose its guiding thread or its raison d'être: the history of psychoanalysis is the story of Freud's autobiography. Or, by extension, the history of psychoanalysis is a family saga, the history of the family he created. Genealogical researches—that mode of historical knowledge dear to aristocrats and those in search of their personal "roots," but a mode that is anathema to professional historians—and accounting of debts and inheritance—more usually the domain of the historians of royalty and of industrial empires—can become the framework for the history of the dissemination of psychoanalysis: informal gossip about analytic filiation—who frequented which couch, who is the analytic mother and father of whom; informal gossip about who is the true legatee of the symbolic legacy of theory and of the true method of psychoanalysis.

This singular and unique importance of Freud for the history of psychoanalysis prompted Derrida to ask a searching question about the distinctive relation of psychoanalysis to its founder: "How can an autobiographical writing, in the abyss of an unterminated self-analysis, give birth to a world-wide institution?"[19] Derrida's numerous writings on psychoanalysis—on the interconnection of autobiography and theory, of telepathy and the analyst's use of the first-person pronoun, of family dynamics and institutional affiliation[20]—raise the question of the distinctiveness of the institutional character of psychoanalysis: Is it a revival of an ancient model of an esoteric therapeutic philosophical sect, à la Ellenberger? Is its insistently reflexive character the harbinger of the deconstructionist or postmodern world of the end of the twentieth century?

In an obvious sense, the institutional history of psychoanalysis begins with Freud's relationships with his followers, and there have been useful and major studies of the family networks and sub-networks, from Roazen's studies of the external forms of discipleship, through Roustang's more psychoanalytically oriented, but no less critical, studies of the structure of relationship, the structure of mastery and slavery, necessary to the formation of psychoanalytic institutions, to more contextually embedded accounts of specific psychoanalytic cultures.[21] And it is when one places these contextualized histories of national cultures of psychoanalysis alongside the studies that focus on Freud that one senses that in the historiography of psychoanalysis there are two distinct genres: on the one hand,

Freud Studies, which is more biography than history, more the struggle over the legacy than a social history of a new profession; and on the other hand, the histories (always plural) of psychoanalysis in its local habitats and micro-cultures.

However, one should not presume too quickly that it is only the figure of Freud that leads to history ending up as a cross between myth and family romance; the most accomplished of psychoanalytic histories to date, Elisabeth Roudinesco's monumental *La Bataille de Cent Ans: L'Histoire de la Psychanalyse en France, 1885–1985*, quickly dispels such an illusion. Each of the two volumes of Roudinesco's generously conceived and culturally catholic history has a hero: the first volume, covering the period from Charcot to the early years of the Société Psychanalytique de Paris, appears to have Freud as its hero. Her study of the early years of French psychoanalysis, from 1885 to 1939, is a study of cultural misappropriation, of the image of the cosmopolitan, universalist Freudian theory refracted in a chauvinistic, anti-Semitic, and sexually repressive French society. Hence the Freud who appears in this history is present only as a negative contrast to the false Freuds, those invoked in France in this period as the inventor of an unconscious that Roudinesco argues is only an "inconscient à la française."

Implicit in the second volume is the possibility of the emergence of a Freud who is now faithfully reflected by his disciples—this is the Freud of Laplanche and Pontalis, of an exegetical attention to detail that has produced a document such as This and Theves' lengthy study of the translation of Freud's "Die Verneinung," a four-page paper he published in 1925. This and Theves scrutinize and compare, line by line, word by word, particle by particle, the seventeen different translations of these four pages that French psychoanalytic culture has produced.[22]

However, the living hero of Roudinesco's second volume is not this textually embalmed and sacred Freud, but Jacques Lacan, magician and charlatan, grand theorist and transgressor of all psychoanalytic etiquette. It is tempting, though not perhaps safe, to draw

the historical conclusion: it is only when there is a figure as domi-
nating as Lacan in any given psychoanalytic culture that the spell
cast by Freud can be conjured away. Perhaps one method of internal
transformation open to psychoanalysis is neither the repudiation nor
the forgetting of Freud; perhaps "Freud" is as flexible as Jesus or
Newton, allowing a plethora of faithful versions to flourish in his
many mansions. Another lesson is equally clear: it is possible for the
story of a psychoanalytic culture to be told that is not a version of
Freud's family romance. Someone else's will do just as well.

Roudinesco's history is by quite a margin the most comprehensive
and subtle general history of a psychoanalytic culture to date. Only
the summation of research done on the early American enthusiasm
for and co-option of Freud's work bears any comparison. Together
the American and French histories raise the question: will the history
of psychoanalysis always be best done within the framework of
national cultures?

Schorske and McGrath had provided an account of the place of
psychoanalysis within Viennese culture that can only hold for a very
specific time and place; at the same time, they supported an older,
Marxisant or *sociologisant,* view of psychoanalysis as the apolitical
discourse that tempts the bourgeoisie away from the privileged arena
of political struggle and conflict. It is as if Vienna exported one
brand of International to subvert the effects of the other. Left-lean-
ing bourgeois groups have, throughout the twentieth century, viewed
with suspicion those who would place their inner personal hygiene
alongside the plight of the masses. The attractions of the theories
and movements associated with both Marx and Freud have been one
of the cultural constants in Western intellectual circles of the twentieth century, as have, inevitably, been the attempts at Freudo–Marxist
synthesis, from Reich to Habermas, from Marcuse to Althusser.

Similarly, it is transnational media that may be extensively implicated in the creation of the image of charismatic scientists, from the
late nineteenth century on. Certainly, in the late 1910s and 1920s
Freud joined Einstein and a few other contemporary scientists in the

novel role of a charismatic figure for the daily press and weekly reviews; an analysis of the function of such charismatic figures, from Darwin to Hawking, will aid in the understanding of the popular dissemination of psychoanalysis. Roudinesco's history of psychoanalysis in France[23] gives ample details of this popularization for one culture, and there is an illuminating study by Rapp of England in the 1920s.[24] There is also a fine study of American psychiatry, concentrating on psychoanalysis, as portrayed in the Hollywood cinema from the 1930s to the 1980s, which shows both how rich a resource for twentieth-century cultural history the cinema is, and how central a part of popular culture psychoanalysis had become from the early 1930s on,[25] one dream industry feeding off the other. Yet the connections *between* these national cultures are essential to explore, a fact which the transcultural media of film should alert us to, together with a sense of the international character of so much of the history of medicine in the period.

If the history of the rise of French psychoanalysis to cultural prominence can be written as the history of a cultural movement, relatively independent of pre-established professional organizations, the American example provides a clear contrast. From the 1920s until 1989, when a civil suit required the American Psychoanalytic Association to change its regulations, the American psychoanalytic profession required all psychoanalysts to be medically qualified. Thus, in the United States, the history of psychoanalysis was intimately part of the history of medicine, in particular of the history of psychiatry. For a period, from the late 1930s (at the latest) to the 1960s, psychoanalysis was an indispensable part of the American psychiatrist's training and authoritative knowledge, and certainly a crucial component of his or her social status. With the introduction of psychotropic drugs in the 1950s and 1960s, with the shift, on the part of those concerned less with symptom alleviation and cure and more with the welfare of patients in institutions (a shift well marked in the historiography of psychiatry with the work of Foucault, Doerner, and Scull)—in other words with the rise of drug psychiatry

199

and social psychiatry as two sides of one coin—the mid-century psychoanalytic hegemony, which had been in part so successful because it appeared to fuse attention to the symptom with concern for the patient, was undermined, set to one side, and, finally, with the rise of a victorious and philistine organic psychiatry of the 1980s, virtually eliminated. Nathan Hale has offered the indispensable account of the decline and fall of American psychiatric psychoanalysis, yet the full significance of this story has yet to be written.

Even before it has been written, its main outlines pose questions for the historiography of psychoanalysis: given that the relations of psychiatry and psychoanalysis were half-hearted on both sides in the beginning of the century, should we reconsider the question of the history of psychoanalysis in its relations to medicine in general? One immediate way to do so would be to consider the relations of psychoanalysis with other branches of medicine, in particular with general practice. However, the background to this exploration would be an analysis of the varieties of medicine that emerged in the late nineteenth century. First, there is the clinical art of medicine, transformed, no doubt, from the beginnings of the nineteenth century on, by the supremacy of the clinical examination, pathological anatomy, and the post mortem, but still dominated by the individual contract between doctor and the patient, no matter how subordinated to general principles and laws governing the behavior of organs; second, the rise of public health medicine, of epidemiology and state-centered sciences of hygiene: sanatory and miasmic medicines, vaccination, the statistical ordering of the population, and the imperative to render the health of the nation visible and public; third, and imperialistically, the rise of scientific laboratory-based medicine, from the laboratories of Bernard, Koch, and Pasteur[26] to the test- and drug-based medicine of the twentieth century, in which the doctor can only act on the patient's behalf once the patient's body has become fully integrated within and tamed by the barrage of tests and safeguards of the laboratory—situated either in a hospital, or in an industrial plant for the manufacture of magic bullets.

However, one of the consequences of the rise of scientific medicine was a crisis in the very idea of the doctor-patient relationship. Doctors refused to be stampeded by the enthusiastic Pasteurians into exchanging the white coats of a scientific priesthood for their more traditional sacerdotal accessories; organizations of doctors opposed to scientific medicine were started, articulating for the first time an ideal of the unique relationship the doctor has with his patient: unique and confidential, to be protected from the universalizing, statistical requirements of populational medicine and hygiene and from the requirements of public testing and standardization of the laboratory. From whence came one reactive modern ideal of the doctor-patient relation, an intimate relation of trust, confidence, and secrecy. This is the doctor we find inhabiting the family dramas of Freud's near contemporaries, Ibsen, Chekhov, and Schnitzler (the last two of whom were practicing physicians). It would be a mistake to conceive of the doctors who are so prominent in these plays—these pillars of bourgeois society, often psychotherapists *avant la lettre*—as traditional doctors; these are the *new* general practitioners of a medical world that is divided and at odds with itself, now scientific, now priestly.

Viewed within this admittedly tentative sketch of the cartography of medicine in the modern era, psychoanalysis would not appear as a wing of the newly professionalizing medical subspecialities such as psychiatry or neurology so much as a reaction to the more widespread problems faced by general practitioners when confronted with a shift toward public and scientific legitimations for their ancient art. Hypnosis and suggestion, quite clearly the historical antecedents of much psychoanalytic practice,[27] can be viewed as revivals of folk medical practices, as the rough-and-ready rural technique of the founder of the Nancy School of suggestion, Ambroise Liébeault, shows. The history of psychoanalytic practice, as shown in Carlo Ginzburg's speculative study of the new sciences of the end of the nineteenth century concerned with clues and signs, derived from medical diagnostics, may owe much to the resurfacing of "popular" practices and rules of thumb, becoming acceptable because of the pressure that the rise of scientific medicine placed on more traditional conceptions of the physician–client relationship.[28]

The work of Michael Balint at the Tavistock Institute in London in the early 1950s is salutary in this respect. Employing a psychoanalysis deprived of all technical terms for their scrutiny of the day-to-day work of general practitioners within the British National Health Service, Balint and his non-analytically trained GP colleagues put together a conception of the long-term function of the doctor as being primarily engaged in establishing working relationships, the joint capital of a medical mutual investment company, with patients that allowed the business of medicine, such as organizing the illness into an agreed-upon diagnosis and finding the correct dosage of the "drug doctor" (the principal element in the GP's pharmacopoeia), to proceed smoothly.[29] Freud's view—often instantiated in later present-centered histories, that psychotherapy was as old as illness and that "we doctors could not give it up if we wanted to, because the other party to our methods of healing—namely the patient—has not the slightest intention of doing without it"[30]—was thus expanded: the demand addressed to each and every doctor has always been initially psychotherapeutic in character, whatever the manifest "presenting symptom." It is one of the principal functions of psychoanalysis to retain and to bring to the center of every doctor's attention the psychotherapeutic function that every visit to the doctor entails and awakens. In this way, instead of the "collusion of anonymity" and ensuing irresponsibility that the modern institutions of hospital, clinic, specialist, and laboratory have created, the GP—whose speciality is "the total personality," or who in the United States practices medicine first and foremost on the family—will serve as a conduit both for modern medical science and for the ancient and perennial medical function that has been crystallized by psychoanalysis: the transference relationship.

Such a historiography—yet to be written in any detail—would pay attention to the vexed question of the relationship between psychoanalysis and deep cultural movements, yet would retain some sense of the relationship between psychoanalysis and the changing character of the medical profession. Psychoanalysis began with the medical interpretation of Aristotle's concept of catharsis that Josef Breuer and Bertha Pappenheim accepted and applied to their relationship. Many interpretations of the cultural significance of psychoanalysis in the twentieth century prefer to align it with ethical transformations and the advance of secularization, rather than with medicine, as if they recognized psychoanalysis to have an ethical rather than a medical lineage. It is to these interpretations that I will now turn.

Ernest Gellner[31] accepts the significance of psychoanalysis—he accepts Auden's view that we live in a Freudian climate; but he locates its significance in the domain of secular anxiety consequent upon the processes of modernization, the luxury of Western societies, and the increasing ineptitude of religious institutions and consolations. Psychoanalysis emerged as a secular procedure with the authority of science that offered hope to those in trouble with their fellow humans. Gellner pinpoints psychoanalysis as the leader, perhaps even the loss leader, of those twentieth-century movements that we can gather together under the name of "therapy service industries." These industries service what Philip Rieff, in one of the most acute of all commentaries on Freud and his institutional creations, called "psychological man." Characterizing psychoanalysis as "a popular science of morals that also teaches a moral system,"[32] Rieff pinpointed its "ethic of honesty" as an alternative to the inefficient and toxic moral commitments of modern society: beyond political man, the public man of action and virtue; beyond religious man, who, in Western society, is always against this world; beyond *homo economicus*, the avaricious self-interested calculator invented by the Enlightenment, is psychological man, whose only ideal is one of experimental insight leading to self-mastery.

Rieff's fruitful essays on Freud and the "triumph of the therapeutic" in the mid- and late twentieth century are extended and placed in a different context by Alasdair MacIntyre's *After Virtue,*[33]

in which he proposes that historical cultures are in part defined by
their stock of characters, which, as the masks worn by moral phi-
losophies, partially define the possibility of public and private action.
These masks constitute the moral and social ideals of the epoch; a
character "morally legitimates a mode of social existence . . . So the
culture of Victorian England was partially defined by the *characters*
of the Public School Headmaster, the Explorer and the Engineer;
and that of Wilhelmine Germany was similarly defined by such
characters as those of the Prussian Officer, the Professor and the
Social Democrat." For the twentieth century, MacIntyre isolates
three characters: the rich aesthete-hedonist, the manager, and the
therapist. "The manager represents in his *character* the obliteration
of the distinction between manipulative and nonmanipulative social
relations; the therapist represents the same obliteration in the sphere
of personal life . . . Neither manager nor therapist, in their roles as
manager and therapist, do or are able to engage in moral debate."[34]
In parallel with MacIntyre, Rieff noted how the analyst is able to
escape from the moral debates of the religious and the nonprofes-
sional precisely because "his is not a therapy of belief but one which
instructs how to live without belief."[35]

MacIntyre pinpoints the same ideal as Rieff perceived in Freud's
vision of the "secular spiritual guide," the analyst functioning as
physician and priest to each and every family;[36] even Lacan could
wax eloquent on the ideal represented by psychoanalysis: "Of all the
undertakings that have been proposed in this century, that of the
psychoanalyst is perhaps the loftiest, because the undertaking of the
psychoanalyst acts in our time as a mediator between the man of
care and the subject of absolute knowledge."[37]

It is instructive, if somewhat surprising, that the final works of
Michel Foucault led him to a similar relocation of the historical
significance of psychoanalysis in the ethical domain. Foucault's odyssey recapitulates, in miniature, some of the main themes in the
historiography of psychoanalysis. In *Madness and Civilization*, he
located Freud as the perfected end-point of the alienation of the

madman—thus as the riposte to and culmination of nineteenth-century psychiatry; in *The Order of Things,* psychoanalysis, through its founding concept of the unconscious and its recognition of the Other, represents "a perpetual principle of dissatisfaction, of calling into question"[38] of the human sciences in general, rather than the medical domain. As Foucault turned away from the archaeology of concepts to the genealogy of practices, so psychoanalysis became less a subversive principle than a propitiously typical, because purged and purified, element in the apparatus of knowledge-power that emerged in the nineteenth century to become dominant in the welfare states of the twentieth. Psychoanalysis is quite clearly the most sophisticated and effective—because so liberal—incitement to talk about sexuality, to codify it and to recognize it as the core of the subject's being. Foucault's projected six-volume history of sexuality was thus conceived of as an archaeology of psychoanalysis, asking how it had become possible for us, we Freudians, to say *this,* to act in *this* way.

However, in seeking the genealogy of psychoanalytic practice in the development of confessional techniques, Foucault was drawn further and further back in time, expanding his notion of the confessional to include larger features of Christianity and its long alliance and conflict with the state. He came to be more concerned with the extended matrix of individualization of intimate knowledge, produced by pastoral techniques, and the methods of subjectivation—a method of producing a subject of moral truth and action. Foucault evoked a long tradition of the hermeneutics of the self, starting with the early Christians and passing through Freud, which required an extended purification of any trace of desire, no matter how distorted, and in the process specified the singularity of that individual. Simply through the juxtaposition of this hermeneutics of the self with the "aesthetics of existence" of the Ancient World, a way of life that depended solely "on certain formal principles in the use of pleasures,"[39] Foucault was in search of an ethic for the conduct of life that was outside that tradition whose modern and ubiquitously influential representative, he implied, was psychoanalysis and the practices it required of the subject. To highlight both the significance and the historical limitations, perhaps even the cultural perversity, of psychoanalysis, Foucault proposed the category of the pastoral as best suited to focus attention on the distinctiveness of the ethos of the post-Ancient moral universe.[40] This distinctive "oriental" (that is, Judeo-Christian) pastoral power—self-sacrificing, salvation-oriented devotion to the individual[41]—eventually separated itself off from political power in the nineteenth century via "an individualizing 'tactic' which characterized a series of powers: those of the family, medicine, psychiatry, education, and employers."[42] Thus psychoanalysis arose as the most distinctively modern "technology of the self."[43]

These analyses by Gellner, MacIntyre, and Foucault, half historical, half moral reflections on the sensibility of the age, are, insofar as they are historical, oriented toward being a characterization of the psychoanalytic clientele: patient-centered history. But the "patient" has been transmuted into a representative, perhaps the quintessential, character of our time: a subject in therapy, in search of authenticity and satisfactions primarily in its private life and its pleasures.[44] This history is, then, part of a panoramic history of sensibilities.[45] The attention of literary and film theorists, of essayists and novelists throughout this century, also points to the fact that the innovative recounting and writing of the individual life made possible by psychoanalysis—in the form of case history, of memoir, of fictionalized analysis, of stream-of-consciousness modernist prose à la Woolf and Joyce, or of the Hollywood movie à la Hitchcock or Brian de Palma and the confessional sexual fantasy à la Nancy Friday[46]—constitutes the mythical genre of our time.[47]

Looking to the other side of the psychoanalytic mirror, to the history of the analyst, it is not yet clear whether, beyond its place in the history of science, of ideas, of sexuality, psychoanalysis belongs to histories of the medical-industrial complex, to those of the service and leisure industries, or is a part of the media. Shamanic doctor, secular priest, unadorned and simple therapist, even scientist, as the early analysts so unproblematically assumed: these are the figures of the history that has been and is in the process of being rewritten. Auden's certainty about Freud's ineluctable presence as the climate of opinion in our culture may meet with our assent; the historians of psychoanalysis have not as yet proved less shaman-like than our meteorologists, both ancient and modern. Whether they will is an interesting question.

6

DISPATCHES FROM THE FREUD WARS

I have two epigraphs for this essay. The first is from James Strachey's editor's introduction to his translation of Freud's *Complete Introductory Lectures.* Freud, he says, was "never rhetorical" and was entirely opposed to laying down his view in an authoritarian fashion. The second is a report by the Wolf-Man of what he thought to himself shortly after he met Freud for the first time: "this man is a Jewish swindler, he wants to use me from behind and shit on my head." This paper is dedicated to the proposition that the Wolf-Man got it right.[1]

This bracing declaration of intent is taken from Stanley Fish's 1987 paper, "Withholding the Missing Portion: Psychoanalysis and Rhetoric," which is a close reading of the "Wolf Man" case history. It demonstrates that Freud was entirely authoritarian in relation to his patient and employed *nothing but* rhetoric both in the treatment and in his relation to the reader of the case history. The truth that the Wolf Man has recognized but Freud does all he can to neutralize is that "the patient, aware at some level that he is being engulfed by the analyst, protests by simulating the analyst's behavior; the analyst in turn looks into a mirror and refuses to recognize what he sees."[2] At the end of the paper Fish cites, now as confirmation of his view of the engulfment of the patient by the analyst, the Wolf Man's opinion of Freud: "Interestingly enough, it is a truth the patient intuited even before the analysis began; after meeting Freud for the first time he recorded these thoughts: 'A Jewish swindler; he wants to use me from behind and shit on my head.'"[3]

So this sentence of the Wolf Man's really does sum up Fish's view of Freud's writing: it is not just a flashy piece of rhetoric. Fish implies that the Wolf Man somehow managed, in a small part of his mind, before the treatment began and before he was totally sucked in and engulfed by the master rhetorician who is Freud, to tell the truth about Freud and psychoanalysis.

Fish's argument—a tour de force of sustained reasoning against the legitimacy of psychoanalysis—concentrates on the anal erotism around which Freud himself organizes the account of his patient's childhood, and highlights how Freud continually delays, like a pre-varicating constipated neurotic, the disclosure of the crucial element of the case. In Fish's view, it is Freud who finally voids his episte-mological bowel onto the patient and thence, through the rhetorical mastery which both Freud and James Strachey so vigorously disavow, onto the reader. The Wolf Man got it right, Fish argues, but he could only get it right at the beginning of the treatment, before he was overwhelmed, engulfed, and shat on by Freud. The rest of his life was spent unsuccessfully trying to come out from under all that psychoanalytic filth. The same is true, by implication, of every reader of the case history, including, one presumes, Stanley Fish. We must conclude, then, that his paper is a cleaning-up operation, and Fish emerges, like a new Antonio extricating himself from the deal he'd done with the Jew, back in business and smelling sweet.

This is not by any means the first time that the Wolf Man's analysis has served as a test case for the truth of psychoanalysis. No doubt it will not be the last. The account was written in 1914, it should not be forgotten, as a test case for deciding between Freud's own views and those of Jung and Adler. Many people came to view the Wolf Man himself as the psychoanalytic patient incarnate. So he was to a young Austrian journalist, Karin Obholzer, who had be-friended the Russian patient known to psychoanalysts as the Wolf

Man. By then, in the mid-1970s, he had become a querulous old man living alone and in straitened circumstances in Vienna. In the course of her discussions with him about his life, about Freud, and about psychoanalysis, she read out to him a passage from Ernest Jones's biography of Freud so that the Wolf Man himself could appraise the truth of what psychoanalysts had written about him. I quote from the transcript of her interviews, which was published in German in 1980, and in English translation in 1982:

O: Here is [the passage from Jones's biography]: "From the age of six he had suffered from obsessive blasphemies against the Almighty, and he initiated the first hour of treatment with the offer to have rectal intercourse with Freud and then to defecate on his head!"[4]
W: And what? His head? I don't understand that. What's the last sentence?
O: Yes, it is curious. "He initiated the first hour of treatment with the offer to have rectal intercourse with Freud and then to defecate on his head." In German, it's something like, to have intercourse with him from behind and to shit on his head.
W: No, that may have been something else. When I was lying on this couch, I turned around when Freud said something that especially interested or struck me. And Freud said, "You turn around because you want to show me you have beautiful eyes." Freud said that to me. Of course I stopped doing it so that he wouldn't think I was vain, or what not. Unconsciously, he meant. But that was the only time I turned around. And Freud explained this situation to me like this: He sits at the head end rather than at the foot of the bed because there was a female patient who wanted to seduce him, and she kept raising her skirt. I still remember that. And he said that was why he sat at the head end. . . .
O: You mean Jones simply invented this?
W: Perhaps Freud wrote something . . .
O: Jones quotes a letter to Ferenczi.
W: I cannot remember Freud writing about it. That I turned

around was inconsequential, wasn't it? But what that fellow writes, I don't know, it seems to me he doesn't have all his marbles.

O: So you know absolutely nothing about this?

W: No, I know nothing. What does he mean? What does intercourse mean?

O: Having intercourse from behind . . .

W: Homosexually?

O: Yes, homosexually, I imagine.

W: For heaven's sake, what nonsense! But that's . . . to write something like that, I don't know, is that fellow crazy or what, writing such nonsense. He explained it to me, he sits with his back to the couch because he had a female patient and he sat at the foot of the bed and she did some sort of gymnastics with her feet and wanted to seduce him or God knows what. That's what he told me. But this? Having intercourse from behind, what does that mean? It's nonsense, utter nonsense. That fellow must have a screw loose. How can he write about a lawyer, since that never came up. Where does he get those ideas?

O: I ask myself the same question.[5]

Unlike Stanley Fish, who gives no footnote for the source of this information about the first hour of the patient's treatment, the passage from Jones's biography which Obholzer was reading out loud had cited a letter from Freud to Ferenczi dated 13 February 1910. In 1974 the Wolf Man was seemingly more interested in a memory of something else Freud had said to him, and had to have his attention drawn back to the passage from Jones's biography. Obholzer did, however, succeed in drawing him into making a definitive statement, indignantly impugning the veracity of Jones's account—aspersions which, it must be said, his interviewer was more than happy to agree with. "I ask myself the same question," she comments darkly and insidiously, as if we have one more reason for doubting the veracity not only of Jones but of anything psychoanalysts say.

Let us take stock of these two discussions. Stanley Fish quotes a sentence from the Wolf Man which, he argues, sums up the truth of the relationship between the patient and Freud, a sentence that thereby becomes an allegory of the relationship between Freud and all patients, and by extension, between psychoanalysis itself and the entire twentieth century. Sixty years after the events took place, Karin Obholzer presents to the Wolf Man Jones's account of the Wolf Man's relationship to Freud; the conclusion to be drawn from her account is that Jones fabricated this evidence. One commentator thinks the statement sums up the truth of the Wolf Man's relationship to Freud; the Wolf Man, under pressure from Obholzer, thinks the statement is fabricated. If the statement is true, then psychoanalysis is impugned; if it is false, then psychoanalysis is impugned. Heads you lose, tails I win.

Stanley Fish states that the Wolf Man made a "report" of this phrase. When he cites the phrase a second time, he amplifies somewhat: there was a truth that "the patient intuited even before the analysis began; after meeting Freud for the first time he recorded these thoughts," and so forth. Notice how Fish is implying that the Wolf Man knew this truth *before the analysis began;* and he implies that the Wolf Man recorded these "thoughts" immediately after meeting Freud for the first time. There is not much to go on here, but the scenario Fish is attempting to evoke is something like the following: there was a preliminary meeting between Freud and the Wolf Man, which produced in the Wolf Man these "thoughts," which he then recorded, *before the analysis proper started.* And it is clear why Fish wants us to accept this implied scenario: he paints a portrait of the Wolf Man about to be deprived forever by Freud of his independence of judgment. Never again, Fish implies, will the Wolf Man be able to see his analyst clearly for what he really is: a Jewish swindler who will cover him forever in shit.

This implied scenario receives support from the absence of a footnote giving Fish's source. How can the absence of a footnote give support for anything? The absence of the footnote allows the reader to infer that, given the construction of Fish's sentences, he does have evidence direct from the Wolf Man that this is what he thought. The rhetoric of the sentence leads the reader to believe that this evidence is independent of Freud. And the absence of a footnote giving a source implies some out-of-the-way connection: perhaps it came to Fish from a relative of the Wolf Man's, or from a secret cache of papers that Fish has access to. Or perhaps Fish has been in telepathic communication with the Wolf Man. The crucial implication is of course that the source is independent of and uncontaminated by— Sigmund Freud.

When Obholzer went to see the Wolf Man in 1974, the only source for this "thought" of the Wolf Man's was the passage in Jones's biography, which did not mention the Jewish swindler. Nor had any other sources been published when Stanley Fish wrote his paper—it is, as we have already seen, an interesting question how Fish got hold of it. We now know for certain *one* source for the entire phrase. That source is, as readers of Jones have grown accustomed to expect, accurately recorded in his biography of Freud—a letter dated 13 February 1910 from Freud to Sándor Ferenczi. In the Freud-Ferenczi correspondence, first published in 1992,[6] a paragraph from the letter written on that date runs as follows:

> On the whole I am only a machine for making money and have been working up a sweat in the last few weeks. A rich young Russian, whom I took on because of compulsive tendencies, admitted the following transferences to me after the first session: Jewish swindler, he would like to use me from behind and shit on my head. At the age of six he experienced his first symptom cursing against God: pig, dog, etc. When he saw three piles of faeces on the street he became uncomfortable because of the Holy Trinity and anxiously sought a fourth in order to destroy the association.[7]

In the light of this letter, let me say a few more words about Obholzer's interview with the Wolf Man. The Wolf Man was perplexed about what Jones had written; clearly he had no recollection of having said anything about sodomy and shitting to Freud. Obholzer took him at his word, and put in serious doubt Ernest Jones's trustworthiness as an accurate historian. She colluded with the Wolf Man's indignant feeling that Jones was making it up. It is of course possible that *someone* was making it up, but, in the light of this published letter, that person would have to be Freud, not Jones.

Let us now consider the following question: what motive could Freud have had for making up this passage, even if it were proved, which it is not, that Freud was the sort of person whom we expect regularly to make up such things? Why would Freud, after his first few sessions with a patient, write a completely fabricated version of that session to one of his close analytic colleagues? That was a question the journalist Obholzer never asked herself, because the implausibility of any possible answer would have put in doubt the trustworthiness of the recollections of the old man she was interviewing. Should she, writing in the late 1970s, trust the recollections of a man aged 86 about events that occurred in 1910, when he was 24? Or should she trust an account that gives a direct reference to a letter dated three days after the event in question and written by the person to whom the words were spoken? The very fact that one can seriously ask this question tells one quite a lot about the curious inversion of historiographic criteria that surrounds the history of psychoanalysis. This one example—Obholzer's seemingly healthy skepticism, which turns out to be pathological suspicion based on a conviction that the psychoanalytic establishment will lie whenever they can get away with it—is, interestingly enough, entirely typical of minor skirmishes in the Freud Wars. There are many similar instances in print. The example also reminds us about the trustworthiness of memory, as if Freud hadn't already told us enough. I will have a lot more to say about trust and trustworthiness later in this chapter.

Despite Jones having got his footnote right, giving the correct date and recipient of the letter, he committed a considerable number of errors in his transcription and summarizing, including the moment when the transference occurred. Jones writes that "the Wolf Man initiated the first hour . . .," when Freud's letter states that the patient "admitted the following transferences to me after the first session"—which could mean at the end of the session, after the session had finished, or perhaps before the second session began, or even at the beginning of the second session.[8] I labor this point for obvious reasons; as we have already seen, Fish claims that the Wolf Man "recorded" his thoughts, or made a "report" of them, after meeting Freud for the first time, and before the analysis started. Fish might have gleaned this from Jones's version, still leaving us with the mystery of his source for the "Jewish swindler." But, more importantly, it is not the Wolf Man who "recorded" his "thoughts," but Freud who recorded the Wolf Man's *words;* it is Freud who made a report to Ferenczi about his interesting new patient, not the Wolf Man who reported his private judgment of his new analyst to some unnamed other (and thereby, through an independent channel, to Fish). It makes a difference.

The difference is the following: where Fish wishes the thought of the Jewish swindler's threat to sodomize and defecate to be an independent judgment made by the Wolf Man *about* Freud, it is quite clear that this "judgment" is a "transference"—in part a clearly negative transference. Freud explicitly called the phrase a set of transferences, and immediately connected them with stories the patient had told him about his childhood: the story of feeling discomfort at the sight of three piles of feces in the street and his search for a fourth to destroy the impious connection to the Trinity.[9] A quick start for an analysis, one might think, and perhaps the precocious emergence of such interesting material was the reason why Freud wrote about it to Ferenczi. Maybe all of Freud's analyses started like this, who knows? A couple of years after beginning this analysis, Freud did write:

The patient's first symptoms or chance actions, like his first resistance, may possess a special interest and may betray a complex which governs his neurosis . . . A young girl will [on] lying down for her first hour . . . hurriedly pull the hem of her skirt over her exposed ankles; in doing this she is giving away the gist of what her analysis will uncover later: her narcissistic pride in her physical beauty and her inclinations to exhibitionism. A particularly large number of patients object to being asked to lie down, while the doctor sits out of sight behind them.[10]

Whatever the exact reason for Freud's writing to Ferenczi about this new patient, however, it is clear that what the Wolf Man said to him was entirely converted into material for analysis. The epithet "Jewish swindler, etc." was for Freud nothing but negative and positive transference mixed in together by the habitual ambivalence of the neurotic.

It is important for Stanley Fish's argument that he detach these words from Freud's pen and detach them from the Wolf Man's analysis altogether, so as to convert them into an independent judgment upon Freud and the analysis. To do so, Fish has to dissemble the source from which the remark comes—it comes from Freud, not direct from the Wolf Man—and detach the phrase concerning Freud from the anal and pious childhood material which immediately follows in the original letter and with which it is, for Freud, the reporter of these words, intimately connected. Let us leave to one side—for good—the question of whether Fish manages to extricate himself entirely, as he so wished the Wolf Man to have once been free, from the clutches of the Jewish swindler and his shit. The point is that Fish got it wrong: the judgment that Freud is a Jewish swindler who will cover his patients and his readers in shit is just as much a part of Freud's rhetoric as any other passage Fish quotes. If the Wolf Man got it right, it is courtesy of Freud. The accusation that Freud used nothing but rhetoric is, in the nature of such an accusation, bound to cut both ways.

There are a number of morals to be drawn from this episode in writing the history of psychoanalysis—an episode which revolves around one transference phantasy, voiced during one particular session in early February 1910. First and most important, what the writer critical of psychoanalysis, Stanley Fish in this instance, takes to be a patient's independent judgment of psychoanalysis is in fact a negative transference. How do you tell the difference, you may well ask? That is the fundamental problem in addressing psychoanalysis, and an answer hinges on one's interpretation of the function of negation in human speech. Leaving that question to one side, we note that there are errors of presentation in all three writers—errors of different sorts, and for different tendentious purposes, but errors nonetheless. Jones omits material; Obholzer puts in doubt an attribution; Fish tendentiously displaces an attribution. With these subtle and small errors, substantially different interpretations emerge.

———————

Such variations in interpretation and purported conclusion are quite typical of recent writings about Freud and psychoanalysis. The fact of this variation has become a central issue in the recent spate of aggressively critical writings. One of the methodological principles of these critical writings is a deep distrust of the evidential basis upon which one judges human beings in general, which manifests itself in a skepticism about the trustworthiness of both analysts and patients. Indeed, I would go so far as to say that the recent criticisms of psychoanalysis concern trustworthiness at many different levels. I wish now to survey these critical writings, to indicate the different forms of distrust of which Obholzer and Fish are in certain ways typical.

Frederick Crews opened his much-read *New York Review of Books* article "The Unknown Freud" with an account of the three fronts upon which recent criticisms of Freud have been operating. First, there is the conviction that psychoanalysis is of no use as a therapy: it is therapeutically inefficacious, no better than any other therapy, and maybe even no better than complete absence of intervention. Second, psychoanalysis has been discarded as a reputable system of

217

scientific explanation, as a theory. Crews cites as the principal source of this view the successful criticism of the epistemology of psychoanalysis mounted by Adolf Grünbaum in his book *The Foundations of Psychoanalysis*. Taking these two views as already proven and widely accepted—a rhetorical opening move of breathtaking aplomb—allows Crews to devote his article to the third wing of criticism, an attack on Freud's own "self-description" as a fearless explorer, a solver of mysteries, an objective thinker, and an ethically scrupulous reporter of his clinical work.

It is this division of the labors of those who criticize psychoanalysis into three principal areas—theory, therapy, and method of discovery or data acquisition—that allows Crews to pass off a deeply personal attack on Freud as part of a scholarly criticism of Freud's psychoanalytic theories and clinical practice. The argument purports to show that psychoanalysis is deeply flawed not only because its therapy does not work, not only because it is a bad and outdated theory, but principally because Freud was untrustworthy, demented, mendacious, and so forth—all these epithets are quotations from Crews's article. Notice how these extremely damaging personal charges about Freud's character slip seamlessly into charges about the empirical basis of Freud's theories. If Freud was a liar, to use Frank Cioffi's epithet from an article written over twenty years ago, then we needn't even bother to think about psychoanalysis, because its empirical foundation is irremediably suspect. In this way, the question of scientificity is intertwined with an ethical question about Freud's honesty.

The one thing historians of science don't usually do is spend much time—in print, and I won't open up the question of private fantasies of historians of science—doubting the trustworthiness of scientists. There are deep and profound reasons why this is so. Let me illustrate with an example, taken from my participation in a seminar for postgraduate students in the history of science in early 1995. A student presented the results of recent research devoted to replicating Charles Coulomb's experiments from the 1780s, which, for the first time, directly established by careful measurement the law governing the attraction and repulsion of electrically charged particles. Despite years of careful work, no modern historians could successfully replicate Coulomb's results. What is more, their application of modern electromagnetic theory led to the view that his results were not at all probable—there were too many interfering factors in the experimental setup he used, factors of which he could not have been aware, for him to have obtained the results he got. In the seminar, I made the suggestion that Coulomb had fiddled his results. As far as I am aware, no historian in the debate has ever made any such suggestion; just as revealingly, no student or scholar in the room was interested in my suggestion.

When Gerald Holton showed some twenty years ago that the American physicist Robert Millikan had arrived at his measurement of the charge on the electron, for which he received the Nobel Prize, by carefully eliminating as untrustworthy certain data which went against his own theory, no historians cried "Foul!"[11] Millikan had been engaged in a controversy over the nature of electrical charge associated with subatomic particles. The issue in dispute was whether these charges were always associated with the particles, and always expressed in integral values, or were in some sense independent, and thus would, when measured, show a continuous range of values. Holton showed that pages from Millikan's laboratory notebooks had comments like: "*Error high* will not use" scrawled on them. In an experiment where the experimental fact to be established is whether *all* measurements are integral multiples of a single value, it would appear that *any* discarding of data looks like a cover-up and a fudge. But historians of science do not interpret Millikan as a fraud. Instead, they have interpreted the new historical evidence to show that, when scientists are engaged in a heated scientific controversy, they often do shift the goalposts of the experimental setup. To begin with, common sense would tell us that Millikan may have been called away—by nature, for instance—from his lab bench at a crucial moment in the experiment. The comment in the margin of the notebook may have been a record of this call of nature rather than signs of a dastardly plan to defraud the Viennese group of physicists who were his "enemies." All scientific data is subject to similar indeterminacy requiring the necessity of judgment which could, to an unfriendly eye, look like fiddling the results. This has been called the "experimenter's regress" by Harry Collins and others.[12] There may always be the additional task of distinguishing what should be attributed to the experimenter's regress and what may be attributed to fraud and fabrication. But Millikan's lesson is that historians do not usually go around trying to do better than the historical actors they are studying; nor do they try and trip up those historical actors. The principles of charity which lead one to interpret human communication generously, on the whole, are applied in history as well.

It is a methodological principle of the history of science that lying and fabricating evidence are the very last hypotheses to be considered. And there is inductive evidence that this is the right interpretive strategy to adopt. Noting how Millikan shifted the goalposts of the experimental setup chimes in extremely well with the recent views of how experiments are conducted, interpreted to make sense, and brought to a conclusion.[13] The setting up and interpretation of experiments are as much subject to the hermeneutic circle as the reading of texts. Under theoretical and competitive pressure from colleagues, the interpretive procedures are transformed more rapidly and with greater boldness than when one is working in a quiet backwater, where the values of bank managers rather than commandos rule. The adage "he who dares wins" applies as much to science as to boys' war-games.

Nonetheless, when it comes to fraud and the fabrication of evidence, the case of psychoanalysis is different, principally, I want to suggest, because questions concerning the trustworthiness of human communication are at the core of its theory and practice. Anyone who has followed one of the major debates about Freud's standing, the debate over the reality of infantile sexual abuse of Freud's patients in the 1890s, will be aware of this dimension. A quick review of the issues: Jeffrey Masson wrote a book whose principal aim was to revive Freud's seduction theory by reasserting the truth—that is, the absolute trustworthiness—of Freud's early patients. Masson accused Freud of scientific cowardice, in that he claimed Freud rejected his own evidence that his patients had been abused in childhood in favor of the view that his patients, and therefore the analyst, had no sure way of knowing whether the events they remembered had actually taken place or not. Masson, in other words, took up the Fish position: in the end, the judgment voiced by the patients is to be trusted, and it is the tendentiousness of psychoanalysis that has distorted the truths they could have told, if only they had been allowed to.

In the other corner of the alternative Freud historiographic tradition is the exact opposite view. This tradition agrees with Masson that Freud was untrustworthy, not because of moral cowardice but because of blatant fabrication. None of Freud's reports concerning what happened to his patients, or indeed of what they said, can be trusted. As Crews put it, closely following Esterson's recent book as well as Israëls and Schatzman's paper, Freud, not his patients, was the principal author of the seduction scenes, and Freud then concealed this fact by attributing these scenes to his patients' fantasy lives.[14] In sum, all of these seduction scenes—and by implication much else that passes for events from the inner lives of Freud's patients—were the fabricated product of Freud's feverish imagination. Crews and most of the other anti-Freudian scholars thus take up the Obholzer/Wolf Man position: the data is untrustworthy because the analyst made it all up.

———

This is inherently implausible. But it is a scenario worth exploring for one moment. Imagine that Freud never had any patients, imagine that he was like the barrister evoked in Frederic Maitland's famous essay "Why the History of English Law Is Not Written" who never receives the knock on the door from the law clerk, and instead writes the definitive history of law in England—Maitland's premise being that it is only failures in the business of living who produce anything of significance in the book business.[15] The critics of Freud do not quite go that far; but they cancel out, in effect, the existence of Freud's patients by making them out to be the fools, the dupes, and the victims of his practice and, more important, of his writing and institutional maneuvering. It was Masson who proclaimed that Freud betrayed the truth of his patients, and his later books declare that no patient can receive a fair hearing, because the practice of psycho-therapy involves imbalances of power between therapist and client which no therapist can resist abusing. On the other side of the fence, among those who are not interested in the patients' truth but only in the fabrication of evidence by the analyst, an equally enormous power is conferred on the analyst. It is not so much that he, like Maitland's barrister, never meets a client, but rather that the analyst literally implants his own fantasies in the mind of the patient.

I think this is the fundamental source of the deep mistrust of psychoanalysis: the view that the power of the psychoanalyst is so great, because of the relationship of power, or the relationship of suggestion, that he exerts over the patient and, by extension, over the whole of twentieth-century culture, that the so-called evidence of analytic sessions is irredeemably contaminated, at best, by the analyst's wishes (as Crews puts it), or is largely the creation of the analyst's malignant imagination and technique. Crews evokes this scenario clearly when he writes:

> So far as we can tell, the only mind [Freud] laid bare for us was his own. Once we have fully grasped that point, we can begin inquiring how such a mind—rich in perverse imaginings and in the multiplying of shadowy concepts, grandiose in its dynastic ambition, atavistic in its affinities with outmoded science, and fiercely stubborn in its resistance to rational criticism—could ever have commanded our blind assent.[16]

This idea that the evidential base of psychoanalysis is contami-nated lies at the heart of Grünbaum's philosophical critique. There is an ideal of purity at stake here, the notion that science must have pure materials to work with—much as analytical chemistry is based on the purity of the materials used for testing and experimenting. In Crews's hands, this emphasis on contamination becomes an ethical concern. Where Grünbaum speaks of contamination, Crews accuses Freud of having "tampered with the record to make himself appear a master detective and healer,"[17] of having "invented"[18] one of the key figures in the Wolf Man's case: his Dora case is described as "one of the worst instances on record of sexist hectoring by a reputed healer,"[19] yet another illustration of the "by now well-established fact that Freud's hypersensitive ear was chiefly attuned to his own fanciful associations."[20] Crews makes a tight link between the claim that Freud was so busy imposing his own ideas and associations on his patients that he could not hear anything his patients said to him and the further claim that Freud mounted an assault on "the very self-hood of insecure female patients."[21] The man who was blind to the corrective of prudent empirical observation almost inevitably became the man who forced his own ideas on others. Note in passing what a bizarre view Crews has of how scientists operate: he thinks that they are akin to nineteenth-century bankers, who view prudence as the highest virtue. One look at the autobiographies of, say, Leo Szilard or Jim Watson would demonstrate that scientists with pretensions to greatness more often pride themselves on being streetwise than penny-wise.[22]

Thus the revisionist criticisms of psychoanalysis that employ these patient-based materials link the question of the status of psychoanalytic evidence closely to the ethical stance of the analyst in the production of such evidence. To provide reliable scientific evidence, the principled scientist must, it is implied, be objective; must not tamper with the evidence; must not impose his or her own preconceptions on the evidence. This is the ethic of the "prudent," "responsible"[23] scientist. It is one of the more curious features of the debate over the scientific standing of psychoanalysis that such an image of the scientist can in all seriousness be proposed as ever having had a real instantiation outside of NSF grant-application forms, when any perusal of the philosophy of science literature— from the discussion of the venerable Duhem-Quine thesis concerning the underdetermination of theory by observation, to the by now noncontroversial claim as to the theory-laden character of all observation—shows it to be strictly obsolescent and the product of excessive idealization of the sciences. If one paraphrases some of the pejorative words used by these critics with more neutral terms (the sort of terms one uses in a paper for *Nature*)—for instance, if we paraphrase "tamper" as "convert," as my computer's thesaurus proposes—we see that any scientist who wants to convert raw data into something scientifically meaningful has fallen victim to every one of Crews's accusations (and there is no good reason to paraphrase this loaded word).

But the theme of contamination goes far deeper than the claim that Freud and, following him, every analyst have contaminated the scientific data. As he demonstrates when he mentions "our blind assent," Crews intends to show how Freud contaminated his patients only as the first stage in Crews's drive to decontaminate ourselves; he casts himself as the Health and Safety Officer, demanding that the men in white coats move in and get rid of the dangerous toxic residues of this early twentieth century scientific experiment.

If we attempt to separate epistemological and ethical issues, we obtain some clarification. If Freud forced his own views on those of his patients, then the evidential basis of psychoanalysis is worthless: this is the epistemological criticism, which relies on the idealized conception of the ethics of the scientist. If Freud forced his own views on those of his patients, then the ethical claims of psychoanalysis are worthless from a different point of view, from that of the patient, since what any practice concerned with human beings requires is a recognition of the independence and autonomy of its objects of study and care. Curiously enough, we have grown more sensitive to the principles invoking autonomy and independence precisely because so many of the professional practices to which we consent as individual clients deprive us of them; the demand that one be allowed to preserve one's autonomy and independence when one is an anesthetized patient on an operating table is not one we seriously entertain, although the introduction of mesmeric and chemical anesthesia in the 1830s and 1840s was often combated precisely on those grounds.[24] The ethics of the modern surgeon, that exemplar of the scientific professional, may require procedures of informed consent, but they do not require the patient's autonomous participation in the operation. And it is the implication of Freud's often quoted and much contested exhortation to the analyst to model himself on the surgeon[25] that the *patient* model himself, or be modeled, upon the surgical patient—giving up his autonomy and independence so as to make possible "free association" and allow the analyst the liberty of interpretation, the possibility of dissecting his mind. It is, after all, one of the most direct consequences of the concept of the unconscious that patients, even those asked for their informed consent, are never autonomous and independent.

It is only in a historical moment that clings to its new shibboleths of autonomy, independence, and informed consent that the stridency of such defensively suspicious, such Hobbesian-inspired ethical concerns could slide so easily into being epistemological concerns. Frederick Crews is by no means alone in his conviction that psychoanalysis is dirty in exactly the ways the anthropologist Mary Douglas anatomized in her classic study *Purity and Danger*. As Ian Hacking notes in his research on the recent literature on post-traumatic stress disorder, multiple personality disorder, and child abuse studies:

> Freud transformed western consciousness more surely than the atomic bomb or the welfare state. It is a curious fact that many of the clinicians now most deeply involved in memoro-politics hate Freud. Therapy by the recall of forgotten memory of real abuse is their stock-in-trade, but the father of the idea must be slain. *"Freud did to the unconscious mind with his theories what New York City does to the ocean with its garbage."*[26] . . . There's an easy explanation for

225

this loathing. Freud is nowhere more detested than in the ranks of the most committed feminists.[27]

While agreeing with Hacking that the hatred of Freud by feminists is a major source of the hatred of Freud in these new scientific debates about hot socio-political issues, I am increasingly convinced that this is by no means the whole story.[28] I suspect the political side of this hatred of Freud is connected to the death of American liberalism of the universalistic, New Deal variety. The identity politics of autonomy and difference is fundamentally antithetical to the universalizing claims of a discipline that puts in doubt the very concept of autonomy.

Whatever the source of the view, there is a widespread conviction that Freud had dirty hands. But as I've already indicated, the view that Freud contaminated his empirical data comes in a weak and a strong form. The weaker argues that he was so in the grip of his own theoretical and personal preconceptions that he could only hear what confirmed them; the stronger argues that he actively and knowingly manipulated the data, willfully constructed it in his own image using his arbitrary interpretive techniques, and ultimately, in full awareness of what he was doing, employed the all-powerful force of suggestion, whether covertly or in a more naked form, to produce whatever he wanted. These two criticisms have in common the elimination of the patient as a source either of significant data or of resistance to the force of the analyst.

But there are important differences between the two views: one sees the patients as made redundant, abandoned, because the theorist is off on his own hobby-horse. The other sees the patient as inexorably turned into the tool of the analyst's theories, either through rhetoric (Fish) or through suggestion (Crews, Borch-Jacobsen).[29] Whether they are willing or unwilling tools, whether they consent or not is beside the point, as we shall see. Derrida goes so far as to explore the hypothesis, in the first person—via the telepathy that may have provided Fish with his evidence—that Freud's writing is the same thing as hypnosis:

> An event can take place which isn't real. My usual distinction between reality and external reality is perhaps not quite adequate at this point. It gestures towards the event which no idea of "reality" can help us think. But so what, I'll say to you, if what is announced in the announcement indeed bears the index "external reality"? Well then, treat it as an index, it can signify, telephone, telesignal another event which takes place before the other, without the other, in accordance with another time, another space, etc. That's the *a, b, c* of my psychoanalysis. When I speak of reality, it's so as to send them to sleep, otherwise you won't understand any of my rhetoric. I've never given up hypnosis, I've simply transferred one mode of induction to another: one might say that I've become a writer and have poured all my powers and hypnagogic desires into the writing, into the rhetoric, into the staging and into the composition of texts. What do you want me to say to you, sleep with me, that's all that interests them, the rest doesn't matter. So the telepathic announcement has come true even if it hasn't come to pass in external reality.[30]

Derrida suggests to us that we think of the twentieth century as having been, without knowing it, or perhaps with Crews's blind assent, entirely under the hypnotic sway of Freud. He thus voices, along with Fish and Crews and many others, this perennial theme in the consideration of psychoanalysis as a discipline. Just as Hitler's voice ruled the radio waves, so Freud's ruled the mind waves.

Both criticisms—the view that psychoanalysis ignores its patients and the view that psychoanalysis smothers its patients—show toward those patients a profound lack of respect for their more or less average trustworthiness, their more or less average skepticism, their more or less average powers of resistance to being manipulated, their more or less average independence as moral agents. These criticisms thus enact, as much as put forward as an argument, a deep distrust of anyone ever being a reliable source of evidence about the mind, a deep distrust of anyone ever being an independent moral agent.

————

Along with other recent works in the history of science, Steven Shapin's *The Social History of Truth* displays acute sensitivity to the way in which the authority of evidence is guaranteed or constructed. How someone becomes a trustworthy witness concerning the evidence of the senses or becomes an authority on matters of theory turns out to play a fundamental role in the development of the sciences. One example of such discussions about the source and authority of evidence can be seen in early nineteenth century debates about the relation between the earth's history as revealed in documents and the history revealed in the evidence of rocks, mountains, seas, and fossils. Conservative history dons at Oxford asked: why abandon the testimony of human history, in language, by intelligent witnesses, in favor of the brutal stupidity of rocks and fossils? William Buckland, a geologist by no means unfavorable to the use of written testimony in constructing the history of the earth, in private would give the reply: because human beings lie, whereas rocks do not. This points in the direction of the problem of trust provoked by psychoanalysis: we need guarantees of the trustworthiness not only of witnesses, not only of practitioners, but also of patients. Freud started off psychoanalysis by putting total trust in his patients, but then withdrew the index of "external reality," as Derrida puts it, from his patients' accounts of the past. The theme of skepticism and trustworthiness figured at the foundation of psychoanalysis: Freud believed the stories his patients told him were true in the sense that the events they remembered had actually happened. When he rejected the seduction theory, he shifted to believing that what they told him was true in the sense that the events they remembered were psychically real. Some critics of psychoanalysis, and some exponents of psychotherapy, regard this procedure as not being worthy of the

228

word "trust"—they think that to trust someone's word means to believe everything they say about the past to be literally true: we could call them fundamentalists because of the obvious analogy with some religious believers' attitude to holy text. And this is why the example of the dream is so educative for analysts and for commentators about analysis: believing in the truth of a dream does not commit one to believing that the events recounted in the dream were real. Freud thus conceived of a practice of speech in which one trusts everything the patient says while withholding belief. In effect, he proposed the methodological rule of thumb that the best way to understand other people is to set to one side when listening to them the entire dimension of truth and lies.

It is, of course, an unexceptional fact of everyday life that we neither take what people say at face value nor its opposite. It is only if we contrast the everyday ambiguous mixture of lies, deceptions, self-deceptions, half-truths, jokes, and ironies with Buckland's ideal of passive objects that cannot deceive, that are obliged to tell the truth because they cannot lie, that we think understanding other human beings is more difficult than understanding things. Karl Popper, Steven Shapin, and the sociobiologists might all agree that understanding human beings is the human being's métier; understanding things is an auxiliary skill, a successful latecomer. It has even been argued by some sociobiologists that human beings have been selected primarily for their abilities to understand other human beings: it is a primary and extremely salient special characteristic of our species.

The skeptical critics of psychoanalysis behave as if understanding other human beings were an entirely hopeless business, rather than being a biological or social activity at which we are supremely accomplished. When a man yells at his loved ones, "I am not angry!" the loved ones have no difficulty understanding that he is angry but wishes, for other perfectly understandable reasons, to deny it at the same time. It is only idealists who hanker after human beings who always tell the truth and an object for science which never deceives;

it is only such idealists who take exception to some of the psychoanalytic rules of thumb which are so akin to this normal hermeneutic
practice of everyday life—I am thinking of the famous opening of
Freud's paper "Negation": "You ask who this person in the dream
can be. It's *not* my mother." We emend this to: "so it *is* his mother."[31]
Note that Freud regarded this achievement of negation of the
previously repressed affirmation as the highest intellectual achievement possible; it is not possible for the subject to affirm that it is his
mother—the closest he can come is to admit his mother to consciousness with the chaperoning negative particle.

It is roughly along these lines that some recent defenses of Freud
have been mounted: psychoanalysis is a legitimate extension of explanations we use in everyday life. The Grünbaumian critique argues
that psychoanalysis claims to be a science, and must be judged by
the standards of scientific explanation, which have nothing to do with
ordinary explanation. But what if psychoanalysis both claims to be
a science and also has much in common with ordinary, nonscientific
explanations of how people work? Then we will have to address the
way in which ordinary explanation and scientific explanation inter-
sect. Hopkins, Nagel, Gardner, and others[32] take it as given that some
(though not necessarily all) psychoanalytic explanations are just like
ordinary explanations of human behavior, built on the basis of
motives, intentions, reasons, and beliefs. In this way, psychoanalysis
shades over into ordinary explanations, which we surely want to
count as explanations, since they give us knowledge, though not
irrefragable knowledge. But what happens to the charge of contamination and the related strict separation of scientific and ordinary
explanations of human behavior? This is the problem that Grünbaum, in strictly epistemological mode, and Crews, in his onslaught
on the ethical and epistemological standing of psychoanalysis, share.
They are required to construct a watertight dike which separates
psychoanalytic explanations, produced by charlatans, mountebanks,
frauds, liars, and so forth, from ordinary explanations produced by
us, ordinary people, who, with a gesture of second-order charity, I

assume Crews and Grünbaum assume are not charlatans, mounte-banks, and so forth.

Here is an illustration of this everyday explanatory strategy, using a hypothetical example:

1. "He is very protective of women because he is so aware of their being and having been victimized."
2. "He is very protective of women because, having a physically handicapped younger sister, he is so aware of the general plight of victims, and of women in particular."
3. "He is very protective of women because, having a physically handicapped younger sister, he is unconsciously guilty about having bullied her when they were small children, and is thus highly sensitive to the general plight of victims, and of women in particular."
4. "He is very protective of women because, having a physically handicapped younger sister, he is unconsciously guilty about having bullied her when they were small children, and is thus highly sensitive to the general plight of victims, and of women in particular; if he were made aware of the ancient source of his unconscious sense of guilt, he might no longer feel so compelled to perceive women so directly as defenseless victims, although he might still choose on reflection to see them in that way."

This is the slippery slope that Nagel suggests psychoanalysis has left us with in this century. At what stage, moving from (1) to (4), has this become a psychoanalytic explanation? Grünbaum would prob-ably argue that it becomes psychoanalytic only at stage (4), when it sets up a prediction on the basis of an implicit causal connection between the bullying experience as a child and the present protec-tiveness. I suggest that one is in a Freudian world by the time one gets to (2), because the connection between the sort of siblings we have and our general moral orientation in the world is what psycho-analysis suggests we should look out for.[33] This is also Hilary Put-nam's view, if the following passage is anything to go by:

We are not free to inhabit the pre-Freudian world . . . If Father Freud and his rebellious sons (Jung, Adler, Lacan, etc.) wished to be viewed as the producers of scientific "theories," that is a fact for cultural historians to note, I am suggesting, but not one to stop us from considering that their "theory" is of value just to the extent that what it becomes for us is not theory but observation . . . The stories are of value, I am suggesting, just to the extent that they suggest ways of constructing other narratives which help us to understand individual people.[34]

What the Nagel thesis concerning the overlap between psychoanalytic and everyday explanation entails is the breakdown of the barrier between scientifically pure data and hopelessly contaminated data. We accord the same measure of trust to patients as sources of evidence as we do to the people we live and work with, and if that is good enough for everyday life, then it should be good enough for psychoanalytic explanation. Another essential feature of ordinary, everyday explanations also has consequences for the attempt to assess psychoanalysis as a scientific explanation: the requirement that an explanation applied to someone else's behavior must in principle be applicable to oneself. All the basic terms of such explanations, known to some philosophers as folk psychology—reasons, motives, interests, love, hate, envy, greed, and so forth—are categories whose scope necessarily includes all human beings. In this domain, there seems to be something like a Kantian epistemological imperative to demand a universal scope for the explanatory categories. We would be rather amused by an empirical finding that there was a tribe in New Guinea or a group of villagers in Dorset who displayed no envy or lacked all signs of having motives for their actions.

What follows from this neo-Kantian epistemological imperative is the necessity of applying one's theories to oneself. It is here that the thesis about contamination, or about the reliability of the clinical data, as Grünbaum puts it, becomes exposed as inapplicable to this domain of ordinary explanation. What sense would it have to say that my self-understanding of myself is irredeemably contaminated? Of course, there are many occasions upon which I distrust my own perceptions, emotions, judgments; but to go from these frequent occasions of mistrust to the idea that I can never have reliable information about myself, or that I regard my own experience as contaminated, is not only unwarranted but counterfactual. The plain fact is that we all do, from Montaigne through Freud and Nietzsche to Adolf Grünbaum, have explanations concerning our own actions and thoughts, explanations which of necessity have the same form and substantive content as those we apply to others. Self-analysis is indispensable for psychoanalysis in the same way as self-understanding is for individual human beings; maybe not sufficient, but absolutely essential.

So for some critics, the errors of psychoanalysis begin with treating patients as trustworthy sources of evidence. They urgently demand that we separate out what really happened from what was only imagined, and thus that we separate out what are the true desires and values of patients from what comes to them from their environments—from their loved ones, from television, and finally from their analysts. This is a demand emanating from an epistemological individualism under siege, requiring to know how I can distinguish my own thoughts from those that have been introduced into my mind without my being aware of it—through reading, talking, subliminal perception, even telepathy. Such a requirement is completely unworkable as a principle for gathering evidence, as well as being exactly the place not to start when one wishes to address questions concerning mental operations. Behind the distinction lurks yet again the postulate of an inviolable core of selfdom and of the essence of an individual, which must not, if knowledge of that individual is to be scientific, be contaminated by unduly influencing the patient's mind—subjecting him to the overwhelming power of suggestion.

It is here that the epistemological problem again shades over into the ethical challenge. Patients cannot be trusted as sources of evidence because they are irredeemably contaminated. And why are they contaminated? Because the analysts, to quote the Wolf Man, shit on their patients. That this is the contention of certain critics, such as Masson, with his emphasis on the abuses of therapists' power, of Crews, with his talk of the sustained assault by Freud on the very selfhood of insecure patients, and of critics of the uncovering of repressed childhood traumas, is crystal-clear. This cycle of suggestion by the analyst and contamination of the patient's evidence looks like the pessimistic vision of the hermeneutic circle. And there have been a number of philosophers and psychoanalysts who defend psychoanalysis by invoking the hermeneutic circle: because psychoanalysis consists in the understanding of one human being by another, the to-ing and fro-ing between the analyst's understanding of the patient and his understanding of himself and his theory is an endless one, in which both ends of the oscillating movement of understanding are implicated. Psychoanalysis, it is claimed, is a discipline of interpretation, and any discipline that involves interpretation cannot be a science.

It was to cut off this line of retreat that Adolf Grünbaum opened *The Foundations of Psychoanalysis* with an exposition of Freud's view that psychoanalysis was a natural science like any other. He then undercuts Habermas's and Ricoeur's reinterpretation of Freud's position as a scientistic misunderstanding of psychoanalysis. Grünbaum's work is, in my view, conducted within the tradition established by logical positivism, namely that there is one model of how scientific explanations work—that there is one ahistorical thing called science. And he assumes, with detailed quotation, that Freud's view was the same. While not fully agreeing with Ricoeur's and Habermas's readings of psychoanalysis, I think that Grünbaum equally gets Freud's view of psychoanalysis wrong. And the reasons why, indeed his methods for arriving at that view, are quite educational.

Grünbaum opens his book thus:

> Throughout his long career, Freud insisted that the psychoanalytic enterprise has the status of a natural science. As he told us at the very end of his life, the explanatory gains from positing uncon-

scious mental processes "enabled psychology to take its place as a natural science like any other."[35] Then he went on to declare: "Psychology, too, is a natural science. What else can it be?"[36]

This energetic rhetorical question of Freud's—what else can it be?—helps Grünbaum put pressure on the Popperians as Grünbaum wishes. If psychoanalysis and evolutionary biology—Popper's other candidate for a pseudo-science—are not sciences, what else can they be? Grünbaum wants to see both evolutionary biology and psychoanalysis, as potential sciences, come before the bar of the positivist philosopher for inquisitorial and adversarial examination, after which judgment will be delivered. In the case of Freud, the judgment is clear: psychoanalysis has every right to aspire to be a science and has, on occasion, produced arguments that can be empirically tested. Where it hasn't, its claims are pitiful and often willfully deceiving; where it has, the final arbiter of empirical testing has declared its theories as falsified.

Even if one were to let Grünbaum construct his extremely unrealistic vision of the sciences and declare psychoanalysis to have failed its entrance examination, the urgent question would not so much be whether psychoanalysis is a science, but rather what kind of discipline is psychoanalysis? Indeed, the more fruitful way around is to find an adequate characterization of psychoanalysis as a discipline, and only then consider whether it is a science or not. I suspect that such a focus on disciplinary-specific methods and concepts would then allow the question of scientificity to lapse for want of interest. For instance, take the example of social anthropology, which has elaborated a number of methods, a range of conceptual approaches, and a variety of literary technologies. It is a stable discipline which produces knowledge—but is it a science? This is not a question that is at the heart of anthropological inquiry or debate. One can well imagine an Adolf Grünbaum look-alike performing the same critical task on social anthropology as this particular Adolf Grünbaum performed on psychoanalysis. But nobody bothers.

An intermediate strategy would be to emphasize the plurality of models of scientificity, in contrast to Grünbaum's and maybe even to Freud's conceptions. One obvious, and at the same time somewhat naive, answer would be to characterize psychoanalysis as an observational, naturalistic science of human beings, somewhat along the lines of ethology. Such observational disciplines conform to one model of what it is to be a science. They also remind us that sciences come in all shapes and sizes.

Which shapes and sizes? I am particularly drawn to a list of modes of scientific reasoning and their accompanying practices proposed by Ian Hacking in his work on the rise of statistical reasoning in the nineteenth century. In his schema there are six different styles of scientific reasoning: postulation and deduction; experimental exploration; hypothetical construction of models by analogy; ordering of variety by comparison and taxonomy; statistical analysis of regularities of populations; and historical derivation of genetic development.[37] The naturalist makes use of a number of these styles, most particularly ordering of variety by comparison and taxonomy, the historical derivation of genetic development, and sometimes the statistical analysis of regularities of populations. A salient feature of the work of the naturalist is the attempt at coping with complexity and variety; the drive to reduce this complexity to simple principles is not necessary to the work of the naturalist. The unraveling of, for instance, the details of the life-cycle of a worm that lives under the tongue of a frog, whose progeny in turn take up residence first in a snail, then at the bottom of a pond, then in the stomach of a predator, moving on to the stomach of a third predator, the pupa of a dragonfly, which is then eaten by a frog to whose tongue the creature then migrates—this is a tour de force of scientific work which would be diminished by any attempt to reduce its eccentricity. True, the very idea of a life-cycle, the very idea of habitat and parasitism are the general concepts with which the naturalist works; but I don't think anyone would argue that the worm's life has been *reduced* to simply being instances of a parasitic life-cycle. That is not how these general concepts function in natural history.

There have, however, always been pressures in this century, stemming from the tradition of logical positivism, to make the sciences conform to one standard model. The demarcation problem is one expression of this tradition: how do you distinguish science from non-science? Like Ian Hacking, like Alistair Crombie, like the tradition of French epistemology from Bachelard and Koyré to Foucault, one may focus less on the demarcation of science from non-science than on the differences between different sciences or modes of reasoning. One may seek the specificity of a science, not its departure from an ideal. It is only when one's principal preoccupation is, like Karl Popper's was, with disciplines that one does not wish to accredit that one highlights that distinction between the sciences and their outside. It is this anxiety about a natural human failing of believing in pseudo-sciences, famously for Popper the pseudo-sciences of Marxism, psychoanalysis, and Darwinism, that led him to place all the weight on explanations that lead to predictions and thus allow falsification: "It is important to show that Darwinism is not a scientific theory, but metaphysical . . . it is metaphysical because it is not testable . . . Darwinism does not really *predict* the evolution of variety. It therefore cannot really *explain* it."[38] For Popper, in the 1920s and 1930s, this was clearly an ideological anxiety. Today, there may well be other, more economic, motivations for such anxieties: the need to be reassured that an industrial corporation's money, or a state-funded medical program's budget, is being used efficiently. And we should not underestimate the need for government agencies to find some criterion for restricting the power of large science-based industries, such as the pharmaceutical industry. Each of these reasons can also lead to a preoccupation with prediction and control. But would they mean that the naturalist who studies the life-cycle of the worm that lives under a frog's tongue must stop calling herself a scientist? Will her voice also become another of the siren calls of the pseudo-sciences which we listen to at our peril?

Like the naturalists, most psychoanalysts are not bothered about the question: is it science? When they are forced to address the question, they have a number of responses. They may well beat a humble retreat, not wishing to become embroiled in semantic debates, whose heat does not derive from a passionate interest in discovering new and difficult things. Such was Robert Stoller's view, writing in 1985:

> Residing in a university and surrounded by colleagues who are scientists, I know not to inflate my work with allegations that it constitutes experiment (for example, "every psychoanalysis is an experiment") or science ("our science"). *Research* is not a synonym for *search* and should not appear in a psychoanalyst's sentence if it is there for propaganda. At our best, we analysts are naturalistic observers of behavior with techniques—unstable but powerful—that no one else has. That's a good start. I shall settle for words such as *work* and *studies*.[39]

Stoller's response recognizes that psychoanalysis arouses hostile, sometimes phobic, responses in "scientists"—as if they themselves consituted a unitary category. Dropping the word *science* is easy enough for him; but note how he describes what he does: "we analysts are naturalistic observers of behavior with techniques—unstable but powerful—that no one else has." That is a plausible description of one part of what psychoanalysis is—how does it differ from science? Of course, it isn't the same as doing experiments on protein synthesis; but it might be more like observing quasars, where, because of the inaccessibility of the object, there are no experiments to be done, only naturalistic observation using unstable but powerful techniques. This does not mean that psychoanalysis is the same sort of science as astronomy—it is just as plausible to compare it, as Freud often did, with surgery on an unconscious, anesthetized patient. But it does mean that it shares with astronomy a belief in simple, repeated, noninterventionist observation.

Take as an example, again from Stoller, his observations on erotic vomiting. He quotes a patient:

When I begin to vomit I get a "rush." My thought about a "rush" is a flood of good feelings throughout my entire body. Usually when you inject a narcotic in the vein you experience a rush and then you dump, which is often pleasurable. I don't put needles in my arm because I get those sensations and much more from simple vomiting . . . I always vomited after going to bed after a stealing session if I'd gone out alone. [The patient was a burglar for several years.] I always slept beautifully after I had stolen something . . . Vomiting for me is like sex or an orgasm in that I'm tensed, I feel the rush or intense flood of good feelings almost continually throughout the vomiting and experience relief and quiet warmth in my body when I'm finished. It is not identical to an orgasm. I do not feel it intensely in my genitals alone, but I do feel it there as well as the rest of my body and feel pleasure in my mouth.[40]

As Stoller himself admits, this is naturalistic observation at the level of the hoary old sexology of Havelock Ellis and Krafft-Ebing. It still, however, takes a psychoanalyst to write this, in the ancient tradition of naturalists' stories of how the other lives. But Stoller does not stop there. He generates an informally couched but nonetheless abstract and general account of sexual excitement, which has powerful predictive consequences:

I suspect that one's erotic excitement—one's preferred erotic script—is an artistic creation at the center of which is a remembered (not often consciously remembered, however) bad experience or relationship in early childhood, which must then be mastered. That mastery process is written into the erotic script. The rule may become: do unto others what (you tell yourself) was done unto you. For the lucky few, that standard allows intimacy, gentleness, and good humor. But for those who were meanly treated, revenge—cruelty and paranoia—is necessary (what we call sadomasochism).[41]

The implicit principle here is that all sexual excitement is founded on bad experiences, that is, traumas. The consequences that follow

239

from this are numerous: among them is the methodological rule that one recognizes bad experiences as more fundamental for the writing of scripts than good ones. And that one should not expect to find any human beings without bad experiences at the core of their erotic life. One cannot divide up humans into two erotic populations: those who had bad experiences in early life, and those who didn't. Everyone has had bad experiences—or, as Stoller quietly but crucially interpolates, all people tell themselves that they have. Psychoanalysts necessarily, then, seek out the bad experiences of a person's remembered childhood, which is why they look like naturalistic investigators of the sexual life of mankind; and if you are seeking out bad infantile experiences because you have at the back of your mind an ideal of an innocent childhood, which can be restored, you are moving in the opposite direction from psychoanalysis.

This plainly is naturalistic observation and inference. And that might be a first answer to the question that Freud posed, "What else can it be?" which Grünbaum quoted, assuming—or letting the reader assume—that it is an entirely rhetorical question. If psychoanalysis is not a science, what else can it be? It can be naturalistic observation and inferences drawn on the basis of those observations. Not all psychoanalysts would welcome such a description; some would vigorously repudiate it. But it might hold for analysts like Stoller, Freud (at times), and Winnicott. Winnicott often viewed his theories of development as an extension of his medical practice of history-taking; indeed he defined a full-scale treatment as a "prolonged history-taking."[42]

But, a critic might retort, the crucial question is not what sort of investigative searching is going on in psychoanalysis, but what the real issue is in the confrontation between psychoanalysis and its scientistic critics. We saw Stoller's response to this confrontation, when he recommended not using the word *science* to describe most of what he does in psychoanalytic treatment and observation. Maybe that would make the confrontation go away; it is more likely that it wouldn't. One of the several reasons why this is so can be seen when we realize that the debate over the scientificity of psychoanalysis has been drawn up, principally by Grünbaum, Macmillan,[43] and others, as if it is the terrain on which Freud placed it—the terrain of the unproblematic scientific enterprise. Grünbaum is quite certain that Freud thought of psychoanalysis as being a natural science in exactly the same sense that he, Grünbaum, understands natural science, and that therefore there was no hint whatsoever of the hermeneutic in Freud. And he then, please recall, quoted Freud: "Psychoanalysis is a part of the mental science of psychology . . . Psychology, too, is a natural science. What else can it be?" But Grünbaum failed to quote the very next sentence, which shows that Freud thought psychoanalysis was in a completely different position from the other sciences. Let me quote the passage in full:

> Psychoanalysis is a part of the mental science of psychology . . .
> Psychology, too, is a natural science. What else can it be? But its
> case is different. Not everyone is bold enough to make judgements
> about questions of physics; but everyone—the philosopher and the
> man in the street alike—has his opinion on psychological questions
> and behaves as if he were at least an amateur psychologist.[44]

This crucial difference—in Freud's eyes—is eliminated and passed over by Grünbaum. What are the implications for Freud of this fact that all people regard themselves as an expert on psychological matters, in particular as an expert on their own personal psychology? The issue is made more complicated by what is to be found in part of the other passage quoted by Grünbaum. Remember that the passage had begun with a contrast between the psychology of consciousness and "our" view, "which held that the psychical is unconscious in itself, [and] enabled psychology to take its place as a natural science like any other." The next paragraph, again not quoted by Grünbaum, continues: "Every science is based on observations and experiences arrived at through the medium of our psychical apparatus. But since *our* science has as its subject that apparatus itself, the analogy ends here."[45] That is, psychoanalysis would *appear* to be like every science, but because its object is also its subject, the analogy between psychoanalysis and every other science abruptly ends there. Not only does every person investigated by psychoanalysis view herself as an expert, so that the person doing the investigation thinks of herself as an expert well before the investigation has begun, but psychoanalysis must differ from other sciences in having to work from and be critical of this expertise. That expertise is both the essential starting-point and the central problem.

In both these passages, Freud's rhetorical movement is the same: he asserts that psychoanalysis is a natural science, and then gives a clinching reason for distinguishing it from other natural sciences. I do not think it is insignificant that Grünbaum twice quotes Freud's seemingly straightforward assertion and then twice omits the second step in the argument, the second step in what is quite literally a dialectical argument that asserts a thesis and then presents the reader with an antithesis which must irreversibly transform the thesis. Freud is pointing very precisely at the inappropriateness of the implicit assumption that Grünbaum holds to: namely, the clean break between the sorts of explanations offered by all sciences and those offered outside science. In matters of psychology, we already have working knowledge that is necessarily our starting-point as well as the principal obstacle to further knowledge. Psychoanalysis is continuous with ordinary everyday explanations, not a break with them. And the plausibility and usefulness of these everyday Freudian or psychoanalytic explanations are to be judged on roughly the same criteria as we judge everyday non-psychoanalytic explanations.

All sciences protect themselves against everyday explanations. There are a number of ways of doing this: constructing esoteric vocabularies; employing equipment and techniques that require virtuosity and dexterity to make them work; institutional requirements of education and competence. How can a psychology that is continuous with everyday explanation and language—necessarily so, since

242

explanations and data are swapped on a daily basis between analyst and patient—achieve this protection? Certainly the psychoanalysts attempted to construct some methods of protection: institutions, sometimes esoteric vocabularies—although Freud and Winnicott are interesting examples of how psychoanalysts can construct esoteric vocabularies that are also entirely open. But the short answer must be that they failed and, so long as they remain responsive to what counts as an explanation in ordinary life, must fail, precisely because of the fact that everybody—whether legitimately or not—regards himself as an expert on himself and on other human beings. But an equally important reason why the psychoanalysts failed to achieve protection is because of the unexpected success of psychoanalysis: namely, its influence over nonscientific culture in the twentieth century. In conclusion, I will turn to examining this alternative answer to the question: what else could psychoanalysis be except science? The answer is: popular culture.

In her interesting book *Freud's Dream: A Complete Interdisciplinary Science of Mind*, Patricia Kitcher quotes from the Harvard neurophysiologist and dream researcher Allan Hobson, also known as a close associate of Grünbaum and Crews in their vociferous criticisms of psychoanalysis: "*The Interpretation of Dreams* was antiscientific because Freud so forcefully dismissed all previous writers that he actually aborted an emerging experimental tradition. Psychiatry and psychology have been in Freud's thrall for almost a century . . . The tenacity of the psychoanalytic view remains impressively obstructive to integrative theorizing."[46] Hobson is complaining that Freud was *too successful* to be a good scientist; his views swept all before him. Kitcher notes that this is a pervasive complaint about Freud. His enormous success is attributed variously to his "magnetic personality, the tight control he exercised over the institutions of psychoanalysis, or his strategy of going over the heads or, perhaps, under the feet[47] of the established scientific community to appeal to an uncritical lay audience." She goes on to repudiate these criticisms:

Although popular, the first two hypotheses are not very plausible. Freud did not have personal contact with the vast majority of people who came to accept psychoanalysis, and he could only control those who already wished to become members of the psychoanalytic community. Insofar as the third hypothesis is meant as a criticism, it is also wide of the mark. As John Dewey pointed out long ago, scholars should try to make their learning available to the larger society.[48]

Kitcher is right to point to the limited efficacy of a charismatic personality, but she does not mention the "defect" that many critics of psychoanalysis do insist on: Freud's literary mastery, his ability to persuade scientist and non-scientist alike through his remarkable writings. Frank Sulloway has even advanced the view that Freud's literary technology—as he calls Freud's writing in following, albeit somewhat waywardly, the influential distinctions introduced by Simon Schaffer and Steven Shapin[49]—covered up for the deficiencies of Freud's material technology, that is, his ability to reproduce psychoanalytic phenomena in a reliable manner. To quote Sulloway: "In short, after 1900 Freud chose to play down the normal role that is performed in modern science by a material technology that can be widely tested and criticized by others."[50] Freud's literary technology did bypass a traditional conception of the regulation of scientific knowledge. As I made clear in Chapter 4, Freud did go over the heads of scientists. But that is because his literary technology *was* his material technology.

Far from playing down the material technology, Freud's writings allowed each and every reader to reproduce the phenomena in the privacy of their own homes, in much the same way as my generation of school children were able to do what Marconi did by making crystal sets at home. Psychoanalysis did bypass the normal scientific forum. In doing so, it embodied an extension of the supposedly democratic and open ethos of science, recognizing that an explanation of human beings must be judged by its objects as well as the scientists. Thus it set a new criterion that any human science—any psychology, sociology, anthropology—might now have to meet: the criterion of being judged by those human beings the discipline purports to describe rather than by the members of the academic community. Any human science that cannot pass this test might be said to have failed to be a science of the human, whatever the academic or "scientific" world might say about it.

What kind of criticism is it to accuse Freud of writing too persuasively? Consider what one would say to a literary critic—this is not an entirely imaginary example—who said: Swann is an aesthete and a prig, Marcel is a do-nothing member of a decadent class, and it is only the literary technology of Proust that makes them interesting characters. One might reply: you are arbitrarily dividing off Proust's characters from his writing. It is through the writing that his characters become infinitely rich, acquire infinite depth, and thus show us the possibility of everyone, even an invalid Parisian snob, being that interesting. Similarly, Freud's writings are a resource for the democratization of the soul; through them, everyone can participate in what Philip Rieff called the "excitement of the wholly interesting life."[51]

As described in Chapter 5, Alasdair MacIntyre suggests that there are three principal characters of the twentieth century; the naturalist no longer figures in our pantheon, but did in the nineteenth century, which is why that aspect of Freud's work, together with figures such as Kinsey and Ellis, seem so quaint and endearingly old-fashioned. MacIntyre lists the hedonist-aesthete, the manager, and the therapist as our century's characters. Each of these escapes from moral discourse, which is MacIntyre's principal concern. I think MacIntyre is right, in that the therapist holds up a vivid mirror to the moral ethos of our time. But therapy, once the haven of the caricatural bleeding-heart liberals, is now asked to perform moral functions extending over into policing and criminal functions for the community, in contrast with the original psychoanalytic ideal of the therapist in alliance with her patient against moral and collective ideals. Put simply, I'm beginning to feel as if I'm acting in bad faith when I ask my students to address the question of the subversive individualism of Freud's theories, when the law, very much at some therapists' behest, now requires a therapist to report to the police any crime or wrongdoing that is mentioned in therapeutic sessions. The question to ask is: is the debate about the scientific status of psychoanalysis linked to the seemingly separate question of the displacement of moral authority and independence of the character of the therapist?

To the question "what else could it be?" I have offered three answers. Psychoanalysis can masquerade as a discipline of naturalistic observation and inference, similar to other disciplines that do not conform to the positivistic criteria so fixated on modes of explanation to be found in physics and the laboratory sciences. The second answer tried to unpack the reply of Freud to his own question—a question overlooked by Grünbaum, who, whatever his other virtues, which are considerable, cannot be said to be a sophisticated reader of texts. I pointed to the fact that psychoanalysis has always started from and opposed the fact that we are all experts on ourselves and each other. It is the science of that individual expertise—both for and against it. And third, I have suggested that psychoanalysis is popular culture, the popular culture not only of films and TV, not only of detective stories and avant-garde art (because today the avant-garde is also popular culture), but also the popular culture of gossip, of sorting out relationships with employers, spouses, and children.

Finally, I will make a point that is so obvious and so fundamental that it is surprising how little it is mentioned or emphasized. It relates to all three of the domains I have discussed: naturalistic observation, ordinary everyday explanation, and popular culture. The claims of psychoanalysis are treated by its critics as if they were claims made by an objective scientific subject about a determinate and separate field of phenomena. Everybody would, nowadays, like to be an objective scientific subject—it is one of the most seductive and persuasive ideals of our time. The higher that ideal is raised, and the weaker the forces of contestation of that ideal, the more difficult it becomes to realize that ideal in psychoanalysis: the more difficult it becomes to examine the underbelly of that ideal, which is what psychoanalysis requires of the investigator—since the field of phenomena under investigation is himself and all his works. But to be a critic of psychoanalysis in the name of that ideal—which includes rigorously following the empiricist rites of passage—requires one to engage as intimately as possible with psychoanalysis. To be a critic worthy of the name, you must lie down on the couch.

To contest Freud's theory of dreams without examining one's own dreams; to contest Freud's theory of infantile sexuality without examining one's own sexuality and its relation to one's own childhood; to contest Stoller's hypothesis that sexual excitement is, for all of us, principally founded on a bad experience in childhood—all these contestations require us to measure psychoanalysis against our own experience, our own sexual excitements, our own childhood experiences. This imperative is the force upon which psychoanalysis became popular culture. It is also the imperative—often evaded by the critics of psychoanalysis—upon which any scientific testing of psychoanalysis should be based: the imperative to test it against one's own experience. To suggest that, in order to be truly objective, one should temporarily set aside the application of psychoanalytic hypotheses to oneself is to miss the force of the psychoanalytic method and of its theories. These theories begin and end at home. To pretend that one can treat home as off-limits for the purposes of official investigation into its territorial claims is both short-sighted—leading to naive puzzlement over the excessive influence of psychoanalysis— and disingenuous, as if the Bishop of Oxford were to declare: Mr. Huxley may well be descended from an ape, but, even if *he* is, I for one know that *I* am descended from Adam and Eve.

This, you may have noticed, makes the principal scientist at work in psychoanalysis the patient. And it has always seemed simple common sense to me that testing such psychoanalytic hypotheses by direct experience, by doing psychoanalysis, by lying on the couch, is

247

what the good, solid, prudent empiricist would do. Those who discount the possibility of any useful information being derived from undergoing that experience appear to me to be unduly mistrusting of themselves, as well as of other people—the other people with whom they might engage in the process. They remind me of commentators on physics who would declare as illicit entering a laboratory in order to see what is done, hear how it is done, participate in the production of a disputed and controversial phenomenon. There will always be critics who think that the physicists will just pull the wool over their eyes and find a way of defending their outlandish theories, so there is no point in venturing onto their territory.[52] But how else is one to test the validity of physics? Certainly philosophical criticism will be of no relevance—it has been ruled out of scientific court for a long time now.[53] The critics of psychoanalysis who disdain the empirical method of testing it by trying it out on themselves are following a path that was once legitimate and open, the path taken by those philosophers skeptical of the discoveries Galileo had made with his telescope on the grounds that using curved glass habitually produces illusions.[54] In our scientistic age, this path is no longer open to anyone who aims to be taken seriously as a critic of science. For some reason, it remains open to those who criticize psychoanalysis.

To be convinced that one can speak from a position of critical strength in these matters without applying psychoanalysis to oneself, I would have to be convinced that I am not qualified to pass judgment on my own person, on my own body, on my own dreams, on my own destiny. In other words, I would have to be convinced that *only* someone other than myself is qualified to judge those things about me. Who will convince me that I am so disqualified?

EPILOGUE

Sigmund Freud was well prepared for posthumous interviews. Surrounded by his books and statues in his old house in London, a mausoleum kindly preserved by his daughter Anna, just as he had left it, expressly for occasions such as this, I nervously eyed the couch on the other side of the room. Perhaps perceiving my uneasiness, he could not resist a sly dig at my refusal of the fat cigar he offered me; he gently rebuked me for my denial of one of the greatest and cheapest enjoyments in a life that is principally filled with frustrations and hardship.

Q: Some sixty years ago, you moved from Vienna to Hampstead, where, as in numerous other well-heeled corners of the world's cities, since your death, a ghetto of susurrating analytic patients has congregated, daily visiting their analysts, faithfully following in your footsteps. Does this please you?

Freud: As the poet says, *Ins jenseits kann man nichts mitnehmen.*[1] None of this is mine, not the house, nor the Freud industry nor the psychoanalytic movement. Let each have his totem; the only alternatives are varieties of sex'n'drugs 'n' rock'n'roll—palliatives that are not to be disdained, I might add.

Q: But aren't you horrified by the bizarre explosion of therapies associated with your name?

Freud: I started out my working life employing hypnotism and, having for years been an enthusiastic zealot of that mysterious

249

craft, I have never underestimated the power of suggestion, nor, it should be said, the attractions of absolute authority and supine dependency that it holds out to practitioners and patients alike. Psychoanalysis was an attempt by a rationalist to harness the fundamental power, the erotic power, underlying suggestion without abusing the liberty of the patient. There was never any guarantee that it would always, or often, achieve that goal. The postmodern therapeutic imperative shows that the idea at least had legs in it. As for abandoning it, healers could not relinquish therapy even if they wanted to, because the patient has not the slightest intention of doing without it. Whether it is American-style therapy or Lourdes is a matter of taste; I've always made my inclinations clear.

Q: Whatever their needs, no one is taken in any longer by your claim that psychoanalysis is the only respectable, the only scientific version.

Freud: I am always condemned in the name of some higher ideal. I've been following the ups and downs of the anti-psychoanalytic majority: in the early 1900s, I was disgusting for hinting that children and women have independent sexual lives—remember my books were treated as pornography by booksellers in London in the 1920s; in the 1930s, I was criticized for having a jaundiced view of the possibilities of socialist revolution. In the 1960s, I was pillaged for not understanding that madness is a political protest. In the 1980s, I was too cowardly to admit that men are natural-born rapists and sexual abusers of children. Now, in the 1990s, I'm not only a purveyor of shoddy goods well past their sell-by date, but a latter-day astrologer and charlatan. What ever will be next?

Do you really want to behave toward truth as if she were your wife, so that the prospect of finding out that she is not as she seems is tantamount to her adultery? Your modern-day apologists for science are, I have noted, particularly horrified at the possibility that truth might be faithless; they seek certainty at all costs, just as the jealous man needs to know every little detail, usually at his own expense. Psychoanalysis continues to flaunt the infidelity of truth. Let the man who is too fearful to entrust himself to the uncertainties of life try to make an honest woman of truth by imprisoning her in his safe yet meager laboratory. Is this the true expression of his love? To him, it always seems like a scandal and a mystification to be told that you can only cure through love, and thus can only discover truth through love.

Q: Judged by today's moral standards, you rate pretty poorly. You never noticed that the civilization whose apologist you sometimes were was imperial and colonial, and founded on racism—except when you talked condescendingly about the habits of primitives. You entirely overlooked the stratification of society by classes and the oppressive economic relations under which the working classes and their neuroses are generated. And your theories of femininity are notorious as the bulwark of the conservative forces that kept women tied to family, babies, and the great god penis.

Freud: Forgive me for saying so, but you are speaking in the cultish dialect of the 1970s, giving you yet another ideal, that of the Trinity of Race, Class, and Gender, by which I am condemned. It is true that I spoke of primitives and overlooked the force of race in human affairs: I was an educated Jew who lived by the universal—and self-evident—ethical standards of Western culture. It is true that I do not side with the revolutionaries: for all the justice of the cause of the poor and propertyless, I see no solution in the egalitarian politics of envy, only newer versions of the *force majeure* of culture exerted on the individual. It is true that I doubted the practicality of women's demands for equality. There I have to admit that perhaps I was wrong: penis envy shows itself to be more capable of sublimation than I thought—and I have to thank my disciple Woody Allen for reminding me that both men and women are equally prey to the ravages of penis envy.

But I find myself perplexed by the criticisms you address to me, which are all belied by your own practice. Whereas you talk of big issues—of race, sex, and class—your world is full of smaller and smaller groups, each with its issue, its unstable identity, its resentful demand to be treated as a special case. From the ugly resurgence of nationalism, with small nation pitted against its neighbor, to the bickering and open warfare of your religious sects, to the sexual politics of the pampered First World, I see nothing but what I once called, obviously in a much too offhand moment, the narcissism of minor differences. To elevate a sexual predilection into a political principle is surprising, though far be it from me to be surprised by the importance you sometimes—but only sometimes, when it suits you—give to sexual pleasure.

Q: You took the words out of my mouth. Because to be called a Freudian is for us to be obsessed with sex, to be continually finding sex in places where it doesn't belong. Would you, in the light of what the late twentieth century has done to sex, reconsider your own obsession with its importance?

Freud: Do you doubt that sexual satisfaction is one of the chief and finest things in life? Why turn on it as a false god, simply because it so often escapes you, and even when you find it, it does not always make you happy? Or are your newfound prudishness and sanctimoniousness due to AIDS having blighted it with fear and provoked in you the desire to deprive others of its pleasures, just as syphilis did for my era? I never thought sex was a path to heaven, nor that it would ever cease to be in conflict with other principles that human beings hold equally dear. However, I must be mindful of the fact that I am in the country that still clings to the principle "no Freud please, we're British." If you are reluctant to admit that sexual desire is to be found at the very heart of your lives, please at the very least recognize that we—and particularly you—are all still sexual hypocrites.

Q: It is not only sex that gives you a bad name. In recent years we have had anti-Freudians accusing you of covering up the sexual abuse of children—and accusing you of fabricating evidence to prove your alternative theories. Then we have the anti-Freudians demonstrating that some therapists, those of your progeny who deny you most vociferously, are implanting false memories in their patients' minds. Most people are quite ready, under these circum-

252

stances, to say: "That's enough! I've had it about up to here with Freud!"

Freud: Whichever side I am on, it is bound to be the wrong one. When therapists protest against the sexual abuse of children, it is like surgeons in casualty militating against the invention of the motor car; to be sure, it is the cause of the injuries they have to heal, but their job is—to heal. I never confounded psychoanalysis with a moral crusade; quite the opposite. Nor should my critics.

And similarly with false memories—though I would like to claim some priority in their discovery: I called them fantasies, daydreams, and screen memories. What strikes me as novel is their being used as weapons in a family grudge match of accusation and counter-accusation. The Oedipus complex I discovered in Sophocles' play is now played out in the law court—on television, for preference. The classic neuroses are cloaked for you in that modern mixture I could never have foreseen: the potent combination of art and bodily intoxicants that goes under the name of the mass media. I always had considerable respect for mankind's creative manipula-tion of the body through its chemistry—I did, don't forget, subject myself to the pleasures and hardships of cocaine, and not only in the interests of science. But it is clear that I underestimated, and am very impressed by, the consolations that can be had through becoming addicted to culture.

Q: The harshest criticisms of you at present are: Freud is all fine words, but in the end he's a liar and a cheat. How do you reply to this verdict?

Freud: We each have our neurotic compulsions. Mine was to tell a little—not too much—of the truth about myself in order to enlighten others and show them a way out of their own private miseries. My critics no doubt have theirs, as they, small-minded clerks in their hearts, bring me before their self-appointed court of truth. Yet this imperative to tell the truth, the whole truth, and nothing but the truth is a pathology peculiar to the latter half of this media-ridden century. As my fellow countryman and pessimist Milan Kundera writes: "The whole moral structure of our time rests on the Eleventh Commandment: Tell the truth! . . . and of course we may ask just what the word 'truth' means to the administrator of the Eleventh Commandment. To prevent misunderstanding we stress that it is not a question of God's truth, for which Jan Hus died at the stake, nor a question of the truth of science and free thought, for which they burned Giordano Bruno. The truth elicited by the Eleventh Commandment is not connected with religion or philosophy, it is truth of the lowest ontological storey, a purely positivist, factual truth: what did C do yesterday? what is he really thinking deep in his heart? what does he talk about when he gets together with A? and does he have intimate contact with B? Nevertheless, even though it is on the lowest ontological storey, it is the truth of our time and contains the same explosive force as did the truth of Hus or Giordano Bruno."[2]

And you are the high priest of the Eleventh Commandment, sufficiently powerful to drag me back from immortality to demand an answer to your impertinent questions. However, even you might well wonder what you are doing demanding truth of a dead man.

Abbreviations
Notes
Acknowledgments
Index

ABBREVIATIONS

E   Jacques Lacan, *Ecrits* (Paris: Seuil, 1966). Where a second figure is given it refers to the English translation, *Ecrits: A Selection*, trans. Alan Sheridan (London: Tavistock/New York: Norton, 1977). Where a reference is given solely to the English translation, the page number will be followed by (Engl.)

FF   *The Complete Letters of Sigmund Freud to Wilhelm Fliess, 1887–1904*, ed. J. M. Masson (Cambridge, Mass.: Harvard University Press, 1984)

FFer 1   *The Correspondence of Sigmund Freud and Sándor Ferenczi, Volume 1, 1908–1914*, ed. Eva Brabant, Ernst Falzeder, and Patrizia Giampieri-Deutsch, trans. Peter T. Hoffer, with an introduction by André Haynal (Cambridge, Mass.: Harvard University Press, 1994)

FFer 2   *The Correspondence of Sigmund Freud and Sándor Ferenczi, Volume 2, 1914–1919*, ed. Ernst Falzeder and Eva Brabant, with the collaboration of Patrizia Giampieri-Deutsch, under the supervision of André Haynal, transcribed by Ingeborg Meyer-Palmedo, trans. Peter T. Hoffer, with an introduction by Axel Hoffer (Cambridge, Mass.: Harvard University Press, 1996)

FJones   *The Complete Correspondence of Sigmund Freud and Ernest Jones, 1908–1939*, ed. R. Andrew Paskauskas, with an introduction by R. Steiner (Cambridge, Mass.: Harvard University Press, 1993)

FJung   *The Freud/Jung Letters*, ed. William McGuire, trans. R. Manheim and R. F. C. Hull (Princeton: Princeton University Press, 1974)

ID   Sigmund Freud, *The Interpretation of Dreams*, Vols. IV and V of *SE*

Int. J. Psa.	*International Journal of Psycho-analysis*
J	Ernest Jones, *Sigmund Freud: Life and Work* (London: Hogarth Press, 1953–1957), Vols. I–III
Letters	Sigmund Freud, *Letters of Sigmund Freud, 1873–1939*, ed. Ernst L. Freud, trans. Tania and James Stern (London: Hogarth, 1970)
Minutes	*Minutes of the Vienna Psychoanalytic Society*, ed. Herman Nunberg and Ernst Federn, trans. M. Nunberg, 4 vols. (New York: International Universities Press, 1962–1976)
SE	Sigmund Freud, *The Standard Edition of the Complete Psychological Works of Sigmund Freud*, 24 vols., edited by James Strachey in collaboration with Anna Freud, assisted by Alix Strachey and Alan Tyson (London: The Hogarth Press and the Institute of Psycho-analysis, 1953–1974)
Stud	Sigmund Freud, *Studienausgabe*, 10 vols. with an unnumbered *Ergänzungsband* (abbreviated as *Erg*) (Frankfurt am Main: Fischer Verlag, 1969–1975)

NOTES

Introduction

1. Mark Edmundson, *Towards Reading Freud: Self-Creation in Milton, Wordsworth, Emerson, and Sigmund Freud* (Princeton: Princeton University Press, 1990), p. 3.

2. Richard Rorty, "Freud and Moral Reflection" (1984), in Rorty, *Essays on Heidegger and Others: Philosophical Papers, Volume 2* (Cambridge: Cambridge University Press, 1991), pp. 143–163, and Rorty, "Something to Steer By," *London Review of Books*, 20 June 1996, pp. 7–8.

3. Even Richard Webster, whose principal criticisms of Freud are for his shortcomings as a scientist and for his promulgation of religious doctrines rather than science, acknowledges that "perhaps the most important critiques of Freud . . . produced in the latter part of the twentieth century" have been those of the feminists. Webster, *Why Freud Was Wrong: Sin, Science, and Psychoanalysis* (London: HarperCollins, 1995), p. 22.

4. Freud, "The Dynamics of Transference" (1912), *SE* XII, 104n1.

5. Frederick Crews and his critics, *The Memory Wars: Freud's Legacy in Dispute* (New York: New York Review of Books, 1995), p. 298; Crews's original celebrated article was published as "The Unknown Freud," *New York Review of Books*, 18 November 1993, pp. 55–66.

6. Milan Kundera, *Testaments Betrayed*, trans. Linda Asher (London and Boston: Faber and Faber, 1995), p. 7.

7. The reference, while not strictly Freudian, is to a famous passage in Michael Balint's *The Basic Fault* (London: Tavistock, 1968), pp. 128–129.

8. "Bad Ideas of the Twentieth Century," originally screened in November 1993 by BBC2 in the United Kingdom.

9. Crews, *The Memory Wars*, p. 295.

10. Frederick Crews, "Scattered Comments on Psychoanalysis," e-mail to Psychoanalysis Listserver, 9 May 1996.

1. Justice, Envy, and Psychoanalysis

1. 1 Kings 3:16–28.

2. Freud, *Group Psychology and the Analysis of the Ego*, SE XVIII, 120–121.

3. Jean Carbonnier, at one point in his discussion (Carbonnier, *Flexible Droit: Pour une Sociologie du Droit sans Rigueur*, 6th ed.; 1st ed., 1969 [Paris: Librairie Générale de Droit et de Jurisprudence, 1988], pp. 361 ff.), notes that "ne pas réclamer l'enfant vivant était reconnaître pour sien l'enfant mort," a formulation which focuses on the same question as Freud's, but eliminates the question central to envy—who has a baby and who doesn't—by substituting the quasi-psychotic imperative: "if I have a baby, it means that I will not have to recognize my loss, my impotence."

4. That this duping is akin to repression is illustrated by Maryse Choisy's experiments, in which she asked her dinner party guests how Solomon recognized the true mother; they invariably answered that the true mother was recognized by her wish to see the child alive and with another rather than dead. Whereupon, on being told Freud's analysis, they were greatly impressed. "Three years later I asked the same people (including psychoanalysts): 'What did Freud say about Solomon's judgement?' They knew Freud had written something about it, but they had all (including the psychoanalysts) forgotten what it was." (Maryse Choisy, *Sigmund Freud: A New Appraisal* [London: Peter Owen, 1963], pp. 66–67.)

5. Jon Elster, "Solomonic Judgements: Against the Best Interests of the Child," in Elster, *Solomonic Judgement: Studies in the Limitations of Rationality* (Cambridge/Paris: Cambridge University Press and Maison des Sciences de l'Homme, 1989), pp. 123–174; this quote from p. 128.

6. Carbonnier, *Flexible Droit*, p. 366.

7. Ibid., p. 367n25.

8. Ibid., p. 330.

9. Ibid., p. 372.

10. Jean Carbonnier, cited as general epigraph in Théodore Ivainer, *L'Interprétation des Faits en Droit: Essai de Mise en Perspective Cybernétique des "Lumières du Magistrat"* (Paris: Librairie générale de droit et de jurisprudence, 1988).

11. Freud, *Group Psychology*, SE XVIII, 119–120.

12. Ibid., p. 121.

13. For a provocative discussion of the importance of this seeing, see Stephen Heath, "Difference," *Screen* 19 (1978): 51–112, and Luce Irigaray, *Speculum* (Paris: Editions de Minuit, 1974), translated as *Speculum* (Ithaca, N.Y.: Cornell University Press, 1985).

14. Freud, "Female Sexuality," *SE* XXI, 232.

15. Freud, "Femininity," *SE* XXII, 124; see also "Female Sexuality," *SE* XXI, 234.

16. "Femininity," *SE* XXII, 122. The importance of the hostility to the mother for Freud is confirmed by his criticisms, both in print and in private correspondence, of Jeanne Lampl-de Groot's account of female development; see Lisa Appignanesi and John Forrester, *Freud's Women* (London: Weidenfeld and Nicolson/New York: Basic Books, 1992), p. 386.

17. "Femininity," *SE* XXII, 123.

18. *ID, SE* IV, 204–205.

19. Teresa Brennan, *The Interpretation of the Flesh: Freud's Theory of Femininity* (London: Routledge, 1992), pp. 103ff.

20. Freud, "Femininity," in *New Introductory Lectures on Psycho-analysis, SE* XXII, 134.

21. Klein, *Envy and Gratitude,* in Melanie Klein, *The Writings of Melanie Klein,* under the general editorship of Roger Money-Kyrle, in collaboration with Betty Joseph, Edna O'Shaughnessy, and Hanna Segal, 4 vols. (London: The Hogarth Press and the Institute of Psycho-analysis, 1975), p. 195.

22. As Juliet Mitchell has pointed out to me, Klein's views in this respect draw considerably on Joan Riviere's classic paper, "Jealousy as a Mechanism of Defence"(1932), reprinted in *The Inner World and Joan Riviere: Collected Papers: 1920–1958,* ed. with a biographical chapter by Athol Hughes, foreword by Hanna Segal (London and New York: Karnac Books, 1991); see particularly p. 111.

23. St. Augustine, *Confessions,* trans. R. S. Pine-Coffin (Harmondsworth: Penguin, 1961), book I, chap. 7, pp. 27–28.

24. Jacques Lacan, *Le Séminaire: Livre XI: Les Quatre Concepts Fondamentaux de la Psychanalyse, 1964* (Paris: Seuil, 1973), pp. 105–106; *The Four Fundamental Concepts of Psychoanalysis.* trans. Alan Sheridan (London: Tavistock, 1977, reprinted in paperback by Penguin, 1986), p. 116.

25. Helmut Schoeck, *Envy: A Theory of Social Behavior,* trans. Michael Glenny and Betty Ross (New York: Harcourt, Brace and World, 1970), p. 19.

26. Diana Fuss, "Identification Papers," unpublished colloquium paper, School of Criticism and Theory, Dartmouth College, Hanover, N.H., June 1995, p. 35.

27. Friedrich Nietzsche, *The Genealogy of Morals,* Essay I, Sections VIII–X, in Nietzsche, *The Birth of Tragedy and The Genealogy of Morals,* trans. Francis Golffing (New York: Doubleday Anchor, 1956), pp. 168–173.

28. Max Scheler, *Ressentiment* (1912), trans. William W. Holdheim, ed. Lewis A. Coser (New York: The Free Press, 1961), p. 52.

29. See also J. Sabine and M. Silver, "Envy," in R. Harré, ed., *The Social*

Construction of the Emotions (New York/Oxford: Blackwell, 1986), pp. 169–170.

30. Friedrich Nietzsche, *Daybreak: Thoughts on the Prejudices of Morality,* trans R. J. Hollingdale, introduction by Michael Tanner (Cambridge: Cambridge University Press, 1982) para. 304, pp. 155–156.

31. Bertrand Russell, *The Conquest of Happiness* (London: George Allen and Unwin, 1930), p. 83.

32. Friedrich Nietzsche, *Beyond Good and Evil,* trans. with commentary by Walter Kaufmann (New York: Vintage, 1966), no. 187, p. 100.

33. I would like to thank José Brunner for pointing out to me the extent to which Rawls's account of justice is sometimes implicitly, sometimes explicitly, geared to avoiding the problems raised by "the problem of envy" (*A Theory of Justice,* p. 530), the most pressing of what Rawls calls "the special psychologies," which "in some way must be reckoned with."

34. For an account that underlines the centrality of Rawls's moral psychology, see Ronald Dworkin, "The Original Position," in Norman Daniels, ed., *Reading Rawls: Critical Studies of "A Theory of Justice"* (New York: Basic Books, 1974), pp. 25ff.

35. John Rawls, *A Theory of Justice* (Oxford: Oxford University Press, 1972), p. 51. Subsequent page references to this book will appear in parentheses in the text.

36. The faint allusion to Shakespeare's famous sonnet is no doubt intentional; the consequences of the allusion are worth reflecting upon:

> When in disgrace with Fortune and men's eyes,
> I all alone beweep my outcast state,
> And trouble deaf heaven with my bootless cries,
> And look upon my self and curse my fate,
> Wishing me like to one more rich in hope,
> Featured like him, like him with friends possessed,
> Desiring this man's art, and that man's scope,
> With what I most enjoy contented least,
> Yet in these thoughts my self almost despising,
> Haply I think on thee, and then my state,
> (Like to the lark at break of day arising
> From sullen earth) sings hymns at heaven's gate,
>> For thy sweet love remembered such wealth brings,
>> That then I scorn to change my state with kings.

Shakespeare melds together a range of sentiments and attitudes to the world that Rawls is keen to distinguish: emulative envy, itself close, as I point out below, to the Lacanian notion of desire; moral resentment; loss of self-respect; self-disgust. The contiguity of these sentiments, so successfully evoked in Shakespeare's poem, places in doubt the plausibility of maintaining Rawls's distinctions. At the very least, it highlights their contrived quality.

37. Rawls first lumps Freud in with those "conservative writers" who "have contended that the tendency to equality in modern social movements is the expression of envy" (p. 538). See Schoeck, *Envy*.

38. Stanford M. Lyman, *The Seven Deadly Sins*, revised and expanded edition (Dix Hills, N.Y.: General Hall, 1989), pp. 189–193.

39. Freud, *Group Psychology, SE* XVIII, 119–120.

40. Ibid., p. 121.

41. In passing let us note that Rawls makes this redescription easier for himself by redescribing Freud's vision of the scene in the nursery in the following, subtly altered light: "If children compete for the attention and affection of their parents, to which one might say that they justly have an equal claim, one cannot assert that their sense of justice springs from jealousy and envy. Certainly children are often envious and jealous; and no doubt their moral notions are so primitive that the necessary distinctions are not grasped by them. But waiving these difficulties, we could equally well say that their social feeling arises from resentment, from a sense that they are unfairly treated" (p. 540). The key shift in the redescription is that Rawls adopts the parent's-eye view of the competition for love and attention, whereas Freud adopts the child's-eye view, whose starting point is a desire to eliminate the other.

42. Though it should be noted that Rawls had addressed the question invoked by Augustine's vision of the abundant breast when he discussed the supposed pervasiveness of envy in peasant societies, noting that such envy is based on the probably erroneous economic theory that "the aggregate of social wealth is more or less fixed, so that one person's gain is another's loss" (p. 539).

43. But Rawls does implicitly admit the correctness of Freud's view of the superego: "Our existing moral feelings may be in many respects irrational and injurious to our good. Freud is right in his view that these attitudes are often punitive and blind, incorporating many of the harsher aspects of the authority situation in which they were first acquired. Resentment and indignation, feelings of guilt and remorse, a sense of duty and the censure of others, often take perverse and destructive forms, and blunt without reason human spontaneity and enjoyment" (p. 489).

44. Gerrard Winstanley, "The Law of Freedom in a Platform; or, True Magistracy Restored" (1652), in George H. Sabine, ed., *The Works of Gerrard Winstanley* (New York: Cornell University Press, 1941, quoted as epigraph in

Carolyn Steedman, *Landscape for a Good Woman: A Story of Two Lives* (London: Virago, 1986).

45. Lyman, *The Seven Deadly Sins*.

46. St. Augustine, *De Mendacio* (Lying) (395) and *Contra mendacium* (Against lying) (420), in *Treatise on Various Subjects*, ed. R. J. Deferrari, Fathers of the Church, vol. XVI (New York: Fathers of the Church, 1952), pp. 51–110 and 121–179. See also, in Shakespeare's *Measure for Measure*, Isabella's willingness to sacrifice her brother's life for her chastity.

47. See Johan Heilbron, "The Tripartite Division of French Social Science: A Long-Term Perspective," in P. Wagner, B. Wittrock, and R. Whitley, eds., *Discourses on Society: The Shaping of the Social Science Disciplines*, vol. XV (Dordrecht: Kluwer, 1990), pp. 73–92.

48. A. Levi, *French Moralists: The Theory of the Passions, 1585 to 1649* (Oxford: Clarendon Press, 1964). See also P. Janet, *Histoire de la Science Politique dans ses Rapports avec la Morale* (1858) (Paris: Alcan, 1913).

49. Louis Hippeau, *Essai sur la Morale de La Rochefoucauld* (Paris: Nizet, 1978); see also H.-J. Fuchs, *Entfremdung und Narzissismus. Semantische Untersuchungen zur Geschichte der "Selbstbezogenheit" als Vorgeschichte von französich "amour-propre"* (Stuttgart: J. B. Metzler, 1977).

50. Marcel Mauss, *The Gift: Forms and Functions of Exchange in Archaic Societies* (1925), trans. Ian Cunnison, introduction by E. E. Evans-Pritchard, reprinted with corrections (London: Routledge and Kegan Paul, 1969), p. 74.

51. Johnson, *Rasselas*, chap. 39, quoted in A. O. Hirschman, *The Passions and the Interests* (Princeton: Princeton University Press, 1977), p. 55.

52. Hume, *A Treatise of Human Nature*, book III, part II, section II, quoted in Hirschman, *The Passions and the Interests*, p. 54.

53. Hutcheson, *A System of Moral Philosophy* (1755), vol. V, p. 12, quoted in Hirschman, *The Passions and the Interests*, p. 65.

54. See for instance Frances Hutcheson, *Inquiry into the Original of our Ideas of Beauty and Virtue* (1725), 2nd ed., 1726, pp. 182–184, and the commentary in Louis I. Bredvold, "The Invention of the Ethical Calculus," in R. F. Jones et al., *The Seventeenth Century* (London: Oxford University Press, 1951), pp. 165–180.

55. Jon Elster, *Sour Grapes: Studies in the Subversion of Rationality* (Cambridge: Cambridge University Press, 1983).

56. Karl Marx, *Economic and Philosophical Manuscripts* (1844), in *Early Writings*, introduction by Lucio Colleti, trans. Rodney Livingstone and Gregor Benton (Harmondsworth: Penguin, 1975), p. 346.

57. See Mark D. Altschule, "Acedia: Its Evolution from Deadly Sin to

Psychiatric Syndrome," *British Journal of Psychiatry* 3 (1965): 117–119; Morton Bloomfield, *The Seven Deadly Sins: An Introduction to the History of a Religious Concept, with Special Reference to Medieval English Literature* (East Lansing: Michigan State University Press, 1967).

58. A similar view, couched in very different language, is arrived at by Bernard Williams, "Formal Structures and Social Reality," in Diego Gambetta, ed., *Trust: The Making and Breaking of Cooperative Relations* (Oxford: Blackwell, 1988), pp. 3–13.

59. W. H. Auden, "Nietzsche," in his *New Year Letter* (London: Faber and Faber, 1941), p. 96, quoted in Patrick Bridgwater, *Nietzsche in Anglosaxony* (Leicester: Leicester University Press, 1972), pp. 206–207.

60. For example, Jacques Lacan, *Ecrits: A Selection,* trans. Alan Sheridan (London: Tavistock, 1977), p. 264; Jacques Lacan, *Le Séminaire. Livre IV. La Relation d'Objet. 1956–1957* (Paris: Seuil, 1994).

61. Jacques Lacan, *Le Séminaire. Livre I. Les écrits techniques de Freud (1953–54)* (Paris: Seuil, 1975), p. 193; *The Seminar. Book I. Freud's Papers on Technique 1953–1954,* trans. with notes by John Forrester (Cambridge: Cambridge University Press/New York: Norton, 1988), p. 170.

62. The idea that it is the woman laying claim to the live baby who might be found behind the veil of ignorance I owe to Elizabeth Goodstein, in the course of a very useful discussion of an earlier draft of this chapter with her and my colleagues in the Cambridge Unofficial Knowledge group (Peter de Bolla, Jonathan Burt, Maud Ellmann, and Simon Goldhill) in June 1995.

63. La Rochefoucauld, *Réflexions ou Sentences et Maximes morales, suivi de Réflexions diverses et des Maximes de Madame de Sablé,* ed. Jean Lafond (Paris: Gallimard, 1976), no. 27, p. 48: "On fait souvent vanité des passions même les plus criminelles; mais l'envie est une passion timide et honteuse que l'on n'ose jamais avouer."

64. William Shakespeare, *Julius Caesar* V.5.68.

2. Casualties of Truth

1. Philip Rieff, *Freud, the Mind of the Moralist,* 3rd ed. (Chicago: University of Chicago Press, 1979), p. 300.

2. Freud, "On Beginning the Treatment," *SE* XII, 135–136.

3. Ibid. Translation modified.

4. *FJones,* Freud to Jones, 21 September 1913, p. 226.

5. *Letters,* Freud to J. J. Putnam, 8 July 1915, p. 314.

6. Adam Phillips, "Women: What Are They For?" *London Review of Books*, 4 January 1996, p. 6.

7. Freud, "'Civilized' Sexual Morality and Modern Nervous Illness," *SE* IX, 192.

8. Rieff, *Freud*, p. 324.

9. Jacques Lacan, *Le Séminaire: Livre XI* (Paris, Seuil, 1973), pp. 230–260.

10. See Lisa Appignanesi and John Forrester, *Freud's Women* (London: Weidenfeld and Nicolson/New York: Basic Books, 1992), pp. 178–180.

11. *FFer 1*, Freud to Ferenczi, 11 February 1908, p. 5.

12. *FJung Letters*, 70F, 17 February 1908, p. 121.

13. *FFer 1*, Freud to Ferenczi, 7 February 1909, pp. 42–43.

14. See *FFer 1*, Ferenczi to Freud, 30 October 1909, p. 91, which consists of an analysis of Gizella's desire to give a coffeepot to Ferenczi's brother-in-law, which she and Ferenczi then decided symbolized the penis; Ferenczi's reply was a veiled desire to give his own coffeepot to his favorite sister, who he felt was neglected by her husband; the coffeepot in question had been a gift from Mathilde Freud, who disliked black coffee—a trait that "at the time, we related to repressions" (see French translation [*FFer 1* (French), p. 98] for a clearer version of this phrase). See Appignanesi and Forrester, *Freud's Women*, pp. 55–56.

15. *FFer 1*, Ferenczi to Freud, 8–11 February 1909, p. 44.

16. *FFer 1*, Ferenczi to Freud, 27 April 1910, p. 167.

17. *FFer 1*, Ferenczi to Freud, 12 May 1913, p. 485, and *FFer 1*, Ferenczi to Freud, 6 November 1913, p. 518.

18. *FFer 1*, Ferenczi to Freud, 12 July 1912, p. 389.

19. Ferenczi, *The Clinical Diary of Sándor Ferenczi*, ed. Judith Dupont, trans. Michael Balint and Nicola Zarday Jackson (Cambridge and London: Harvard University Press, 1988), 4 August 1932, p. 186.

20. *FFer 1*, Ferenczi to Freud, 10 June 1909, p. 65.

21. *FFer 1*, Ferenczi to Freud, 26 October 1909, pp. 87–88.

22. *FFer 1*, Ferenczi to Freud, 2 January 1910, p. 119.

23. *FFer 1*, Ferenczi to Freud, 5 February 1910, p. 130.

24. *FFer 1*, Ferenczi to Freud, 9 July 1910, p. 186.

25. *FFer 1*, Freud to Ferenczi, 10 July 1910, p. 189: "Jetzt in der Müdigkeit des Jahresendes ist nicht die Zeit dazu." (*Briefwechsel*, Band I/1, 1908–1911, p. 273).

26. *FFer 1*, Ferenczi to Freud, 28 September 1910, p. 214n1, and *Sándor Ferenczi–Georg Groddeck Briefwechsel 1921–1933* (Frankfurt: Fischer Taschenbuch Verlag, 1986), Ferenczi to Groddeck, 25 December 1921, p. 37.

27. Perhaps Ferenczi's attempt to persuade Freud of his kinship with Goethe

in 1913 and 1914 also stemmed from this incident: he surmised that Freud's behavior was tantamount to an attempt to turn his young admirer into an Eckermann. As late as 17 January 1930, Ferenczi reflected on that incident and asked Freud: "Wouldn't mildness and indulgence have been more appropriate from the side of the person of authority?" (Quoted in Ferenczi, *Clinical Diary*, p. xiii; see also his comments on the Palermo incident in a diary entry of 4 August 1932, *Clinical Diary*, p. 185.)

28. *FJung*, Freud to Jung, 24 September 1910, p. 353.

29. *FFer 1*, Freud to Ferenczi, 2 October 1910, p. 215.

30. *FFer 1*, Ferenczi to Freud, 3 October 1910, p. 218.

31. *FFer 1*, Ferenczi to Freud, 3 October 1910, pp. 219–220.

32. *FFer 1*, Freud to Ferenczi, 6 October 1910, p. 221; the German text is: "Ganz richtig es war Schäche von mir, ich bin auch [nicht] jener ψα Übermensch, den wir konstruiert haben, habe auch die Gegenübertragung nicht überwunden. Ich konnte es nicht, wie ich es bei meinen drei Söhnen nicht kann, weil ich sie gerne habe und sie mir dabei leid tun." (*Briefwechsel*, Band I/1, 1908–1911, p. 312).

33. *FFer 1*, Freud to Ferenczi, 6 October 1910, p. 221.

34. *FFer 1*, Freud to Ferenczi, 6 October 1910, p. 222.

35. *FFer 1*, p. 224, gives "unimpeachable therapist"; the German is "ein unverbesserlicher Therapeut" (*Briefwechsel*, Band I/1, 1908–1911, p. 316). While the word "unverbesserliche" might seem to mean (literally) "unsurpassable," dictionaries give as its actual meaning: "incorrigible, inveterate," as in "unverbesserliche Trinker"—inveterate drinker.

36. *FFer 1*, Ferenczi to Freud, 12 October 1910, p. 224.

37. *FFer 1*, Freud to Ferenczi, 16 December 1910, p. 243.

38. Sigmund Freud and Karl Abraham, *A Psycho-analytic Dialogue: The Letters of Sigmund Freud and Karl Abraham, 1907–1926*, ed. Hilda C. Abraham and Ernst L. Freud (London: The Hogarth Press and the Institute of Psycho-analysis, 1965), Freud to Abraham, 18 December 1910, p. 97: "A paper of my own that I have just finished deals with Schreber's book and uses him as a point of departure to try and solve the riddle of paranoia. As you can imagine, I followed the path shown by your paper on the psycho-sexual differences between hysteria and dementia praecox. When I worked out these ideas at Palermo I particularly liked the proposition that megalomania was the sexual over-estimation of the ego. In Vienna I found that you had already very trenchantly said the same thing. I have of course had to plagiarise you very extensively in this paper." See also *Sigmund Freud/Ludwig Binswanger: Correspondance 1908–1938* (Paris: Calmann-Lévy, 1995), Freud to Binswanger, 3 December 1910, p. 118,

and Freud to Binswanger, 1 January 1911, p. 121. For an interesting commentary on Freud's relations to Jung and Ferenczi at this time, see Herbert Lehmann, "A Dream of Freud in the Year 1910," *International Journal of Psycho-Analysis* 59 (1978): 181–187.

39. *FFer 1*, Freud to Ferenczi, 10 January 1910, p. 122, also quoted in *J* II, 495.

40. See Appignanesi and Forrester, *Freud's Women*, p. 35.

41. *Letters*, Freud to Martha Bernays, 25 September 1882, p. 47.

42. *Letters*, Freud to Martha Bernays, 2 February 1886, p. 214.

43. *FFer 1*, Ferenczi to Freud, 3 January 1911, p. 248 gives: "I am much too interested in it to be able to judge and act quite calmly"—which is poor English, and a poor translation: "ich bin dabei viel zu sehr interessiert, als dass ich ganz kühl urteilen und handlen könnte." (*Briefwechsel*, Band I/1, 1908–1911, p. 344.) Compare the French edition, p. 261.

44. *FFer 1*, Ferenczi to Freud, 14 November 1911, p. 312.

45. *FFer 1*, Freud to Ferenczi, 17 November 1911, p. 314.

46. *FFer 1*, Ferenczi to Freud, 26 November 1911, p. 315.

47. *FFer 1*, Ferenczi to Freud, 3 December 1911, p. 318.

48. *FFer 1*, Ferenczi to Freud, 3 December 1911, p. 318.

49. *FFer 1*, Ferenczi to Freud, 3 December 1911, p. 318.

50. *FFer 1*, Ferenczi to Freud, 3 January 1912, p. 326.

51. *FFer 1*, Freud to Gizella Pálos, 17 December 1911, p. 320.

52. *FFer 1*, Freud to Gizella Pálos, 17 December 1911, p. 319.

53. *FFer 1*, Freud to Gizella Pálos, 17 December 1911, p. 320.

54. *FFer 1*, Freud to Gizella Pálos, 17 December 1911, p. 320.

55. *ID, SE* IV, 257.

56. *FFer 1*, Freud to Gizella Pálos, 17 December 1911, p. 321; "Die arme Mutter muss man ihrem zweifachen Leiden überlassen" (*Briefwechsel*, Band I/1, 1908–1911, p. 432); *FFer 1* (French), p. 337 gives a subtly different tenor to this phrase: "On doit laisser la pauvre mère à sa double souffrance."

57. *FFer 1*, Freud to Gizella Pálos, 17 December 1911, p. 320.

58. Freud, "On a Special Type of Choice of Object Made by Men" (1910h), SE XI, 165–175.

59. *The Letters of Sigmund Freud to Eduard Silberstein, 1871–1881*, ed. Walter Boehlich, trans. Arnold J. Pomerans (Cambridge, Mass.: Harvard University Press, 1990), 4 September 1872, p. 17.

60. Freud, "Femininity," *SE* XXII, 134.

61. Freud, "A Case of Paranoia Running Counter to the Psycho-analytical Theory of the Disease" (1915), *SE* XIV, 267–268.

62. Freud, "The Psychogenesis of a Case of Homosexuality in a Woman," *SE* XVIII, 157–158.

63. *FFer 1*, Freud to Gizella Pálos, 17 December 1911, p. 321.

64. *FFer 1*, Freud to Gizella Pálos, 17 December 1911, p. 321.

65. *FFer 1*, Freud to Gizella Pálos, 17 December 1911, p. 320.

66. *FFer 1*, Ferenczi to Freud, 18 December 1911, pp. 321–322.

67. *FFer 1*, Freud to Ferenczi, 26 December 1911, p. 322; "ich habe nichts mehr zu sagen, habe vielleicht mehr gesagt, als zu rechtfertigen war, und will es mir mit Ihrer Zukunft nicht ganz verderben." (*Briefwechsel*, Band I/1, 1908–1911, p. 433). *FFer 1* (French), pp. 338–339, has a significantly different syntax: "je ne veux pas me gâcher tout à fait l'avenir avec vous." The English thus omits the reference to himself ("mir"). A plausible translation would be: "it is not for me to spoil your future completely."

68. *FFer 1*, Ferenczi to Freud, 1 January 1912, p. 324.

69. *FFer 1*, Freud to Ferenczi, 2 January 1912, p. 325.

70. Shakespeare, *Richard III*, Act I, Scene 2.

71. See Freud's remarks concerning the character of Richard III in "Some Character-Types Met with in Psycho-analytic Work," *SE* XIV, 314–315.

72. *FFer 1*, Freud to Ferenczi, 13 January 1912, pp. 326–327.

73. *FFer 1*, Freud to Ferenczi, 13 March 1912, p. 357; the phrase "utterly indifferent" is in English in the original.

74. *FFer 1*, Freud to Ferenczi, 24 March 1912, p. 362.

75. *FFer 1*, Ferenczi to Freud, 17 April 1912, pp. 364–365.

76. *FFer 1*, Ferenczi to Freud, 23 April 1912, p. 368.

77. *FFer 1*, Ferenczi to Freud, 26 April 1912, p. 370.

78. *FFer 1*, Ferenczi to Freud, 27 May 1912, p. 375.

79. *FFer 1*, Ferenczi to Freud, 8 August 1912, p. 402.

80. *FFer 1*, Freud to Ferenczi, 12 August 1912, p. 403.

81. *FFer 1*, Ferenczi to Freud, 3 May 1913, pp. 481–482.

82. *FFer 1*, Ferenczi to Freud, 7 July 1913, p. 497.

83. *FFer 1*, Freud to Gizella Pálos, 17 December 1911, p. 321.

84. For the parallel story of the Jones–Loë Kann–Freud analytic triangle, see Appignanesi and Forrester, *Freud's Women*, pp. 226–239.

85. *FFer 1*, Ferenczi to Freud, 26 December 1912, p. 450; it is of the greatest significance that this demand for analysis surfaced explicitly at the time of the break with Jung, when Ferenczi was comparing his own rebellious impulses with Jung's actual "rebellion."

86. *FFer 2*, Freud to Ferenczi, 24 October 1916, p. 149.

87. See *FFer 2*, Ferenczi to Freud, 18 December 1914, p. 39.

88. *FFer 2*, Ferenczi to Freud, 16 December 1915, p. 95–96.
89. *FFer 2*, Freud to Ferenczi, 18 January 1916, p. 105.
90. *FFer 2*, Ferenczi to Freud, 24 January 1916, p. 107.
91. *FFer 2*, Ferenczi to Freud, 2 February 1916, p. 109.
92. *FFer 2*, Freud to Ferenczi, 12 March 1916, p. 119.
93. Gisella in text; note misspelling (Gizella) but, more important, this is the first letter in which Ferenczi refers to her with her name rather than as Frau G.
94. *FFer 2*, Ferenczi to Freud, 10 July 1916, pp. 132–133.
95. *FFer 2*, Freud to Gizella Pálos, 31 July 1916, p. 136.
96. *FFer 2*, Freud to Gizella Pálos, 31 July 1916, p. 136.
97. *FFer 2*, Freud to Gizella Pálos, 31 July 1916, pp. 136–7.
98. *FFer 2*, Freud to Gizella Pálos, 31 July 1916, pp. 136–137.
99. *FFer 2*, Ferenczi to Freud, 19/20 December 1917, p. 254.
100. The exact date of the marriage is not given in the correspondence, but it must have taken place between 1905 and 1909: see *FFer 1*, Ferenczi to Freud, 8 November 1909, p. 93, reproducing a letter from Ferenczi to Gizella of 20 August 1905, and *FFer 1*, Ferenczi to Freud, 14 October 1909, p. 82, which refers to Gizella as Lajos' "present mother-in-law."
101. *FFer 2*, Ferenczi to Freud, 23 October 1916, p. 148.
102. *FFer 2*, p. 156, Ferenczi to Freud, 18 November 1916, pp. 154–155.
103. *FFer 2*, Ferenczi to Freud, 18 November 1916, p. 155.
104. *FFer 2*, Ferenczi to Freud, 24 November 1916, p. 160.
105. *FFer 2*, Freud to Ferenczi, 26 November 1916, p. 162.
106. *FFer 2*, Freud to Gizella Pálos, 23 January 1917, p. 176.
107. *FFer 2*, Freud to Gizella Pálos, 11 February 1917, p. 181.
108. *FFer 2*, Ferenczi to Freud, 18 November 1916, pp. 154–155, p. 156.
109. *FFer 2*, Ferenczi to Freud, 24 March 1917, p. 189.
110. *FFer 2*, Ferenczi to Freud, 24 March 1917, p. 189.
111. *FFer 2*, Freud to Ferenczi, 25 March 1917, p. 190.
112. Jean Allouch, "Sincérités libertines," *Etudes Freudiennes No. 34* (September 1993): 205–224; this quote is from p. 210.
113. *FFer 2*, Freud to Gizella Pálos, 25 March 1917, pp. 191–192.
114. *FFer 2*, Ferenczi to Freud, 11 April 1917, p. 195.
115. *FFer 2*, Ferenczi to Freud, 25 April 1917, p. 196.
116. *FFer 2*, Ferenczi to Freud, 6 July 1917, p. 226.
117. *FFer 2*, Ferenczi to Freud, 18 August 1917, p. 234.
118. *FFer 2*, Ferenczi to Freud, 18 November 1917, p. 246.
119. *FFer 2*, Freud to Ferenczi, 20 November 1917, p. 249.

120. *FFer 2*, Ferenczi to Freud, 1 March 1919, p. 333.

121. *FFer 2*, Ferenczi to Freud, 12 May 1919, pp. 356–357.

122. Ferenczi to Groddeck, 25 December 1921, in *Sándor Ferenczi–Georg Groddeck: Briefwechsel 1921–1933*, p. 39.

123. Letter from Frederic to Vilma Kovacs, 8 January 1927, included in Ferenczi and Groddeck, *Briefwechsel*, p. 94.

124. Ilse Grubrich-Simitis, "Six Letters of Sigmund Freud and Sándor Ferenczi on the Interrelationship of Psychoanalytic Theory and Technique," *International Review of Psycho-Analysis* 13 (1986): 259–277.

125. Freud, "Analysis Terminable and Interminable," *SE* XXIII, 221.

126. Ibid., p. 222.

127. One suitably "incestuous" telepathic experiment took place in 1909, when Ferenczi's brother, already married to Gizella's other daughter, was delegated to hand over to the female medium being experimented on a letter that Ferenczi had written in Hungarian to Gizella; in this way, Ferenczi hoped to find out, through the telepathic powers of the medium, what his brother thought of his relationship to Gizella, his mother-in-law. See *FFer 1*, Ferenczi to Freud, 14 October 1909, p. 82.

128. Freud, "Psycho-analysis and Telepathy," *SE* XVIII, 191.

129. Ibid., pp. 192–193.

130. *FFer 1*, Freud to Gizella Pálos, 17 December 1911, pp. 320–321.

131. *FFer 2*, Ferenczi to Freud, 16 December 1915, pp. 95–96.

132. *FFer 1*, Freud to Gizella Pálos, 17 December 1911, p. 320.

133. Helene Deutsch, *Confrontations with Myself* (New York: Norton, 1973), p. 135.

134. *FFer 1*, Freud to Gizella Pálos, 17 December 1911, p. 320.

135. See, for example, *FFer 2*, Freud to Ferenczi, 17 October 1915, p. 83.

136. *FFer 2*, Ferenczi to Freud, 8 April 1918, pp. 276–277.

137. Freud, "On the Universal Tendency to Debasement in the Sphere of Love" (1912d), *SE* XI, 186. See *FFer 1*, Freud to Ferenczi, 26 December 1911, p. 322, and *FJung*, 290F, 31 December 1911, p. 475. Drafted a year before, it was an entirely suitable moment for him to return to a paper devoted to the effects of incestuous fixations on the mother.

138. There is still no better account of this aspect of Freud's thought than Rieff, *Freud*.

139. Celia Bertin, *Marie Bonaparte: A Life* (New York: Harcourt Brace Jovanovich, 1982; London and Melbourne: Quartet, 1983), p. 184.

140. *J* III, 484, quoting Freud to Marie Bonaparte, 30 April 1932.

141. Freud, *The Future of an Illusion*, *SE* XXI, 11.

142. See Appignanesi and Forrester, *Freud's Women,* pp. 329–348.

143. A theme picked up in the final chapter of J. M. Masson, *The Assault on Truth: Freud's Suppression of the Seduction Theory* (London: Faber and Faber, 1984). See also Martin Stanton, *Sándor Ferenczi: Reconsidering Active Intervention* (London: Free Association Books, 1990); Claude Lorin, *Sandor Ferenczi: De la médicine à la psychose* (Paris: Presses Universitaires de France, 1993); W. B. Lum, "Sandor Ferenczi (1873–1933): The Father of the Empathic-Interpersonal Approach. Part Two: Evolving Technique, Final Contributions and Legacy," *Journal of the American Academy of Psychoanalysis* 16 (1988): 317–347.

144. *FJones,* Freud to Jones, 10 February 1913, p. 192; emphasis added.

145. *FFer 1,* Freud to Ferenczi, 13 March 1912, p. 357.

146. *FFer 1,* Freud to Ferenczi, 13 March 1912, p. 357; the phrase "utterly indifferent" is in English in the original.

147. Freud, *Introductory Lectures, SE* XVI, 459–460.

148. Ibid.

149. Ernest Gellner, *The Psychoanalytic Movement or the Cunning of Unreason* (London: Paladin, 1985).

150. Rieff, *Freud,* p. 319.

151. I will speculate in passing that this particularity of Jewish rules concerning prohibited sexual relations may explain why Freud, in the 1890s, sometimes concealed the identity of the sexually rapacious father by replacing him with the "uncle"; see, for example, the case of Katharina in *Studies on Hysteria, SE* II, 134n2.

152. Sander Gilman, *Freud, Race and Gender* (Princeton: Princeton University Press, 1993), pp. 109ff.

153. Freud, *Totem and Taboo, SE* XIII, 9.

154. See Appignanesi and Forrester, *Freud's Women,* chap. 4.

155. *FFer 1,* Ferenczi to Freud, 11 January 1909, p. 35.

156. *FFer 2,* Ferenczi to Freud, 17 October 1916, p. 141.

157. *FFer 1,* Ferenczi to Freud, 14 October 1909, p. 82.

158. This unorthodox dating of the Oedipus complex is argued in detail in my *Language and the Origins of Psychoanalysis* (London: Macmillan/New York: Columbia University Press, 1980), pp. 84–96.

159. *FFer 1,* Freud to Ferenczi, 23 May 1913, p. 486.

160. Freud, *Totem and Taboo, SE* XIII, 4.

161. *FFer 1,* Freud to Ferenczi, 12 June 1913, p. 491.

162. James George Frazer, *The Golden Bough,* 2nd ed., (London: Macmillan, 1900), I, 288.

163. Freud, *Totem and Taboo, SE* XIII, 15.

164. Ibid., pp. 12–16.

165. Ferenczi, *Clinical Diary*, 4 August 1932, p. 185.

166. Wladimir Granoff, *Filiations* (Paris: Editions de Minuit, 1975).

167. *FFer 2*, Ferenczi to Freud, 6 July 1917, p. 226.

168. *FFer 1*, Ferenczi to Freud, 12 May 1913, p. 485; *FFer 2*, Ferenczi to Freud, 22 October 1916, p. 145; *FFer 2*, Ferenczi to Freud, 13 November 1916, p. 151; *FFer 2*, Freud to Gizella Pálos, 31 July 1916, pp. 136–137.

169. *J* III, 209, Freud to Marie Bonaparte, 27 September 1936.

170. *FFer 1*, Ferenczi to Freud, 16 October 1913, p. 514.

171. *FFer 1*, Ferenczi to Freud, 18 January 1912, p. 329.

172. *FFer 2*, Freud to Gizella Pálos, 23 January 1917, p. 176.

173. The definition of negative capability is from John Keats, Letter to George and Thomas Keats, 21 December 1817, in Lionel Trilling, ed., *The Selected Letters of John Keats* (New York: Farrar, Straus and Young, 1951), p. 92; the continuation of the thought is quoted in Trilling's Introduction, p. 29.

174. Freud, *Introductory Lectures*, SE XVI, 385.

175. Freud, "The Future Prospects of Psycho-analytic Therapy" (1910), *SE* XI, 150.

176. *FFer 2*, Freud to Ferenczi, 16 October 1918, p. 302.

177. Ferenczi, *Clinical Diary*, 4 August 1932, p. 186.

178. Ferenczi, "Child Analysis in the Analysis of Adults" (1931), in Ferenczi, *Final Contributions to the Problems and Methods of Psycho-analysis*, ed. Michael Balint, trans. Eric Mosbacher et al. (London: Hogarth Press and the Institute of Psycho-analysis, 1955), p. 128.

179. Ferenczi, *Clinical Diary*, 1 May 1932, p. 94.

180. *Letters*, Freud to J. J. Putnam, 8 July 1915, p. 314.

181. Freud, *Introductory Lectures*, SE XVI, 434.

182. Adam Phillips, "Women: What Are They For?" *London Review of Books*, 4 January 1996, pp. 7–8.

183. Immanuel Kant, *Groundwork of the Metaphysic of Morals*, trans. H. J. Paton (New York: Harper and Row, 1964), p. 88.

184. Freud, "'Civilized' Sexual Morality and Modern Nervous Illness," *SE* IX, 192.

185. Sigmund Freud and Oskar Pfister, *Psycho-analysis and Faith: The Letters of Sigmund Freud and Oskar Pfister*, ed. Heinrich Meng and Ernst L. Freud, trans. Eric Mosbacher (London: The Hogarth Press and the Institute of Psycho-analysis, 1963), Freud to Pfister, 16 February 1929, p. 129.

186. *Freud/Pfister*, Freud to Pfister, 24 February 1928, p. 123.

187. Freud, *Civilization and Its Discontents*, SE XXI, 95.

188. Freud, "Thoughts for the Time on War and Death," *SE* XIV, 288.

189. Rieff, *Freud,* pp. 322–323.

190. Freud, "Observations on Transference-love," *SE* XII, 169.

191. Ibid., p. 165.

192. *J* III, 174–176; see also Stanton, *Sándor Ferenczi,* p. 125, and Maria Torok, "La correspondance Freud-Ferenczi," *Confrontation* 12 (Autumn 1984): 97.

193. Ferenczi, *Clinical Diary,* Ferenczi to Freud, 27 December 1931, p. 4.

194. Ferenczi, "Confusion of Tongues between Adults and the Child" (1933), *Final Contributions,* pp. 156–167.

195. Ferenczi, "The Problem of the Termination of Analysis" (1927), *Final Contributions,* p. 83.

196. *Vogue,* 1 November 1952.

197. *Sigmund Freud/Ludwig Binswanger: Correspondance 1908–1938* (Paris: Calmann-Lévy, 1995), pp. 304–305. On 21 November 1939, Binswanger had written to Freud's wife, confessing that "I only truly got to know him through certain of his letters," and suggesting that a collection of Freud's letters be published at some future date, in order to "show this great man in the most human of lights." Anna Freud replied on 29 December 1939 that she had already initiated the same project with Bibring and Kris.

198. *Sigmund Freud/Ludwig Binswanger. Correspondance,* Anna Freud to Ludwig Binswanger, 29 December 1939, p. 305.

199. *FFer 1,* Anna Freud to Gizella Ferenczi, 2 April 1948, p. xxix.

200. *FFer 1,* Michael Balint to Elma Laurvik, 28 April 1966, p. xxxii.

201. *FFer 1,* Michael Balint to Elma Laurvik, 10 December 1968, p. xxxiii.

202. *FFer 1,* p. xxxii.

203. Elisabeth Young-Bruehl, *Anna Freud: A Biography* (London: Macmillan, 1988), pp. 295–297.

204. Freud, *Introductory Lectures, SE* XVI, 433.

205. Young-Bruehl, *Anna Freud,* Anna Freud to Clifford Yorke, 12 March 1980, p. 435.

206. Freud to André Breton, 26 December 1932, in *Les Rêves: La voie royale de l'inconscient* (Paris: Laffont/Tchou, 1979), pp. 56–57; see also *J* II, 455–456, Jack J. Spector, *The Aesthetics of Freud: A Study of Psychoanalysis and Art* (New York: Praeger, 1972), pp. 153–154, and Peter Gay, *Freud: A Life for Our Time* (London: Dent, 1988), p. 585.

207. *FFer 1,* Freud to Ferenczi, 13 January 1912, pp. 326–327.

208. *FFer 1,* p. xxxi (my translation).

3. Collector, Naturalist, Surrealist

1. Sigmund Freud, "Notes upon a Case of Obsessional Neurosis" (1909), *SE* X, 176.

2. Freud, *Civilization and Its Discontents*, *SE* XXI, 70–71.

3. Freud, "The Aetiology of Hysteria," *SE* III, 192.

4. Freud, *Studies on Hysteria*, *SE* II, 139.

5. *FF*, 6 December 1896, pp. 207–208. For the evolutionary dialect, see Frank Sulloway, *Freud: Biologist of the Mind* (London, Burnett Books, 1979); for the philological dialect, see John Forrester, *Language and the Origins of Psychoanalysis* (London: Macmillan/New York: Columbia University Press, 1980).

6. And the fact that the portion of his library that Freud sold was the "professional" portion of mainly psychiatric, neurological, and psychoanalytic books—very little was sold of archaeology or the classics—is an indication of what reading lay closest to his heart; see Edward Timms, "Freud's Library and His Private Reading," in Edward Timms and Naomi Segal, eds., *Freud in Exile: Psychoanalysis and Its Vicissitudes* (New Haven and London: Yale University Press, 1988), pp. 65–79.

7. Peter Gay, *Freud: A Life for Our Time* (London: Dent, 1988), p. 635.

8. Freud to Jeanne Lampl de Groot, 8 October 1938, quoted in Ernst Freud, Lucie Freud, and Ilse Grubrich-Simitis, eds., *Sigmund Freud: His Life in Words and Pictures*, with a biographical sketch by K. R. Eissler, trans. Christine Trollope (London: André Deutsch, 1978), p. 313.

9. Bruno Bettelheim, "Berggasse 19," in Bettelheim, *Recollections and Reflections* (London: Thames and Hudson, 1990), pp. 18–23; this passage from p. 22.

10. *Letters*, Freud to Stefan Zweig, 7 February 1931, p. 402.

11. Maryse Choisy, *Sigmund Freud: A New Appraisal* (London: Peter Owen, 1963), p. 47.

12. See Eilean Hooper-Greenhill, *Museums and the Shaping of Knowledge* (London: Routledge, 1992); Robert Lumley, ed., *Museum Time Machine: Putting Cultures on Display* (London: Routledge, 1988); Susan M. Pearce, ed., *Objects of Knowledge* (London: Athlone, 1990); Krzysztof Pomian, *Collectors and Curiosities: Paris and Venice, 1500–1800* (1987), trans. Elizabeth Wiles-Portier (Cambridge: Polity, 1990); Thomas Richards, *The Commodity Culture of Victorian England* (London: Verso, 1991); David K. Van Keuren, "Cabinets and Culture:

Victorian Anthropology and the Museum Context," *Journal of the History of the Behavioral Sciences* 25 (1989): 26–39.

13. Jack J. Spector, *The Aesthetics of Freud: A Study of Psychoanalysis and Art* (New York: Praeger, 1972), p. 17.

14. See Susan M. Pearce, *Museum Objects and Collections: A Cultural Study* (Leicester and London: Leicester University Press, 1992), pp. 34–35.

15. Sigmund Freud and Karl Abraham, *A Psycho-analytic Dialogue: The Letters of Sigmund Freud and Karl Abraham, 1907–1926*, ed. Hilda C. Abraham and Ernst L. Freud (London: The Hogarth Press and the Institute of Psychoanalysis, 1965), Freud to Abraham, 18 December 1916, p. 244.

16. *FF,* 6 December 1896, p. 214; translation adapted in accordance with Lynn Gamwell, "Freud's Antiquities Collection," in Lynn Gamwell and Richard Wells, eds., *Sigmund Freud and Art: His Personal Collection of Antiquities*, introduction by Peter Gay (London: Freud Museum/State University of New York, Binghamton, 1989), p. 24.

17. *ID, SE* IV, xxvi.

18. *FF,* 24 January 1895, Draft H, p. 110; the juxtaposition of old maids and bachelors is repeated, within the context of a somewhat different argument, in *ID, SE* IV, 177.

19. *FF,* 24 January 1895, Draft H, p. 110.

20. See Marie Balmary, *Psychoanalyzing Psychoanalysis: Freud and the Hidden Fault of the Father* trans. with an introduction by Ned Lukacher (Baltimore: Johns Hopkins University Press, 1982).

21. See Lisa Appignanesi and John Forrester, *Freud's Women* (London: Weidenfeld and Nicolson/New York: Basic Books, 1992), esp. chap. 4; "sexual megalomania" is the phrase Freud used in a letter to Karl Abraham, *Freud-Abraham Letters*, 9 January 1908, p. 20.

22. It should be noted that Krafft-Ebing borrowed these terms from an anonymous Berlin correspondent; see Richard Krafft-Ebing, *Neue Forschungen auf dem Gebiet der Psychopathia Sexualis: Eine medizinische-psychologische Studie* (Stuttgart, 1890), pp. 19–20, quoted in Renate I. Hauser, "Sexuality, Neurasthenia and the Law: Richard von Krafft-Ebing (1840–1902)," Ph.D. dissertation, University College, University of London, 1992, p. 240.

23. Moriz Benedikt, *Hypnotismus und Suggestion: Eine klinisch-psychologische Studie* (Leipzig, 1894), p. 76, quoted in Hauser, *Sexuality, Neurasthenia and the Law*, p. 45.

24. *FF,* 22 June 1987, p. 254.

25. *ID, SE* IV, 194–195; the series of "Rome" dreams of which these anecdotes form a part are dated by Anzieu to January 1897; see Didier Anzieu,

Freud's Self-analysis (1975), trans. Peter Graham (London: Hogarth Press and Institute of Psycho-Analysis, 1986), p. 182.

26. See Freud, *The Psychopathology of Everyday Life, SE* VI, and John Forrester, "What the Psychoanalyst Does with Words: Austin, Lacan and the Speech Acts of Psychoanalysis," in Forrester, *The Seductions of Psychoanalysis: Freud, Lacan and Derrida* (Cambridge: Cambridge University Press, 1990), p. 152.

27. Freud, "Screen-Memories," *SE* III, 304.

28. *FF,* 6 August 1899, p. 366.

29. *FF,* 28 May 1899, p. 353.

30. Anna Freud Bernays, "My Brother, Sigmund Freud," in H. Ruitenbeek, *Freud As We Knew Him* (Detroit, Mich.: Wayne State University Press, 1973), pp. 140–147; this passage from p. 141.

31. Freud, "Psycho-analytic Notes on an Autobiographical Account of a Case of Paranoia (Dementia Paranoides)," *SE* XII, 71.

32. *Minutes of the Vienna Psychoanalytic Society,* ed. Herman Nunberg and Ernst Federn, trans. M. Nunberg, 4 vols. (New York: International Universities Press, 1962–1976), Vol. I, 19 February 1908.

33. Freud, "On Narcissism: An Introduction," *SE* XIV, 89.

34. Lou Andreas-Salomé, *The Freud Journal,* trans. Stanley A. Leavy, with an introduction by Mary-Kay Wilmers (London: Quartet, 1987), p. 89.

35. Jean Baudrillard, *Le Système des Objets* (Paris: Gallimard, 1968), p. 126.

36. One might connect this with Freud's often quoted account (*FFer 1,* Freud to Ferenczi, 6 October 1910, p. 221; see Chapter 2, p. 54) of how he had employed his homosexual drives to enlarge his ego, whereas his friend Fliess had failed in this task and thus succumbed to a paranoia; the accent is as much on Freud's transformation of his homosexual bond with the close friend as it is on Fliess's paranoia.

37. Freud, "Notes upon a Case of Obsessional Neurosis" (1909), *SE* X, 176.

38. H.D., *Tribute to Freud: Writing on the Wall: Advent,* foreword by Norman Holmes Pearson (London: Carcanet, 1985) pp. 96–98.

39. Ibid., p. 14.

40. Ibid., p. 9.

41. W. H. Auden, "In Memory of Sigmund Freud," in *W. H. Auden: Collected Poems,* ed. E. Mendelson (London: Faber and Faber, 1976), pp. 215–218.

42. See Spector, *The Aesthetics of Freud,* and Ernst Gombrich, "Freud's Aesthetics," *Encounter* (January 1966), pp. 30–40.

43. Carlo Ginzburg, "Clues: Morelli, Freud and Sherlock Holmes: Clues and Scientific Method," in Umberto Eco and Thomas A. Sebeok, eds., *The Sign of*

Three: Dupin, Holmes, Pierce (Bloomington: Indiana University Press, 1983), pp. 81–118.

44. The closest Freud came to making up such a catalogue was in the very early days of the First World War, when, during a time of frenzied boredom and suspenseful waiting, he "thought up a . . . little game: I take my antiquities and study and describe every piece" (*FFer 2*, Freud to Ferenczi, 23 August 1914, p. 13).

45. *ID, SE* IV, 217n1.

46. Philip Rieff's classic work, *Freud: The Mind of the Moralist* (1959) (2nd ed., Chicago: University of Chicago Press, 1975) is the indispensable guide to this aspect of psychoanalysis.

47. See Richard Wells, "Preface," in Gamwell and Wells, eds., *Sigmund Freud and Art*, p. 11.

48. Adam Phillips, *Terrors and Experts* (London and Boston: Faber and Faber, 1995), p. 12.

49. Freud, "Thoughts for the Time on War and Death," *SE* XIV, 277.

50. Karl Marx, *Grundrisse: Foundations of the Critique of Political Economy (rough draft)*, trans with foreword by Martin Nicolaus (Harmondsworth: Penguin, 1973), p. 218.

51. Freud, "Thoughts for the Time on War and Death," *SE* XIV, 279.

52. Baudrillard, *Le Système des Objets*, p. 139.

53. See D. E. Allen, *The Naturalist in Britain: A Social History* (London: Allen Lane, 1976).

54. Susan Stewart, *On Longing: Narratives of the Miniature, the Gigantic, the Souvenir, the Collection* (Baltimore: Johns Hopkins University Press, 1984), p. 152.

55. Excellently analyzed in Adam Phillips, "Freud and the Uses of Forgetting," in Phillips, *On Flirtation* (London: Faber and Faber, 1993), pp. 22–38.

56. Freud, "Negation," *SE* XIX, 235–239.

57. *FJung*, 147F, 18 June 1909, p. 235.

58. H.D., *Tribute to Freud*, p. 14.

59. Marx, *Grundrisse*, p. 221.

60. Ibid., p. 216.

61. Georg Simmel, *The Philosophy of Money*, ed. David Frisby, trans. by Tom Bottomore and David Frisby from a first draft by Kaethe Mengelberg, 2nd enlarged ed. (London and New York: Routledge, 1990), p. 239.

62. See Justin Miller, "Interpretation of Freud's Jewishness, 1924–1974," *Journal of the History of the Behavioral Sciences* 17 (1981): 357–374; E. Oring, *The Jokes of Sigmund Freud: A Study in Jewish Humor and Jewish Identity* (Philadelphia: University of Pennsylvania Press, 1984).

63. Baudrillard, *Le Système des Objets*, p. 124.

64. Gay, *Freud*, p. 543; Freud included the moment of discovery of the forgotten *location* of the dream in a paragraph added to the 1909 edition of *ID*, *SE* IV, 15.

65. *ID*, *SE* V, 583.

4. Dream Readers

1. For representative substantial works on these topics, see Theodore M. Porter, *The Rise of Statistical Thinking, 1820–1900* (Princeton: Princeton University Press, 1986); Bruno Latour, *The Pasteurization of France* (1984) (Cambridge and London: Harvard University Press, 1988); David Kohn, ed., *The Darwinian Heritage* (Princeton: Princeton University Press, 1985); Alan Gauld, *A History of Hypnotism* (Cambridge: Cambridge University Press, 1992).

2. See Phyllis Grosskurth, *The Secret Ring: Freud's Inner Circle and the Politics of Psychoanalysis* (London: Jonathan Cape, 1991).

3. Jacques Derrida, "Spéculer—sur Freud," in Derrida, *La Carte Postale* (Paris: Flammarion, 1980), pp. 277–437, this passage from p. 325; *The Post Card: From Socrates to Freud and Beyond*, trans. Alan Bass (Chicago: University of Chicago Press, 1987), pp. 257–409, this passage from p. 305, translation modified. This is not the first time I have considered the question that Derrida so penetratingly asks; see my "Who Is in Analysis with Whom?" in John Forrester, *The Seductions of Psychoanalysis: Freud, Lacan and Derrida* (Cambridge: Cambridge University Press, 1990), esp. pp. 233ff.

4. *ID*, *SE* IV, xxvi; added to the 1909 edition.

5. *ID*, *SE* IV, xxvi (Preface to 2nd edition), translation modified. The last sentence reads: "Für den Leser mag es aber gleichgültig sein, an welchem Material er Träume würdigen und deuten lernt," which Strachey translates as: "To my readers, however, it will be a matter of indifference upon what particular material they learn to appreciate the importance of dreams and how to interpret them." This elegant translation introduces, somewhat superfluously, the term "particular," which evokes an implicit reference to the "general"; it is my contention later in my argument that such an implication is *not* present in Freud's text here. In addition, the translation of *würdigen* as "to appreciate the importance," and its consequent separation from *deuten* ("interpret"), obscures the fact that Freud's German links very closely the valuing and interpreting of dreams; dreams are not distant objects to be valued and appraised, but become valuable for what their interpretation may yield.

6. *J* I, 351 (2nd English edition, 1954).

7. Didier Anzieu, *L'Auto-analyse de Freud* (Paris: Presses Universitaires de

France, 1975), translated as *Freud's Self-analysis,* by Peter Graham (London: Hogarth Press and the Institute of Psycho-analysis, 1986); Alexander Grinstein, *Sigmund Freud's Dreams,* 2nd ed, (New York: International Universities Press, 1980); Alexander Grinstein, *Freud's Rules of Dream Interpretation* (New York: International Universities Press, 1983); Alexander Grinstein, *Freud at the Crossroads* (Madison, Conn.: International Universities Press, 1990).

8. An example of this attitude to Freud's correspondence with Fliess is the following judgment of Masson's: "[The lost letter about a dream relating to Martha Freud] would no doubt be the most important letter of the collection, since it contains the only dream Freud ever analyzed completely." *FF,* Introduction, p. 10.

9. *FF,* 14 August 1897, p. 261.

10. *FF,* 27 October 1897, p. 274.

11. *FF,* 14 November 1897, p. 281.

12. *ID, SE* IV, 103.

13. *FF,* 23 February 1898, p. 300. References to the Dreckology were censored from the 1950 edition of the *Letters* prepared by Anna Freud and her colleagues. Apparently Anna and Martin Freud felt that these letters were not of value for the history of Freud's early discoveries and would be found "sensational" by readers; therefore they should not be published (see Elizabeth Young-Bruehl, *Anna Freud: A Biography* [London: Macmillan, 1988], pp. 296–297).

14. *FF,* 9 February 1898, p. 299.

15. *FF,* 5 March 1898, p. 301.

16. Jacques Lacan, *The Seminar: Book II: The Ego in Freud's Theory and in the Technique of Psychoanalysis, 1954–1955* (1978), ed. J.-A. Miller, trans. Sylvana Tomaselli, with notes by John Forrester (Cambridge: Cambridge University Press/New York: Norton, 1988), p. 170.

17. *FF,* 22 December 1897, p. 289. Anzieu, *Freud's Self-Analysis,* p. 465, notes that this is the first use of the word "censorship" in the correspondence with Fliess.

18. *FF,* 18 May 1898, p. 313.

19. *FF,* 24 May 1898, p. 315.

20. *FF,* 9 June 1898, p. 315.

21. *FF,* 20 June 1898, p. 317.

22. For a comparison of the first and second version of the book, see Anzieu, *Freud's Self-Analysis,* pp. 267ff.

23. *FF,* 28 May 1899, p. 353.

24. *FF,* 27 August 1899, p. 368.

25. *FF,* 1 August 1899, p. 364.

26. *FF,* 9 February 1898, p. 298.

27. *FF,* 4 October 1899, p. 377.

28. *FF,* 7 November 1899, p. 383; for further details concerning this incident and this friendship, see Lisa Appignanesi and John Forrester, *Freud's Women* (London: Weidenfeld and Nicolson/New York: Basic Books, 1992), esp. chap. 4.

29. *ID, SE* V, 487.

30. Freud to André Breton, 26 December 1932, in *Les Rêves: La voie royale de l'inconscient* (Paris: Laffont/Tchou, 1979), pp. 56–57, originally reproduced in André Breton, *Les vases communicants* (Paris: Gallimard, 1932). See also Jack Spector, *The Aesthetics of Freud: A Study of Psychoanalysis and Art* (New York: Praeger, 1972), pp. 153–154, and Peter Gay, *Freud: A Life for Our Time* (London: Dent, 1988), p. 585.

31. *FF,* 7 July 1897, p. 255.

32. *FF,* 7 July 1897, p. 255.

33. *FF,* 31 May 1897, p. 249.

34. *ID, SE* V, 246.

35. *ID, SE* V, 337.

36. See Appignanesi and Forrester, *Freud's Women,* pp. 131–133.

37. Jacques Derrida, "Le Facteur de la Vérité, in *The Post Card,* pp. 414–419.

38. *ID, SE* IV, xxiii–xxiv.

39. Ibid., p. xxiv.

40. Ibid., pp. 104–105.

41. *Stud* II, 125.

42. *ID, SE* IV, 105–106.

43. I use the pronoun "he" to refer to the "reader" of *The Interpretation of Dreams* throughout, partly following the masculine gender of the German word "der Leser" whose fortunes I will be following, and partly to avoid the clumsiness of frequent repetitions of the phrase "he or she."

44. *ID, SE* IV, 105.

45. See Alexander Welsh, *Freud's Wishful Dream Theory* (Princeton: Princeton University Press, 1994), pp. 30–32.

46. *FF,* 6 August 1899, p. 365.

47. The literature re-examining this dream is substantial; much of it is drawn upon in Appignanesi and Forrester, *Freud's Women,* chap. 4, "The Dream of Psychoanalysis," pp. 117–145; see in particular Erik H. Erikson, "The Dream Specimen of Psychoanalysis," *Journal of the American Psychoanalytical Association* 2 (1954): 5–56; Frank R. Hartman, "A Reappraisal of the Emma Episode and the Specimen Dream," *Journal of the American Psychoanalytic Association*

31 (1983): 555–585; Robert Langs, "Freud's Irma Dream and the Origins of Psychoanalysis," *Psychoanalytic Review* 71 (1984): 591–617; Carl Schorske, "Politics and Patricide in Freud's *Interpretation of Dreams*," in *Fin-de-Siècle Vienna: Politics and Culture* (New York: Knopf, 1980); Max Schur, "Some Additional 'Day Residues' of the Specimen Dream of Psychoanalysis," in Rudolph M. Loewenstein, Lottie M. Newman, Max Schur, and Albert J. Solnit, eds., *Psychoanalysis: A General Psychology: Essays in Honor of Heinz Hartmann* (New York: International Universities Press, 1966), pp. 45–85.

48. *ID, SE* IV, 122.

49. Didier Anzieu, "Préface" to Sigmund Freud, *Sur le Rêve*, French translation of *Über den Traum*, trans. Cornélius Heim (Paris: Gallimard, 1988), p. 10.

50. *ID, SE* IV, 191.

51. *On Dreams, SE* V, 640.

52. *ID, SE* IV, 468–469.

53. Ibid., p. 297f. Note in passing Freud's challenge to the reader, when he modestly acquits himself of the charge of being a funny man in waking reality. If readers find his book singularly lacking in wit or charm, they will reluctantly have to agree with his argument that the ingenuity of dreams is not *his* responsibility; if readers are, in fact, charmed and amused by the book, it is less likely that they will really hold Freud's ingenious wit against him. Nonetheless, a considerable number of the charges leveled against Freud by skeptics of dream interpretation and psychoanalysis in general do have this form: they consist in finding Freud too clever for the good of his own claims concerning the meaning of dreams.

54. Ibid., p. 523.

55. See *FF*, 24 March 1898, p. 305: "Fortunately I can answer your objections by referring to later chapters. I have just stopped before one such chapter, which will deal with the somatic stimuli of dreams. It will also touch upon anxiety dreams, on which light will be shed once again in the last chapter on "Dreams and Neurosis." But in the account you have read I shall include cross-references, to avoid the impression it gave you that the author is making things too easy for himself here."

56. *ID, SE* IV, 121.

57. Ibid., p. 134.

58. Ibid., p. 135; note that the *Studienausgabe* edition of *Die Traumdeutung* fails to signal with quotation marks where exactly the critic's contradiction ends; in fact, Strachey in the Standard Edition closes the quotation marks exactly where the first edition of *Die Traumdeutung* does.

59. *FF*, 12 June 1900, p. 417.

60. *ID, SE* IV, 142.

61. Paul Ricoeur, *Freud and Philosophy: An Essay on Interpretation*, trans. Denis Savage (New Haven: Yale University Press, 1970), p. 7.

62. *ID, SE* IV, 142.

63. It is not possible for me here to explore extensively the analogy between political struggle and the inner psychic world of Freud's theories; the connection between politics and psyche has been explored by Schorske (see above) and by William McGrath in his book *Freud's Discovery of Psychoanalysis: The Politics of Hysteria* (Ithaca and London: Cornell University Press, 1986); see also the discussion in Welsh, *Freud's Wishful Dream Book*, pp. 80ff.

64. *ID, SE* IV, 146.

65. Ibid.

66. Ibid., p. 151.

67. Ibid., pp. 151–152.

68. Ibid., pp. 157–158 (incorporating part of a footnote added in 1911).

69. Freud, *Introductory Lectures on Psycho-analysis, SE* XV, 214.

70. Ibid.

71. "We are only lies, duplicity, contrariness and we hide and disguise this from ourselves." Blaise Pascal, *Pensées* (Paris: Editions Garnier, 1961), No. 377, p. 167.

72. La Rochefoucauld, *Maximes et Réflexions Diverses*, Preface by John Lafond (Paris: Gallimard, 1976), No. 366, p. 104.

73. See my "Contracting the Disease of Love: Authority and Freedom in the Origins of Psychoanalysis," in John Forrester, *The Seductions of Psychoanalysis: Freud, Lacan and Derrida* (Cambridge: Cambridge University Press, 1990), pp. 30–47.

74. *FF,* 31 May 1897, p. 249.

75. See *J* I, 354; Anzieu, *Freud's Self-Analysis,* p. 224; Octave Mannoni, *Freud: The Theory of the Unconscious* (1968), trans. Renauld Bruce (London: Pantheon, 1971), pp. 44–45; and Juliet Mitchell, *Psychoanalysis and Feminism* (London: Allen Lane, 1974), p. 9n3.

76. *FF,* 9 June 1898, p. 315.

77. *ID, SE* IV, 238.

78. *FF,* 27 June 1899, p. 357.

79. *FF,* 26 November 1899, p. 389. See also Appignanesi and Forrester, *Freud's Women,* pp. 172–173.

80. Hanns Sachs, "Review of Second Edition of *Autobiographical Study*," *Psychoanalytic Quarterly* 5 (1936): 280–283, reprinted in Norman Kiell, ed., *Freud without Hindsight: Reviews of His Work (1893–1939)*, with translations

from the German by Vladimir Rus and French by Denise Boneau (Madison, Conn.: International Universities Press, 1988), pp. 511–514; this quote from p. 511.

81. On the rise of statistical thinking, see Alain Desrosières, *La Politique des Grands Nombres: Histoire de la Raison Statistique* (Paris: La Découverte, 1993); Ian Hacking, *The Emergence of Probability* (Cambridge: Cambridge University Press, 1975) and Hacking, *The Taming of Chance* (Cambridge: Cambridge University Press, 1990); Porter, *The Rise of Statistical Thinking;* Stephen M. Stigler, *The History of Statistics: The Measurement of Uncertainty before 1900* (Cambridge, Mass.: Harvard University Press, 1986).

82. This anti-statistical, universalistic presumption of significant scientific findings is also the source of a difference of view between Freud and some of his critics concerning the number of cases it takes to establish generalizations or concepts. Given the detailed work Freud engaged in with individual patients, it is unrealistic to expect him or any other psychoanalyst to have "data" that could yield statistically significant findings. More important, for Freud it would have been as significant to count *sessions* as *individual cases*—for which he would have had many thousands of units of data. But his probable confidence in sessions rather than cases indicates how far he was from requiring a significant accounting of the diversity of corporeal individuals, rather than of psychoanalytic "events."

83. *FJones*, Jones to Freud, 2 January 1910, pp. 38–39.

84. *J* I, 352, quoting a letter to Martha Bernays, 29 October 1882.

85. *ID, SE* IV, xxv (Preface to 2nd edition of 1909).

86. Ibid., p. 93 (Postscript to Chapter 1, added 1909).

87. Paul J. Möbius, "Review of *On Dreams,*" *Schmidt's Jahrbucher* 269 (1901): 271, trans. in Kiell, *Freud without Hindsight,* p. 228.

88. *FF,* 8 January 1900, p. 394.

89. Max Burckhard, "A Modern Dream Book: Review of *The Interpretation of Dreams,*" *Die Zeit,* 275 and 276 (6 and 13 January, 1900), in Kiell, *Freud without Hindsight,* pp. 103–114; this passage from p. 108.

90. *FF,* 8 January 1900, p. 394.

91. "Notes on a Case of Obsessional Neurosis," *SE* X, 178–179.

92. *FJones*, Jones to Freud, 17 October 1911, pp. 117–118.

93. For example, *FJones*, Jones to Freud, 7 February 1909, p. 13.

94. See John Forrester, *Language and the Origins of Psychoanalysis* (London: Macmillan, 1980), chap. 3, "Symbolism," pp. 63–130.

95. *ID, SE* IV, 214n4.

96. *FJones*, Jones to Freud, 17 July 1914, pp. 293.

97. *FJones*, Jones to Freud, 25 May 1914, p. 282.

98. *ID, SE* IV, 517–518.

99. *FFer 1*, Ferenczi to Freud, 3 October 1910, pp. 219–220.

100. *FJones*, Jones to Freud, 17 February 1925, p. 569.

101. *ID, SE* IV, 470.

102. *FFer 1*, Ferenczi to Freud, 2 January 1910, p. 119.

103. E. H. Erikson, "Reality and Actuality, an Address," *Journal of the American Psychoanalytical Association* 10 (1962): 454–461.

104. Heinz Kohut, "Creativeness, Charisma, Group Psychology: Reflections on the Self-analysis of Freud" (1976), first published in J. E. Gedo and G. H. Pollock, eds., *Freud: The Fusion of Science and Humanism, Psychological Issues*, Monograph 34/35 (New York: International Universities Press, 1976), pp. 379–425. I would like to thank Sonu Shamdasani for drawing my attention to this paper.

105. Welsh, *Freud's Wishful Dream Theory*, p. 65.

106. Sigmund Freud and Karl Abraham, *A Psycho-analytic Dialogue: The Letters of Sigmund Freud and Karl Abraham, 1907–1926*, ed. Hilda C. Abraham and Ernst L. Freud (London: The Hogarth Press and the Institute of Psychoanalysis, 1965), Abraham to Freud, 8 January 1908, p. 18.

107. Ibid., Freud to Abraham, 9 January 1908, p. 20; Freud's emphasis and exclamation mark.

108. The relevant discussion of "Propyläeen" takes place in *ID, SE* IV, 294–295. The details of Fliess's illness in Munich in 1894 and of Freud's reaction to it are not clear; there is an inexplicable gap in the Freud-Fliess correspondence from 13 September 1894, a letter written just before their meeting in Munich, to 24 January 1895.

109. *FJones*, 8 December 1912, p. 182; written in English—hence the peculiar neologism and the syntax.

110. *FJung*, 330J, 3 December 1912, p. 526.

111. *FJung*, 233F, 9 February 1911, p. 390.

112. All emphases in passages from Jung are in the original.

113. *FJung*, 235J, 14 February 1911, pp. 392–393.

114. *FJung*, 236F, 17 February 1911, pp. 394–396.

115. *FF*, 21 September 1899, p. 374.

116. *ID, SE* IV, 422.

117. Ibid., p. 485.

118. *FF*, 21 September 1899, p. 374.

119. *ID, SE* IV, 487.

120. Welsh, *Freud's Wishful Dream Theory*, argues that the concept of "wish"

stands in place of Freud's "ambition." While agreeing that Freud's ambition to be acknowledged as a great discoverer and scientist is the fundamental wish of the dream book, I see no reason to substitute "ambition" for "wish" in the inner structure of Freud's theory; it is enough to say that ambition is the principal desire underlying many of Freud's dreams as portrayed in the book.

121. *FF,* 7 August 1901, p. 447.

122. *FF,* 19 September 1901, p. 450.

123. Lacan attempted to distance himself from this urge: "I am not engaged in redoing the analysis of Freud's dream after Freud himself. That would be absurd. Just as it is out of the question to analyse dead authors, so it is out of the question to analyse his own dream better than Freud. Freud has his reasons for breaking off his associations . . . It is not a matter of carrying out an exegesis where Freud interrupts himself but for us to take the whole of the dream and its interpretation. That's where we are in a different position from that of Freud." (Lacan, *Seminar II,* p. 152.) It is a moot point whether the two seminars he devoted to the dream of Irma's injection conform to these strictures.

124. *ID, SE* IV, 522.

125. Freud, *Five Lectures on Psycho-analysis, SE* XI, 33.

126. Freud, "The Future Prospects of Psycho-analytic Therapy," *SE* XI, 145.

127. Freud, *On the History of the Psycho-analytic Movement, SE* XIV, 20.

128. *FJones,* exchange of letters of 7 and 16 November 1924, pp. 560–562.

129. Freud, "Prefatory Note to a Paper by E. Pickworth Farrow" (1926), *SE* XX, 280.

130. As was recognized by Michel Foucault, when he noted that the movements spawned by Marx and Freud were distinctive creators of new discursive practices, which "produced not only their own work, but the possibility and the rules of the formation of other texts." Michel Foucault, "What Is an Author?" in Foucault, *Language, Counter-memory, Practice,* ed. D. Bouchard (Ithaca: Cornell University Press, 1977), p. 131.

131. For the theory of obligatory passage points, see Bruno Latour, *Science in Action* (Milton Keynes: Open University Press, 1987).

132. On Darwin's writing, see Gillian Beer, *Darwin's Plots* (London: Fontana, 1982).

5. "A Whole Climate of Opinion"

1. See Lisa Appignanesi and John Forrester, *Freud's Women* (London: Weidenfeld and Nicolson; New York: Basic Books, 1992), pp. 397–429.

2. See Carroll Smith-Rosenberg, "The Hysterical Woman: Sex Roles and

Role Conflict in Nineteenth-Century America" (1972), in Smith-Rosenberg, *Disorderly Conduct: Visions of Gender in Victorian America* (New York: Knopf, 1985; New York and London: Oxford University Press, 1985), pp. 197–216; A. de Swaan, "On the Sociogenesis of the Psychoanalytic Situation," *Psychoanalysis and Contemporary Thought* 3 (1980): 381–413.

3. Henri F. Ellenberger, *The Discovery of the Unconscious: The History and Evolution of Dynamic Psychiatry* (London: Allen Lane, 1970).

4. Jean Laplanche and J.-B. Pontalis, *The Language of Psychoanalysis* (1967), trans. Donald Nicholson-Smith (London: Hogarth Press and the Institute of Psycho-analysis, 1973).

5. Wladimir Granoff, *Filiations* (Paris: Editions de Minuit, 1975).

6. Ola Andersson, *Studies in the Prehistory of Psychoanalysis* (Stockholm: Scandinavian University Books, Svenska Bokförlaget/Norstedts-Bonniers, 1962); Ola Andersson, "A Supplement to Freud's Case History of 'Frau Emmy v. N.' in *Studies on Hysteria* 1895," *Scandinavian Psychoanalytic Review* 2 (1979): 5–15; Henri F. Ellenberger, "The Story of 'Anna O.': A Critical Review with New Data," *Journal of the History of the Behavioral Sciences* 8 (1972): 267–279.

7. Gerhard Fichtner, "Freuds Patienten" (Tübingen: Institut für Geschichte der Medizin, December 1979), mimeo; G. Fichtner and A. Hirschmüller, "Freuds 'Katherina'—Hintergrund, Entstehungsgeschichte und Bedeutung einer frühen psychoanalytischen Krankengeschichte," *Psyche* 39 (1985): 220–240; Albrecht Hirschmüller, *Freuds Begegnung mit der Psychiatrie: Von der Hirnmythologie zur Neurosenlehre* (Tübingen: Edition Diskord, 1991); Hirschmüller, "Freuds 'Mathilde': Ein weiterer Tagesrest zum Irma Traum," *Jahrbuch der Psychoanalyse* 24 (1989): 128–159; Hirschmüller, *Physiologie und Psychoanalyse in Leben und Werk Josef Breuers* [*Jahrbuch der Psychoanalyse*, Suppl. 4], (Bern: Hans Huber, 1978), trans. as *The Life and Work of Josef Breuer: Physiology and Psychoanalysis* (New York and London: New York University Press, 1989).

8. See Peter Swales, "A Fascination with Witches," *The Sciences* 22, No. 8 (November 1982): 21–25; "Freud, Breuer and the Blessed Virgin" (privately printed, 1986); "Freud, His Teacher, and the Birth of Psychoanalysis," in Paul E. Stepansky, ed., *Freud: Appraisals and Reappraisals: Contributions to Freud Studies, Vol. 1* (Hillsdale, N.J.: The Analytic Press, 1986), pp. 3–82; "Freud, Katharina, and the First 'Wild analysis,'" in Stepansky, ed., *Freud: Appraisals and Reappraisals, Vol. 3* (1988), pp. 79–164; and a series of Swales's papers, previously privately printed, now published in Laurence Spurling, ed., *Sigmund Freud: Critical Assessments. Volume 1: Freud and the Origins of Psychoanalysis* (London and New York: Routledge, 1989).

9. Peter Swales, "Freud, Minna Bernays and the Conquest of Rome: New

Light on the Origins of Psychoanalysis," *The New American Review* 1 (1982): 1–23; Swales, "Freud, Martha Bernays and the Language of Flowers, Masturbation, Cocaine, and the Inflation of Fantasy" (privately printed, 1983).

10. Swales, "Freud, Fliess and Fratricide: The Role of Fliess in Freud's Conception of Paranoia" (1982), in Spurling, ed., *Sigmund Freud: Critical Assessments. Volume 1*, pp. 302–329.

11. Carl E. Schorske, *Fin de Siècle Vienna: Politics and Culture* (New York: Knopf, 1979); William J. McGrath, *Freud's Discovery of Psychoanalysis: The Politics of Hysteria* (Ithaca and London: Cornell University Press, 1986).

12. Steven Beller, "Class, Culture and the Jews of Vienna, 1900," in Ivar Oxaal, Michael Pollak, and Gerhard Botz, eds., *Jews, Antisemitism and Culture in Vienna* (London and New York: Routledge and Kegan Paul, 1987), pp. 39–58, this passage from pp. 57–58; see also Michael Pollak, "Cultural Innovation and Social Identity in *Fin-de-Siècle* Vienna," in: Oxaal, Pollak, and Botz, eds., *Jews, Antisemitism and Culture in Vienna*, pp. 59–74.

13. Pollak, "Cultural Innovation and Social identity," pp. 69–70.

14. L. Whyte, *The Unconscious before Freud* (London: Methuen, 1962).

15. K. Codell Carter, "Infantile Hysteria and Infantile Sexuality in Late Nineteenth-Century German-language Medical Literature," *Medical History* 27 (1983): 186–196; Stephen Kern, "The Discovery of Child Sexuality: Freud and the Emergence of Child Psychology, 1880–1910" (Ph.D. diss., Columbia University, 1972), *Diss Abs X1970*, p. 205; Stephen Kern, "Freud and the Discovery of Child Sexuality," *History of Childhood Quarterly: The Journal of Psychohistory* 1 (1973): 117–141; see also Frank Sulloway, *Freud: Biologist of the Mind* (London: Burnett Books, 1979).

16. See, for instance, the thoughtful Arnold I. Davidson, "How to Do the History of Psychoanalysis: A Reading of Freud's *Three Essays on the Theory of Sexuality*," in Françoise Meltzer, ed., *The Trial(s) of Psychoanalysis* (Chicago and London: University of Chicago Press, 1988), pp. 39–64; on the distinctive character of the unconscious, see John Forrester, *Language and the Origins of Psychoanalysis* (London: Macmillan/New York: Columbia University Press, 1980), pp. 4–6, 57ff., 179–180.

17. "What Is an Author?" in Michel Foucault, *Language, Counter-memory, Practice*, ed. D. Bouchard, trans. S. Simon (Ithaca: Cornell University Press, 1977), p. 131.

18. See Elizabeth Young-Bruehl, "A History of Freud Biographies," in Mark S. Micale and Roy Porter, eds., *Discovering the History of Psychiatry* (Oxford and New York: Oxford University Press, 1994), pp. 157–173.

19. Derrida, "Spéculer—sur Freud," in Jacques Derrida, *La Carte Postale*

(Paris: Flammarion, 1980), pp. 277–437, this passage from p. 325; *The Post Card: From Socrates to Freud and Beyond*, trans. Alan Bass (Chicago: University of Chicago Press, 1987), pp. 257–409, this passage from p. 305, trans. modified.

20. Jacques Derrida, "Freud and the Scene of Writing" (1965), *Yale French Studies* 48 (1972): 74–117; "Le Facteur de la vérité," in Derrida, *La Carte Postale*, pp. 441–524; *The Post Card*, trans. Alan Bass, pp. 411–496; "Télépathie," *Cahiers Confrontation* 10 (Autumn 1983): 201–230, reprinted in Derrida, *Psyché: Inventions de l'Autre* (Paris: Editions Galilée, 1987), pp. 237–270; Derrida, "My Chances/*Mes Chances:* A Rendezvous with Some Epicurean Stereophonies," in Joseph H. Smith and William Kerrigan, eds., *Taking Chances: Derrida, Psychoanalysis and Literature* (Baltimore and London: The Johns Hopkins University Press, 1984), pp. 1–32.

21. For the United States, see J. C. Burnham, *Psychoanalysis and American Medicine, 1894–1918: Medicine, Science and Culture* (New York: International Universities Press, 1967); G. E. Gifford, ed., *Psychoanalysis, Psychotherapy and the New England Medical Scene, 1894–1944* (New York: Science History Publications, 1978); Nathan G. Hale, *Freud and the Americans* (New York: Oxford University Press, 1971), and Hale, *The Rise and Crisis of Psychoanalysis in the United States: Freud and the Americans, 1917–1985* (New York and Oxford: Oxford University Press, 1995); John Seeley, *The Americanization of the Unconscious* (New York: International Universities Press, 1967). For the recent history, see Nathan G. Hale, Jr., *The Rise and Crisis of Psychoanalysis in the United States: Freud and the Americans, 1917–1985* (New York and Oxford: Oxford University Press, 1995), pp. 300–379.

22. Bernard This and P. Theves, *Die Verneinung: S. Freud (1925–1975): Nouvelle traduction, étude comparée de quelques traductions et commentaires sur la traduction en générale, Le Coq-Heron No. 52,* Bulletin du group d'étude du Centre Etienne Marcel, Paris, 1975.

23. Elizabeth Roudinesco, *La Bataille de Cent Ans: L'Histoire de la Psychanalyse en France, Vol. I, 1886–1925* (Paris: Editions Ramsey, 1983; reprinted by Seuil, 1986).

24. D. Rapp, "The Reception of Freud by the British Press: General Interest and Literary Magazines, 1920–1925," *Journal for the History of the Behavioral Sciences* 24 (1988): 191–201.

25. Krin Gabbard and Glen O. Gabbard, *Psychiatry and the Cinema,* foreword by Irving Schneider (Chicago and London: University of Chicago Press, 1987).

26. See Bruno Latour, *The Pasteurization of France* (Cambridge, Mass.: Harvard University Press, 1988).

27. See Ellenberger, *The Discovery of the Unconscious;* Allan Gauld, *The*

History of Hypnotism (Cambridge: Cambridge University Press, 1993); Mark Micale, "Hysteria and Its Historiography: A Review of Past and Present Writings I and II," *History of Science* 27 (1989): 223–261, 319–351; Micale, "Hysteria and Its Historiography: The Future perspective," *History of Psychiatry* 1 (1990): 33–124; Micale, *Approaching Hysteria: Disease and Its Interpretations* (Princeton: Princeton University Press, 1995).

28. Carlo Ginzburg, "Morelli, Freud and Sherlock Holmes: Clues and Scientific Method," in Umberto Eco and Thomas A. Sebeok, eds., *The Sign of Three: Dupin, Holmes, Pierce* (Bloomington: Indiana University Press, 1983), pp. 81–118.

29. Michael Balint, *The Doctor, His Patient and the Illness* (London: Pitman Medical, 1957); see Thomas Osborne, "Mobilizing Psychoanalysis: Michael Balint and the General Practitioners," *Social Studies of Science* 23 (1993): 175–200.

30. Freud, "Interview with Adelbert Albrecht," *Boston Transcript,* 11 September 1909, reprinted in Hendrik M. Ruitenbeek, ed., *Freud As We Knew Him* (Detroit: Wayne State University Press, 1973), pp. 22–27, this passage from p. 23.

31. Ernest Gellner, *The Psychoanalytic Movement, or the Cunning of Unreason* (London: Paladin, 1985).

32. Philip Rieff, *Freud: The Mind of the Moralist* (New York: Viking, 1959), p. 300.

33. Alasdair MacIntyre, *After Virtue* (London: Duckworth, 1985), pp. 27ff.

34. Ibid., p. 30.

35. Rieff, *Freud,* p. 305.

36. Ibid., p. 302.

37. Jacques Lacan, "The Function and Field of Speech and Language in Psychoanalysis" (1953), in Lacan, *Ecrits* (Paris: Seuil, 1966), p. 321; translated in Lacan, *Ecrits: A Selection,* trans. Alan Sheridan (London: Tavistock, 1977), p. 105.

38. Michel Foucault, *The Order of Things* (1966; London: Tavistock, 1970), p. 373.

39. Ibid., p. 89.

40. John Forrester, "Michel Foucault and the History of Psychoanalysis," in Forrester, *The Seductions of Psychoanalysis: Freud, Lacan and Derrida* (Cambridge: Cambridge University Press, 1990), pp. 286–316.

41. Michel Foucault, "The Subject and Power" (1983), in Hubert L. Dreyfus and Paul Rabinow, *Michel Foucault: Beyond Structuralism and Hermeneutics,* 2nd ed., with an afterword and interview with Michel Foucault (Chicago: University of Chicago Press, 1983), p. 214.

42. Ibid., p. 215.

43. See Michel Foucault, "Technologies of the Self," in Luther H. Martin, Huck Gutman, and Patrick H. Hutton, eds., *Technologies of the Self: A Seminar with Michel Foucault* (London: Tavistock, 1988), pp. 16–49.

44. Richard Rorty, "Freud and Moral Reflection," in Rorty, *Essays on Heidegger and Others: Philosophical Papers, Volume 2* (Cambridge: Cambridge University Press, 1991), p. 154.

45. See Peter Gay, *The Bourgeois Experience: Victoria to Freud*, 2 vols. (New York and Oxford: Oxford University Press, 1985–1987).

46. Nancy Friday, *Women on Top: How Real Life has Changed Women's Fantasies* (London: Hutchinson, 1991).

47. The recent literary study of psychoanalysis and its literary deployment is too extensive to survey here; two important contributions are Shoshana Felman, ed., *Yale French Studies Nos. 55/56; Literature and Psychoanalysis. The Question of Reading: Otherwise* (New Haven and London: Yale University Press, 1977), and Daniel Gunn, *Psychoanalysis and Fiction* (Cambridge: Cambridge University Press, 1990).

6. Dispatches from the Freud Wars

1. Stanley Fish, "Withholding the Missing Portion: Psychoanalysis and Rhetoric," in Fish, *Doing What Comes Naturally: Change, Rhetoric, and the Practice of Theory in Literary and Legal Studies* (Durham and London: Duke University Press; Oxford: Clarendon Press, 1989), p. 526. The publication history of Fish's paper is a complex one. The first version of it that I came across was somewhat shorter and published under the title "Withholding the Missing Portion: Power, Meaning, and Persuasion in Freud's 'The Wolf-Man,'" *Times Literary Supplement*, 29 August 1986, pp. 935–938. Another version can be found in Nigel Fabb et al., eds., *The Linguistics of Writing: Arguments between Language and Literature* (Manchester: Manchester University Press, 1987). An expanded version was then published in a book version of a special issue of the journal *Critical Inquiry* as "Withholding the Missing Portion: Psychoanalysis and Rhetoric," in Françoise Meltzer, ed., *The Trial(s) of Psychoanalysis* (Chicago and London: University of Chicago Press, 1988), pp. 183–210—although Fish's paper did not appear in the special issue of *Critical Inquiry* (Winter 1987, vol. 13, no. 2). The version to be found in Fish's own collection of papers, *Doing What Comes Naturally*, is the one that I will cite here, although it should be noted that it too varies somewhat from the version found in *The Trial(s) of Psychoanalysis*. Where it is relevant, I have checked to ascertain whether the earlier version(s) contain the passages I am discussing in detail here.

2. Stanley Fish, "Withholding the Missing Portion," *Doing What Comes Naturally,* p. 548.

3. Ibid.

4. *J* II, 308 (English edition); 274 (American edition, Basic Books).

5. See Karin Obholzer, *The Wolf-Man Sixty Years Later: Conversations with Freud's Controversial Patient,* trans. Michael Shaw (London: Routledge and Kegan Paul, 1982), pp. 168–170. Ellipses in the original. The reference to the lawyer stems from an earlier part of the conversation, in which the Wolf Man disputes Jones's description of his father as a lawyer ("The patient was the son of a Russian lawyer in Odessa who was also a very wealthy landowner"; *J* II, 309), exclaiming: "And how can he write that my father was a lawyer? My father was an honorary judge." (Obholzer, *The Wolf-Man* p. 168).

6. The French edition of Vol. I of the *Correspondance 1908–1914* was published in 1992 (Paris: Calman-Lévy); the *Briefwechsel, Band I/1, 1908–1911* was published in 1993 (Wien/Köln/Weimar: Böhlau Verlag); *The Correspondence of Sigmund Freud and Sándor Ferenczi, Volume I, 1908–1914* was published in 1994 (see Abbreviations).

7. *FFer 1,* Freud to Ferenczi, Sunday 13 February 1910, p. 138. The Freud-Ferenczi correspondence, together with the Wolf Man's own memoirs, helps us establish a plausible chronology: the Wolf Man first met Freud between the 1st and 8th February. The patient's first sessions took place, at the Cottage Sanatorium, on or between Tuesday the 9th and Saturday the 12th February, 1910.

8. There is an ambiguity here which Fish might point to, and which might explain Jones's reading: the Wolf Man might have had some thoughts after the first session which he then admitted to Freud during the second session. If "the first session" was actually the preliminary interview, then Fish's implication that the Wolf Man's view of Freud was arrived at "on the edge" of analysis, before analysis had started, is more plausible. But this would involve Freud having been the one to decide to call the preliminary interview "the first session," when it is clear from the way the analysis was managed that there was a preliminary interview at Freud's consulting-room, and then the first session took place at the Cottage Sanatorium. This dislocation of place makes the distinction between the preliminary interview and the first session a more clear-cut one. The key question for Fish, the source of this sentence, still remains: as far as we know, the only source is via Freud.

9. Note the interesting manner in which this association is presented in the published case history; Freud refers to a change in the boy's character, including the sinking away of his piety, when he came under the influence of a new,

irreligious tutor. Freud adds: "This did not take place, however, without one last flicker of the obsessional neurosis; and from this he particularly remembered the obsession of having to think of the Holy Trinity whenever he saw three heaps of dung lying together in the road." (*SE* XVII, 68).

10. Freud, "On Beginning the Treatment," *SE* XII, 138–139. Notice the similarity between Freud's examples here and the story the Wolf Man remembered Freud telling him, both about the young girl and about his turning around to look at Freud. It would be entirely characteristic of the Wolf Man to have confused Freud's writings with his own analysis—although this can only be speculation. In this way, what Freud *wrote* about beginning the treatment came to stand in for what *actually* began the treatment in the Wolf Man's case.

11. Gerald Holton, *The Scientific Imagination: Case Studies* (Cambridge: Cambridge University Press, 1978), pp. 63–69. For an example of a distinguished historian straightforwardly oblivious to the possibility of crying "Foul!" in his discussion of Millikan's work, see Geoffrey Cantor, "The Rhetoric of Experiment," in David Gooding, Trevor Pinch, and Simon Schaffer, eds., *The Uses of Experiment: Studies in the Natural Sciences* (Cambridge: Cambridge University Press, 1989), pp. 159–180.

12. Harry Collins, *Changing Order* (London: Sage, 1985), pp. 73–84.

13. See Collins, *Changing Order,* and Peter Galison, *How Experiments End* (Chicago: University of Chicago Press, 1987), and Gooding, Pinch, and Schaffer, eds., *The Uses of Experiment.*

14. Morton Schatzman, "Freud: Who Seduced Whom?" *New Scientist,* 21 March 1992, pp. 34–37; Han Israëls and Morton Schatzman, "The Seduction Theory," *History of Psychiatry* 4 (1993): 23–59. Allen Esterson, *Seductive Mirage: An Exploration of the Work of Sigmund Freud* (Chicago and La Salle, Ill.: Open Court, 1993).

15. Frederick W. Maitland, *Why the History of English Law Is Not Written,* Inaugural Lecture, 13 October 1888 (Cambridge: Cambridge University Press, 1888).

16. Frederick Crews, *Skeptical Engagements* (New York and Oxford: Oxford University Press, 1986), p. 86.

17. Frederick Crews, "The Unknown Freud," *New York Review of Books,* 18 November 1993, pp. 55–66, this passage from p. 58.

18. Ibid., p. 61.

19. Ibid., p. 60.

20. Ibid.

21. Ibid.

22. See Spencer R. Weart and Gertrud Weiss Szilard, eds., *Leo Szilard: His*

Version of the Facts, Selected Recollections and Correspondence (Cambridge, Mass.: MIT Press, 1978) and William Lanouette, with Bela Szilard, *A Biography of Leo Szilard: The Man behind the Bomb* (New York: Robert Stewart, 1992); James Watson, *The Double Helix* (1967), reprinted with Commentary, Reviews, and Original Papers in Gunther S. Stent, ed., *The Double Helix* (New York: Norton, 1980).

23. Crews, "The Unknown Freud," p. 55.

24. See Alison Winter, "Ethereal Epidemics: Mesmerism and the Introduction of Inhalation Anaesthesia to Early Victorian London," *Social History of Medicine* 4 (1991): 1–33.

25. Freud, "Recommendations to Physicians Practising Psycho-analysis," *SE* XII, 115: "I cannot advise my colleagues too urgently to model themselves during psycho-analytic treatment on the surgeon, who puts aside all feelings, even his human sympathy, and concentrates his mental forces on the single aim of performing the operation as skilfully as possible." Freud wrote this paper in early 1912.

26. C. A. Ross, *Multiple Personality Disorder: Diagnosis, Clinical Features, and Treatment* (New York: Wiley, 1989), p. 181.

27. Ian Hacking, "Memoro-politics, Trauma and the Soul," *History of the Human Sciences* 7 (1994): 29–52, this passage from pp. 40–41.

28. On the debates between psychoanalysis and feminism, see Lisa Appignanesi and John Forrester, *Freud's Women* (London: Weidenfeld and Nicolson/New York: Basic Books, 1992), pp. 430–474; Teresa Brennan, ed., *Between Feminism and Psychoanalysis* (London: Routledge, 1989).

29. See, for instance, Mikkel Borch-Jacobsen, *Souvenirs d'Anna O.* (Paris: Aubier, 1995).

30. Jacques Derrida, "Télépathie," *Cahiers Confrontation* 10 (Autumn 1983): 201–230; this passage from p. 219. See also Nicholas Royle, *After Derrida* (Manchester and New York: Manchester University Press, 1995), "The Remains of Psychoanalysis (i): Telepathy," pp. 61–84.

31. Freud, "Negation," *SE* XIX, 235.

32. James Hopkins, "The Interpretation of Dreams," in Jerome Neu, ed., *The Cambridge Companion to Freud* (Cambridge: Cambridge University Press, 1991), pp. 86–135; David Sachs, "In Fairness to Freud: A Critical Notice of *The Foundations of Psychoanalysis,* by Adolf Grünbaum," in Neu, ed., *The Cambridge Companion to Freud,* pp. 309–338; Sebastian Gardner, *Irrationality and the Philosophy of Psychoanalysis* (Cambridge: Cambridge University Press, 1993); Thomas Nagel, "Freud's Permanent Revolution," *New York Review of Books,* 12 May 1994, pp. 34–38; Sebastian Gardner, "Psychoanalysis, Science, and Commonsense," *Philosophy, Psychology and Psychiatry* 2 (1995): 93–113.

33. See Chapter 1.

34. Hilary Putnam, "Psychoanalysis: A Copernican Revolution or a Pseudo-science?" *Kos* 10 (1984): 3–6.

35. Freud, *An Outline of Psycho-analysis, SE* XXIII, 158.

36. Freud, "Some Elementary Lessons in Psycho-analysis," *SE* XXIII, 282; entire quote from Adolf Grünbaum, *The Foundations of Psychoanalysis* (Berkeley: University of California Press, 1984), p. 2.

37. Ian Hacking, *The Taming of Chance* (Cambridge: Cambridge University Press, 1990), p. 7.

38. Karl Popper, "Darwinism as Metaphysics," in P. A. Schilpp, ed., *The Philosophy of Sir Karl Popper* (La Salle, Ill.: Open Court, 1974), pp. 135–138, quoting from Jim Hopkins, "Psychoanalysis, Interpretation, and Science," in Jim Hopkins and Anthony Savile, eds., *Psychoanalysis, Mind and Art: Perspectives on Richard Wollheim* (Oxford: Blackwell, 1992), pp. 24–25.

39. Robert J. Stoller, "Naturalistic Observation in Psychoanalysis: Search is Not Research," in Stoller, *Presentations of Gender* (New Haven and London: Yale University Press, 1985), this passage from p. 2.

40. Stoller, "Erotic Vomiting," in *Observing the Erotic Imagination* (New Haven and London: Yale University Press, 1985), p. 159.

41. Robert J. Stoller and I. S. Levine, *Coming Attractions: The Making of an X-rated Video* (New Haven and London: Yale University Press, 1993), p. 239; see also Robert J. Stoller, *Sexual Excitement: Dynamics of Erotic Life* (New York: Pantheon, 1979/London: Karnac Books, 1986), pp. 3–35.

42. Winnicott, "The Concept of Trauma in Relation to the Development of the Individual within the Family," in *Psycho-Analytic Explorations*, ed. Clare Winnicott, Ray Shepherd, and Madeleine Davis (London: Karnac, 1989), p. 140.

43. Malcolm Macmillan, *Freud Evaluated* (Amsterdam: North-Holland, 1991).

44. Freud, "Some Elementary Lessons in Psycho-analysis," *SE* XXIII, 282.

45. Freud, *An Outline of Psycho-Analysis, SE* XXIII, 158–159; emphasis in text.

46. J. Allan Hobson, *The Dreaming Brain* (New York: Basic Books, 1988), p. 51.

47. She might also have added "below the belt."

48. Patricia Kitcher, *Freud's Dream: A Complete Interdisciplinary Science of Mind* (Cambridge, Mass.: MIT Press, 1992), p. 148.

49. Steven Shapin and Simon Schaffer, *Leviathan and the Air Pump: Hobbes, Boyle and the Experimental Life* (Princeton: Princeton University Press, 1985).

50. Frank Sulloway, "Reassessing Freud's Case Histories: The Social

Construction of Psychoanalysis," *Isis* 82 (1991): 245–275, this passage from p. 265.

51. Rieff, *Freud: The Mind of the Moralist,* p. 304.

52. The *locus classicus* for the demonstration of how science deals with its critics is the opening hundred pages of Bruno Latour, *Science in Action* (Milton Keynes: Open University Press, 1987).

53. And this is the real point of the admirable work of Shapin and Schaffer that Sulloway so misrepresents in his critique of psychoanalysis.

54. See Paul Feyerabend, *Against Method* (London: NLB, 1975), pp. 99–108.

Epilogue

1. "You can't take it with you."

2. Milan Kundera, *Immortality,* trans. Peter Kussi (London and Boston: Faber and Faber, 1991), pp. 122–124.

ACKNOWLEDGMENTS

A shorter version of Chapter 1, "Justice, Envy, and Psychoanalysis," was originally delivered at the invitation of John O'Neill as part of a panel on "Psychoanalysis and the Passions" at the conference entitled "Passions, Persons, Powers," Berkeley, California, April 30–May 3, 1992. I am most grateful to José Brunner for reading that version and stimulating me into considerable revision and expansion in the light of Rawls's discussion of envy. A much revised version was delivered in the welcoming environment of the Dartmouth College Public Lecture Series in July 1995; I would like to thank Michael Riffaterre, Judith Butler, Diana Fuss, and Donald Pease for their useful comments, and my colleagues in the Unofficial Knowledge group, Jonathan Burt, Peter de Bolla, Maud Ellmann, and Simon Goldhill, together with Elizabeth Goodstein, for comments in a discussion of the paper held in Cambridge in June 1995. Another version appears in *Freud and the Passions*, ed. John O'Neill (University Park: The Pennsylvania State University Press, 1996); copyright 1996 by The Pennsylvania State University, reproduced by permission of the publisher.

A first version of Chapter 2, "Casualties of Truth," was prepared, at the invitation of Conrad Stein and Danièle Brun, for the *Journées d'Etudes Freudiennes* of September 26–27, 1992, devoted to the publication in French of the first volume of the *Freud/Ferenczi Correspondance*. That version was published as "L'inceste psychanalytique et l'idéal de l'amour libre," *Etudes Freudiennes* 34 (Spring 1993): 35–55. A heavily revised version was presented at the colloquium entitled "Proof and Persuasion: The Early Psychoanalytic Case: Patients and Narratives," Shelby Cullom Davis Center for Historical Studies, Princeton University, April 8, 1994, organized by Elizabeth

Lunbeck and Natalie Zemon Davis. The chapter published here is a much extended version of that paper and includes material presented at the Humanities Research Center, University of California at Berkeley, May 1992, by the kind invitation of Martin Jay; I would like to thank Frederick Crews for his intervention on that occasion, which helped me clarify the "amoral" character of psychoanalysis. For their generous comments on the earlier versions, I would like to thank Conrad Stein, Danièle Brun, Tim Kendall, Geraldine Shipton, Michael Roth, John Toews, Elizabeth Lunbeck, Stephanie Kiceluk, and, in particular, Jan Goldstein.

A first version of Chapter 3 "Collector, Naturalist, Surrealist," was originally given as a lecture in a seminar entitled "Museums and Collecting" in the Faculty of Classics, University of Cambridge, May 27, 1991, at the invitation of Simon Goldhill—a particularly happy invitation, since it provoked me into thinking about Freud's collecting activities from a new angle. The version published here is lightly revised from that published under the title *"Mille e tre:* Freud as a Collector" in *The Cultures of Collecting,* ed. John Elsner and Roger Cardinal, first published in the U.K. in 1994, copyright Reaktion Books, 1994. I would also like to thank the staff of the Freud Museum, London, and in particular Erica Carter, its director, for their generous and unstinting assistance in the preparation of this chapter.

Chapter 4, "Dream Readers," was commissioned by Laura Marcus in 1991 for a forthcoming volume of essays reassessing Freud's *The Interpretation of Dreams,* to be published by Manchester University Press, whom I thank for permission to reprint the essay here. I would like to thank Frank Kermode for upholding his long tradition, begun in 1975 when I first met him in his seminar in Cambridge on *The Interpretation of Dreams,* of keeping me up to date on Freud's book. I would also like to thank Routledge, Sigmund Freud Copyrights, and HarperCollins for permission to quote from Sigmund Freud, *The Interpretation of Dreams,* as published in *The Standard Edition of the Complete Psychological Works of Sigmund Freud.*

Chapter 5, "'A Whole Climate of Opinion,'" was commissioned

by Roy Porter and Mark Micale in 1991 for their volume *Discovering the History of Psychiatry* (Oxford: Oxford University Press, 1994); the present version has been lightly revised. I would like to thank Oxford University Press for permission to reprint the chapter here.

Drafts which eventually became Chapter 6, "Dispatches from the Freud Wars," were delivered in early 1995 as lectures to the British Psycho-Analytic Society; to the Department of Philosophy at the University of Essex, courtesy of Peter Dews, Stephen Mulhall, and Jay Bernstein; to my home Department of History and Philosophy of Science at Cambridge; to the Centre for Psychoanalytic Studies at the University of Kent, courtesy of Julia Borossa; and to the conference held in March 1995 entitled "The End of Psychoanalysis?" organized by my colleagues and friends in the Psychoanalytic Forum, Eleanor Armstrong-Perlman, Malcolm Bowie, Jacqueline Rose, Andrew Samuels, and Sonu Shamdasani. Part of the text was published in the *Bulletin of the British Psycho-Analytic Society* in March 1995.

The Epilogue was published in somewhat different form in *The Independent*, London, on October 10, 1994.

Parts of this book were written and parts were revised while I was on research leave in Paris in 1993–94. I would like to thank the University of Cambridge and my philosophical colleagues in the Department of History and Philosophy of Science for allowing me the luxury of a year's leave. The welcome time for research and writing was also made possible by the Nuffield Foundation, who awarded me a Nuffield Foundation Social Science Research Fellowship for part of 1994; I would like to express my gratitude to them.

Finally, I would like to thank my editor, Angela von der Lippe, whose enthusiasm and boldness certainly contributed more than is usual to the creation of this book. The final stages went as smoothly, as dreamlike as such things ever can, thanks to Mary Ellen Geer and Kimberly Nelson.

Cambridge, England
October 1996

INDEX